£32.00
D
KD

D0539073

Spectacular Shakespeare

Spectacular Shakespeare

Critical Theory and Popular Cinema

Edited by
Courtney Lehmann and Lisa S. Starks

Madison • Teaneck
Fairleigh Dickinson University Press
London: Associated University Presses

Associated University Presses
440 Forsgate Drive
Cranbury, NJ 08512

Associated University Presses
16 Barter Street
London WC1A 2AH, England

Associated University Presses
P.O. Box 338, Port Credit
Mississauga, Ontario
Canada L5G 4L8

The paper used in this publication meets the requirements
of the American National Standard for Permanence of Paper
for Printed Library Materials Z39.48–1984.

Library of Congress Cataloging-in-Publication Data

Spectacular Shakespeare: critical theory and popular cinema / edited by Courtney Lehmann and Lisa S. Starks.
    p. cm.
Includes bibliographical references and index.
ISBN 0-8386-3910-0 (alk. paper)
  1. Shakespeare, William, 1564–1616—Film and video adaptations. 2. Motion pictures—History and criticism—Theory, etc. 3. English drama—Film and video adaptations. 4. Film adaptations. I. Lehmann, Courtney, 1969– II. Starks, Lisa S., 1960–

PR3093 .S64 2002
791.43'6—dc21   2001023843

Contents

Part III: The Politics of the Popular: From Class to Classroom

Acknowledgments

WE WISH TO EXPRESS OUR GRATITUDE TO GERALD DUCHOVNAY, THE EDITOR OF *Post Script: Essays in Film and the Humanities*, for supporting the two special issues on Shakespeare and Film that provided the impetus for this project; José Ramón Díaz-Fernández, for inviting us to deliver a presentation on this collaboration at his international conference on Shakespeare and cinema, held in Malaga, Spain, 1999; and to Lena Cowen Orlin with the Shakespeare Association of America, for giving us the opportunity to direct a seminar on Shakespearean films, which generated interest in this volume.

Introduction:
Are We in Love with Shakespeare?

COURTNEY LEHMANN AND LISA S. STARKS

WHAT SHOCKED MILLIONS OF PEOPLE IN 1999—WHOOPI GOLDBERG'S QUIP AT the Oscars that "Little Willy is very large"—now seems anything but surprising, for in the years following the spectacular success of *Shakespeare in Love* (dir. John Madden, 1998), "Little Willy" has become Hollywood's biggest screenwriting sensation.[1] On the heels of this blockbuster about the Bard's lost years, a long list of Shakespeare-inspired films have been released, including *10 Things I Hate about You*, a teenage adaptation of *The Taming of the Shrew* (dir. Gil Junger, 1999); *Never Been Kissed*, a loose adaptation of *As You Like It* (dir. Raja Gosnell, 1999); *A Midsummer Night's Dream* (dir. Michael Hoffman, 1999); *Titus* (dir. Julie Taymor, 1999); *Love's Labour's Lost* (dir. Kenneth Branagh, 2000); and a contemporary adaptation of *Hamlet* (dir. Michael Almereyda, 2000). Now more than ever, it seems as though we are hopelessly in love with Shakespeare.

And this love shows no signs of fading as Shakespeare becomes ingrained in our everyday lives, entering our homes *not* through the library, but through the living room, courtesy of video technology and the rise of the "home theater." But just what is the nature of this love? Whereas the marriage of Shakespeare and Hollywood is certainly profitable, what are its politics? Is this an arranged marriage or a meeting of the minds? What is the real "bottom line" driving recent cinematic representations of Shakespeare, and where is the line drawn between historical agency and Hollywood agents? If romance and history imply two diametrically opposed narrative modes, then what will happen to our sense of the "real" Shakespeare in the age of this romanticized "reel" Shakespeare? Indeed, what becomes of Shakespeare in the classroom when it is increasingly clear that to teach Shakespeare today, we must teach today's Shakespeare—as refigured through the distorting lens of the movie camera?

According to Oscar and Whoopi, the marriage of Shakespeare and Hol-

9

lywood is a happy, healthy one. In the midst of millennial madness, the 1999 Academy Awards presentation promised to be a gala event that would out-Hollywood Hollywood, marking the culmination of seventy-one years of Oscar; it turned out, however, to be less of a Hollywood extravaganza than a Shakespearean spectacle. In full costume and makeup as Elizabeth I, hostess Whoopi Goldberg entered the stage to roaring applause and laughs as she proclaimed herself to be the "African Queen." Mocking Hollywood's lack of "African Queens" and its recent obsession with the Virgin Queen, Whoopi opened the Oscar festivities by exclaiming, in an exaggerated English accent, that "It is my solemn task this evening to welcome you to the 71st Annual Academy Awards ceremony, a ceremony devoted to rewarding the many, many people this year who played me . . . or wrote about me . . . or designed lovely frocks for me. Because, darling, it's all about me!" Of course, to be all about Elizabeth is to be all about Shakespeare, as Whoopi was quick to point out: "You know who's having the biggest year—again? Shakespeare!"[2] But beneath the sequined surface of Whoopi's encomium to Shakespeare and Elizabeth was a more subtle and serious point about Hollywood's racial politics and its preference for dead and distinctly white males. Hollywood may be in love with Shakespeare, but whose Shakespeare?

The big winner that night, *Shakespeare in Love*, convinced us that anyone could love Shakespeare, provided they take lessons from the Bard himself. The film's message was well-received, as evidenced by the fact that this semitragic, semicomic love story about Shakespeare's rise from sexual impotence to poetic mastery won seven Oscars, including Best Supporting Actress, Best Actress, Best Original Screenplay, and Best Picture. Joining the company of legendary Hollywood films such as *All About Eve* (dir. Joseph L. Mankiewicz, 1950), *From Here to Eternity* (dir. Fred Zinnemann, 1953), and *Gone with the Wind* (dir. Victor Fleming, 1939), as well as recent box office hits like *Titanic* (dir. James Cameron, 1997), *Shakespeare in Love* was added to the list of seven elite films that have received thirteen or more Oscar nominations. An undeniable element of the film's success is its clever manipulation of the mystique of Shakespearean authorship, a mystique which the film perpetuates by redefining Shakespearean drama as a labor of love. However, while "the very truth and nature of love," like the truth of authorship, remains an unsolved mystery, the truth about *Shakespeare in Love* is transparent, for the film's vision of a romance that "creates riot in the heart" is anything but revolutionary. Rather, as Courtney Lehmann argues in her essay, this highly acclaimed film uses love to mystify the reality of alienated labor, which is writ large on the sexualized body of Will's collaborator-turned-chattel: Viola. If we squint our eyes at the end of the film, however, we can imagine a happy, healthy ending in which rapture wins out over ruin, as Viola treks across a sandy shoreline that looks surprisingly like Southern California and, by extension, Hollywood—a landscape eagerly awaiting its conversion to cinescape, as well as the second coming of Shakespeare—no longer as starving author, but as movie star.

Ushering in a new age of Bardolatry in Hollywood, *Shakespeare in Love* recreates Shakespeare as both cultural icon and cult figure, underscoring the way in which the Bard's plays, characters, and preoccupations have been reconstituted in contemporary cinema to shape current notions of "Shakespeare"—and of film itself. This illusion of timeless complementarity between Shakespeare and cinema is achieved principally through the film's dehistoricized, romantic vision of the Author. Indeed, underlying the plethora of witty allusions to Elizabethan figures and events that screenplay writers Marc Norman and Tom Stoppard use to create a postmodern pastiche of the Shakespearean stage-world are, oddly enough, Romantic notions of literature and authorship, notions that have been naturalized through conventional depictions of the writer in Hollywood film. These myths of authorship are neatly condensed by the film's producer, Harvey Weinstein, upon acceptance of the Academy Award for Best Picture: "This is a movie about life and art—and art and life combining is called magic."[3]

This idea that the author expresses true life through the "magic" of art is developed in the film through cinematic conventions of editing and narrative, which work together to reinforce the myth of Shakespeare as sublime "Author." Perhaps the most clichéd rendering of the Hollywood myth of the Author occurs when Will (Joseph Fiennes) struggles with writer's block in his study, his fingers stained with ink and his quarters littered with crumpled paper. This Romantic Will lacks inspiration but regains it in the female muse made flesh, Viola. With the help of his muse, Will is able to write "truth" from his own experience of "real" love, which then becomes the film's raison d'être. Viola de Lesseps (Gwyneth Paltrow) makes a bet with the formidable Elizabeth I (Judi Dench) that she can, indeed, prove that a play can "show us the truth and nature of love." But what emerges as the narrative unfolds is twentieth-century America's idea of love, nature, truth, and art—via Hollywood "magic." Because Will Shakespeare himself experiences the true love that he then, in an unmediated, transparent act of composition, transforms faithfully in his "original" story of *Romeo and Juliet*, the stage and screen audience is stunned by the "truth" of his representation of love.

Norman and Stoppard eliminate factors that would challenge this expressive realist idea of authorship, eclipsing Shakespeare's use of source material in his composition of *Romeo and Juliet* and his more fluid sense of dramatic structure, which did not correspond to modern division of acts and scenes. Will appears to write his "original" love story as he lives it, offering his script to his actors in its modern, edited form—act by act—just as Classic Hollywood cinema presents movies to us as a seamless sequence of "real" events. It is not surprising, then, as Lehmann argues, that *Shakespeare in Love* ultimately coopts Shakespearean drama as an endorsement of the Hollywood film industry, even as it mystifies the exploitative labor practices that underlie the industrial process itself.

In our visual culture, the fate of "Shakespeare" not only as Author but as cultural icon depends upon the Bard's continual reinscription in film and popular media. Addressing the recent popularization of Shakespeare in Kenneth Branagh's films, Douglas Lanier claims that Shakespeare's historical signification as theater or "high art" can no longer be sustained in a culture that is increasingly "mass." In this context, the elitist Shakespeare of old is relegated to the status of historical artifact, "the relic of a once popular, now residual cultural institution [theatre]." What defines Shakespeare's popularity now, as Richard Burt argues, is the "teensploitation" movie, which accounts for the fact that many of the upcoming Shakespeare films are clearly written for and marketed to pre-teen and teenage audiences. This trend really began with Baz Luhrmann's MTV-inspired *William Shakespeare's Romeo + Juliet*, which reframed Shakespeare for intellectually tuned-out but technologically plugged-in Generations X and Y. Besides refashioning the Bard to meet the demands of changing cultural tastes and technology, the movies perform the function of "translating" Shakespeare's plays for contemporary audiences who, as suggested above, might otherwise feel alienated by the less accessible historicity and premodern construction of plot and character found in the playtexts. Through film editing, for example, early modern characters become refigured as "fully developed" characters that fulfill modern expectations of identity, as Laurie Osborne explains in her discussion of Trevor Nunn's *Twelfth Night*. To put it simply, Shakespeare needs the movies not only to insure the ongoing cultural relevance of his plays, but also to render them accessible to postmodern audiences, bridging the gap that separates us from early modern England.

While Shakespeare clearly needs the movies to survive in the new millennium, why do the movies need Shakespeare? One hundred years ago, when cinema sought to establish itself as a legitimate art form distinct from theater, Shakespeare was called upon to invest this new industry with an aura of instant authority. But now that cinema has displaced theater as a purveyor of both high and popular culture, what *more* can Shakespeare do for the movies? Why is it that even the most radical of recent art-house and popular adaptations—from Peter Greenaway's *Prospero's Books* (1991) to Luhrmann's *Romeo + Juliet*—use Shakespeare's signature to evoke the idea of the Author as transcendent cultural authority? Though critical theory continues to insist that the figure of the Author is "dead," popular cinema replies in no uncertain terms that Shakespeare is alive and kicking. Are we, then, a postmodern culture on the verge of a modernist breakdown? Or are we simply a culture in search of someone to lend meaning to our own claims to "truth" in an age in which everyone—from T.V. evangelists to telemarketers—assumes the posture of an instant authority? In this context, what do Hollywood's recent appeals to and representations of Shakespeare's "transcendent" cultural authority imply and justify? Determining the nature, uses, and abuses of this authority is the purpose of the essays in this volume, which offer timely critical explorations of both the magic *and* monstrosity that Shakespeare and Hollywood combine to create for the new millennium.

Spectacular Shakespeare: Critical Theory and Popular Cinema brings these issues into focus through three areas of critical inquiry, "Media Imperialism: Appropriating Culture, Race, and Authority"; "Reframing Romance: Sex, Love, and Subjectivity"; and "The Politics of the Popular: From Class to Classroom." Part 1 investigates the ways in which images, identities, and even countries become objects of conquest in the name of Shakespeare, interrogating this practice from African American, British, and Mexican cultural perspectives. In "All Our *Othellos*: Black Monsters and White Masks on the American Screen," Marguerite Hailey Rippy explores the making of a distinctly "American" *Othello* in two fascinating but infrequently discussed spinoffs of Shakespeare's *Othello*: George Cukor's 1947 film *A Double Life* and a 1983 episode of the television sitcom *Cheers*. Using cultural psychoanalysis, Rippy reads these retellings of Shakespeare's play as a symptom of crisis within the white masculine psyche of 1940s and 1980s America. In their elimination of Iago's role as external agitator, both versions focus on the psychic fragmentation of a white protagonist who "becomes" the racial Other embodied in Othello. Set against the cultural backdrop of immigration, *A Double Life* performs this race change as a means of discovering an "authentic," that is, assimilated, American male identity. Similarly, in the context of Reagan's remasculinization of America, *Cheers* creates a 1980s version of the minstrel show, attempting to convert contemporary anxieties about the racially and sexually aberrant into comic entertainment. Here the Othello character is not an immigrant but an ex-con, whose questionable sexuality must be redefined through a descent into primitivism as he plays Othello to Diane's Desdemona. In both versions of *Othello*, assimilation can only occur after an Americanizing and, indeed, masculinizing ritual of racial and sexual exorcism. Appropriating the age-old authority of the Bard as a guarantor of new forms of psychic imperialism, these versions of Othello, Rippy concludes, attest to the fact that the "name of Shakespeare adds a sense of cultural legitimacy to these fundamentally contemporary interpretations of blackness and femininity."

Reversing this "Americanization" of Shakespeare on screen, Lisa Hopkins explores Shakespeare's legitimating authority from the perspective of British culture. In "'How very like the home life of our own dear queen': Ian McKellen's *Richard III*," Hopkins examines this story of a fifteenth-century upstart as a history of the present, arguing that "it is the Windsors, not the Plantagenets, whom this film represents." Set during the Abdication Crisis of 1936, McKellen's *Richard III* (dir. Richard Loncraine, 1995) multiplies the play's preoccupation with problems of legitimate rule by drawing conspicuous attention to this inaugural crisis within the House of Windsor. Designed to incite both pleasure and pain in the British collective memory, the film capitalizes on the British viewer's familiarity not only with the persons, locations, and events associated with the actual history of the royal family, but also with its representation in media forms ranging from the tabloids to the British television series *Blackadder*. It is almost as if, in McKellen's *Richard III*, Shakespeare becomes an honorary member of the paparazzi—both critical of and complicit in the ongoing history of internecine conflict which the film and play conspire to document. But McKellen's pursuit of an unrelenting British referentiality also stages a coup that transcends this conflict; as Hopkins demonstrates, McKellen is attempting to usurp Hollywood's hold on Shakespeare, reappropriating the Bard's cultural authority in hopes of redeeming a struggling British film industry.

Rather than reinforcing cultural boundaries, Baz Luhrmann ruptures them, offering *William Shakespeare's Romeo + Juliet* (1996) as a consumer-friendly tour de force of contemporary visual media. In "(Un)doing the Book 'without Verona walls': A View from the Receiving End of Baz Luhrmann's *William Shakespeare's Romeo + Juliet*," Alfredo Michel Modenessi explores the idea of the cinema spectator as "tourist" in Luhrmann's film, taking us on a frenetic trip through postmodern inter-textuality that begins with the Montague boys sporting *Magnum P.I.* shirts and ends with the "interactive trip" offered by the film's CD-ROM accompaniment. But Luhrmann's dexterous solicitations of the viewer's participation in this interactive trip stop short of acknowledging the film's debt to the rich Mexican culture that provides much of its imagery, as well as its shooting location. In an exhaustive inventory of the distinctly Mexican icons and artistry woven into the postmodern fabric of Luhrmann's film, Modenessi demonstrates the ways in which this cultural backdrop functions as "a rarefied atmosphere capable of exercising a certain fascination over the viewer—without specifying its Mexican 'source.'" As a result, Mexico becomes an icon of the failure of the postmodern aesthetic to generate—from the dissident threads of its resistance to received authority, grand narratives, and totalizing meanings—anything more than "depletion through saturation": "In Luhrmann's film, what seems to begin as an interesting take on how living conditions in Verona Beach reflect intra- and inter- social, ethnic,

and cultural conflicts, ends up being very close in spirit to the oldest stereotypes of a land inhabited by big-sombreroed and *mucho-macho* bandidos."

Part 2, "Reframing Romance: Sex, Love, and Subjectivity," shifts the
angle of critique from the national to the individual, examining the process
of early modern identity-formation through the erotic commerce of courtship and marriage. Much like postmodern notions of fragmented identity,
early modern subjectivity, as Laurie Osborne demonstrates, emerged from
the intersection of conflicting discursive and historical forces. Yet just as
Shakespeare's plays manage to produce the illusion of coherent characters
from discontinuous fragments, so too, cinematic editing creates an illusion
of continuity from cutting, splicing, and rearranging film footage. In "Cutting up Characters: The Erotic Politics of Trevor Nunn's *Twelfth Night*"
(1996), Osborne exposes the impossibility of bringing these special effects
to bear on a character like Cesario/Viola, who, in Nunn's adaptation, becomes the site of a clash between competing ideologies of gender and romantic love. While Cesario is framed through a twentieth-century ideology
based on an equality of the sexes, Viola is framed by the more traditional
ideology of romantic love, which is predicated on hierarchical relationships between men and women. Ironically, then, despite Nunn's masterful
cutting up and redistribution of Shakespeare's text, he ultimately undermines his own continuity effects. As Osborne concludes, Cesario/Viola
emerges as "an unreadably complex figure, whose 'depth' becomes obscure when too many pieces of cinematic behavior are attributed to 'him,'"
thus exposing—in both early modern playtexts and postmodern cinema—
"the process and problems of fragments producing character."

In contrast to Nunn, Branagh, according to Samuel Crowl, creates a masterful synthesis between the ideologies of gender and romantic love. In
"The Marriage of Shakespeare and Hollywood: Kenneth Branagh's *Much
Ado about Nothing*" (1993), Crowl reads Shakespeare's play and Branagh's
film through the ideological and filmic conventions of the Hollywood
"screwball" comedies of the 1940s, analyzing Branagh's unique ability to
tap into "the structure and romantic energy of Shakespearean comedy buried in the heart of these remarkable films." This energy, as Stanley Cavell
characterizes it in his classic redefinition of the "screwball" genre as "comedies of remarriage," stems from the insistent dramatization of "equality of
consciousness between a man and a woman." By emphasizing Beatrice
and Benedick's prior involvement and their shared decision to reunite, the
film generates "a singular social revolution" against the conventional and
repressive patriarchal social order embodied in figures like Claudio and
Don Pedro. With the help of Emma Thompson's personal brilliance,
Branagh's *Much Ado* creates "a perfectly realized Shakespearean antecedent" to the twentieth-century ideology of gender equality. This synthesiz-

ing move between the early modern and the postmodern in turn suggests the ideal metaphor for Branagh's larger project of producing "a marriage, resembling that of Beatrice and Benedick, between Shakespeare and Hollywood."

In "*Shakespeare in Love*: Romancing the Author, Mastering the Body," Courtney Lehmann critiques precisely this "marriage" by exposing the gender and labor exploitation that underlies Hollywood's romance with Shakespeare the Author. The refrain that has become virtually synonymous with *Shakespeare in Love*'s erotic theory of authorship is the phrase "it's a mystery," an expression that connects the very real mystery of Shakespearean authorship to the less ponderous magic of Hollywood film. But mystery is closely aligned with mystification and, as Marx has famously argued, with commodity fetishism, which reduces social relations between people to relations between things. At first glance, *Shakespeare in Love* reverses this formula, offering a vision of people who have "relations" in order to produce "things"—specifically, the play of *Romeo and Juliet*—the commodity destined to save Henslowe from indigence and Will from impotence. Upon closer examination, however, we find that the film's representation of the Author as a figure who *consumes* as a prelude to and a condition of production imitates the cycle of commodification in its purest, *late* capitalistic form. For Will's love, like the deterritorializing logic of Capital, is a love that respects no boundaries: it traverses the institutionalized limits of sexuality, class, gender, and theater. The logic that the film consumer is encouraged to buy into, then, is that by consuming without limits, we actually become more creative, more (re)productive individuals. But in so doing, we also become complicit in an exploitative, erotic commerce that demands not merely passive buying, but ultimately, the selling of Viola into domestic slavery. By the end of *Shakespeare in Love*, it is no mystery that Viola, and not the play, is the "thing" to be consumed, enjoyed, and reproduced for profit. Thus, what *Shakespeare in Love* teaches us is that the play is *not* the thing, for only cinema can duplicate the efficiency of this process, and only Hollywood can create such a pleasing mystification of labor in the name of love.

Further demystifying the commodity logic of Hollywood cinema, Part 3, "The Politics of the Popular: From Class to Classroom," analyzes the reception of Shakespeare on screen in settings ranging from the cineplex to the classroom. Exploring the changing dynamics of Shakespeare's popularity within mainstream culture, these essays attest to the fact that despite the monolithic nature of the terms "mass" and "popular," there is nothing singular about the audience they imply, for both concepts are continually redefined by the contingent interaction of historical forces, market trends, and directorial discretion. In "'Art thou base, common, and popular?': The Cultural Politics of Kenneth Branagh's *Hamlet*," Douglas Lanier analyzes the contradictory ideological investments of this actor/director's popularizing approach to Shakespeare. While Branagh has become synonymous with a concept of Shakespeare liberated from the taint of elitism, his work, Lanier argues, is also inflected with a competing expression of "actor militancy" that seeks a community of patrons weaned on British theater and versed in the appreciation of Shakespearean artistry. Thus, art-house films like *Swan Song* (1992) and *A Midwinter's Tale* (1995) lament the passing of the golden age of the British theatrical community even as they attempt to recreate theater's trademark connection between actor and audience through a filmic medium. But as Lanier explains, these films nervously suggest that this new audience may not be able to grasp the artistry of the Shakespearean actor, and it is at this juncture that Branagh's commitment to "populism" collides with his "actor-militancy." These tensions culminate in Branagh's adaptation of *Hamlet* (1996). Though shamelessly commercial, Branagh's *Hamlet* generates a far more complex shuffle of production values, market values, and human values than its market-orientation implies, for it attempts to extend the problem of community-building to larger political structures of state and nation. Ironically, though, what the film ultimately endorses is a return to the "aristocratic codes of conduct" associated with the family life of the Danish court, which "offers the only viable possibility for passion and affective bonding so central to Branagh's vision of cultural and political community, no matter how corrupt or class-coded order may have become under Claudius's rule."

In her analysis of Hamlet's recent "cameo appearances" in *Last Action Hero* (dir. John McTiernan, 1993), *Renaissance Man* (dir. Penny Marshall, 1994), and *Clueless* (dir. Amy Heckerling, 1995), Elizabeth A. Deitchman focuses on Hollywood's surprising efficacy as a teacher of Shakespeare in "From the Cinema to the Classroom: Hollywood Teaches *Hamlet*." Inspired by Mel Gibson's action-hero reinvention of Shakespeare's gloomy Dane in Zeffirelli's 1990 film, Hamlet emerges in these three films as a Renaissance man turned man of action, who teaches students valuable lessons in self-improvement. These *Hamlet*-inspired lessons range from learning to distinguish between good and bad parenting in *Last Action Hero* to learning how to maximize physical and intellectual potential in *Renaissance Man* and *Clueless*. Additionally, all three of these films feature Shakespearean classroom settings wherein important issues pertaining to contemporary pedagogy are elicited. *Last Action Hero* revolves around the problem of the short-attention span generation and the role of cinema and wish-fulfillment in engaging students' interest in Shakespeare, while *Renaissance Man* explicitly addresses Shakespeare's suitability for students of below-average abilities, as well as the Bard's appropriation by disempowered members of society. Finally, *Clueless*, which explicitly cites Mel Gibson's performance as Hamlet, serves as an extensive comment on Shakespeare's cinematic potential to break down the barriers between elite and popular culture that once rendered Shakespeare inaccessible to students. Thus, Deitchman concludes, "while Shakespeare's cameo appearances in these three films may suggest that we see more of Mel Gibson than Shakespeare at the movies, Hollywood's pedagogical resourcefulness plays a crucial role in helping to redefine cultural ideologies for students and teachers alike."

Annalisa Castaldo explores this potential of cinematic renderings of Shakespeare to engage students' understanding of the fascinating instability of the Renaissance text in "The Film's the Thing: Using Film in the Shakespearean Classroom." Complementing Deitchman's analysis of the multiple meanings that accompany a play with a complex textual history like *Hamlet*, Castaldo considers the pedagogical value of "dissonance" as a constitutive feature of Shakespearean textuality. As recent breakthroughs in editing theories have demonstrated, just as there is no singular Shakespearean author-function, there is also no such thing as an authoritative Shakespearean text. Accordingly, by drawing attention to the ways in which shot-construction, composition, and editing practices disassemble Shakespeare's plays in their effort to reassemble them, film adaptations actually simulate the contingent production and preservation of Renaissance texts.

The most promising locus for the ongoing reproduction and preservation of these texts is the subgenre of the Shakespearean "teen movie," which has increased in popularity in recent years. In his afterword, entitled "T(e)en Things I Hate about Girlene Shakesploitation Flicks in the Late 1990s, or, Not so Fast Times at Shakespeare High," Richard Burt speculates about where this Shakespeare and cinema craze is headed, focusing on a new generation of potential Bardolaters. Examining the gamut of "teensploitation" films that either cite or adapt Shakespeare, including Almereyda's *Hamlet*, Burt contextualizes this flood of films in light of pop culture precedents like *Clueless* and Luhrmann's *Romeo + Juliet*, as well as "high culture" antecedents like *Shakespeare in Love*, the new *Midsummer Night's Dream*, and *Titus*. However, Burt concentrates his analysis of Shakespearean market and audience trends on two recent films: *10 Things I Hate about You* and *Never Been Kissed*. The tendency of these films, he argues, is not merely to "dumb down" Shakespeare's language and plots, but also to reorient the social complexities of Shakespearean drama within pre-teen fantasies of popularity, wherein class issues are reduced to a classroom divided between "losers" and "hotties." Consequently, these films "neuter" Shakespeare's plays, undoing their feminist and homoerotic potential by overemphasizing traditional male authority and positioning Shakespeare as a ticket to exclusively heterosexual success. Rather than using Shakespeare to critique the cultural repression that has led to staggering levels of adolescent violence, the "teensploi" films of the late 1990s use

Shakespeare as a timeless resource for sexually aggressive teens. Thus, as teen sex is made safe through Shakespeare, Shakespeare is made safe for a new generation of teens.

Who would have thought that Shakespeare, the ultimate "Renaissance man," would become *the* man of the new millennium in Hollywood? The recent barrage of Shakespeare films serves as a reminder of the codependency between Bard and screen that has existed since the inception of cinema itself. And clearly, the destinies of both are intertwined, though not even *Shakespeare in Love* can answer the question: "How does it end?" Preferring theoretical inquiry to "mystery," the essays in this volume initiate timely considerations of the cultural ends and the cinematic means of Shakespeare's sudden celebrity in popular film. As *Shakespeare in Love* suggests, Shakespeare may be the once and future Author, but the time for generating critical and pedagogical practices for interrogating the spectacle of his authority is, as Iago puts it, "now, now, very now."

NOTES

1. 71st Annual Academy Awards, dir. Louis J. Horvitz, 4 hr. 30 min., ABC, 21 March 1999.

2. 71st Annual Academy Awards.

3. 71st Annual Academy Awards

FILMS CITED

Clueless. Directed by Amy Heckerling. 1 hr. 37 min. Paramount Pictures, 1995. Videocassette.

A Double Life. Directed by George Cukor. 1 hr. 47 min. Universal International/Kanin Productions, 1947. Videocassette.

Hamlet. Directed by Kenneth Branagh. 3 hr. 58 min. Castle Rock Entertainment, 1996. Videocassette.

"Homicidal Ham." Episode of *Cheers*. Directed by James Burrows. 30 min. NBC Television, 27 October, 1983.

The Last Action Hero. Directed by John McTiernan. 2 hr. 11 min. Columbia/Tri Star Pictures. 1993. Videocassette.

A Midwinter's Tale. Directed by Kenneth Branagh. 1 hr. 39 min. Castle Rock Entertainment and Midwinter Films, 1995. Laserdisc.

Much Ado about Nothing. Directed by Kenneth Branagh. 1 hr. 51 min. Renaissance Films and Samuel Goldwyn, 1993. DVD.

Never Been Kissed. Directed by Raja Gosnell. 1 hr. 48 min. Twentieth Century Fox, 1999. DVD.

Renaissance Man. Produced and directed by Penny Marchall. 2 hr. 8 min. Touchstone Pictures, 1994. Videocassette.

Richard III. directed by Richard Loncraine. 1 hr. 44 min. MGM/UA, 1995.

71st Annual Academy Awards. Directed by Louis J. Horvitz. 4 hr. 30 min. ABC Television, 21 March 1999.

Shakespeare in Love. Directed by John Madden. 2 hr. 2 min. Miramax Films/Universal Pictures, 1998. Videocassette.

Swan Song. Directed by Kenneth Branagh. 23 min. Samual Goldwyn, 1992. Videocassette.

10 Things I Hate about You. Directed by Gil Junger. 1 hr. 37 min. Touchstone, 1999. DVD.

Twelfth Night. Directed by Trevor Nunn. 2 hr. 13 min. Fine Line Features/New Line Cinema, 1996. Videocassette.

William Shakespeare's Romeo + Juliet. Directed by Baz Luhrmann. 2 hr. Twentieth Century Fox/Bazmar, Films, 1996. Videocassette.

Spectacular Shakespeare

Part I
Media Imperialism:
Appropriating Culture, Race, and Authority

All Our *Othellos*:
Black Monsters and White Masks
on the American Screen

MARGUERITE HAILEY RIPPY

Othello . . . endures all contemporary reworkings—and it always seems
relevant. Whatever we do to *Othello*, the play will survive.
> —Jude Kelly, Director

O. J. Simpson was supposed to have transcended race. Yet racial issues
now swirl all around him. He is no longer Hermes hurtling through an
airport, but the tragic Moor, tortured by the imagined betrayal of his
alabaster bride. Never mind that Iago is nowhere to be found, or that
this Othello failed to fall on his blade: commentators, searching for
Shakespearean analogues, have found one with a racial subtext.
> —Ellis Cose, "Caught between Two Worlds"

It is the cause, it is the cause, my soul,
Let me not name it to you, you chaste stars:
It is the cause. Yet I'll not shed her blood,
Nor scar that whiter skin of hers than snow,
And smooth as monumental alabaster.
Yet she must die, else she'll betray more men.
Put out the light, and then put out the light.
> —William Shakespeare, *Othello*

THERE ARE CERTAIN STORIES WE CANNOT RESIST TELLING AND RETELLING AS A
culture, altering the terms slightly, but retaining the fundamental structure
of the narrative. These stories are transformed in their reiteration from anecdote to archetype, from entertainment to myth. *Othello* has become such
a tale, retold by the media, political leaders, and frequently invoked to conjure visual representations of a taboo image in American culture: the vio-

lent black man contrasted to a passive white female victim. Director Jude
Kelly raises an interesting question in the quotation that opens this essay—
does Shakespeare's Othello "survive" any adaptation? This essay suggests
that Othello lives on in American popular culture, but that he has traded
performative complexity for stereotypical brutality in the American mind,
in no small part because of the mysterious disappearance of his confidant,
Iago.

   Othello, retold in twentieth-century American terms, embodies the simultaneous attraction to and repulsion from blackness as a sexual image, a
quality that Toni Morrison has described as "delicious sensuality coupled
with demands for purity and restraint."[1] But Othello also reflects back into
American society its fascination with the black body as a site of displacement for the guilt and anxiety of the white American subject, a process
popularized through a variety of texts preoccupied with the threat of lynch-
ing and castration in relation to white femininity.[2] These castration texts
reveal a cultural fascination with the threat of black masculinity in relation
to white femininity in which blackness and femininity are used not as binary opposites, but as interrelated and mutually oppressive constructions.
Following the tradition of the castration text, twentieth-century American
adaptations focus on the skin rather than the soul.

   Looking on Desdemona before he murders her, Othello is obsessed with
the whiteness of her skin and her relationship to his own self-definition as
a man. He is both allured and repulsed by the paradox of sexuality within
white femininity, and the speech that opens act 5, scene 2, garners the most
attention in American versions of *Othello*. The moral associations of race
are not unique to the twentieth century; Anthony Barthelemy observes that
"In the Christian tradition whiteness is desired, blackness is condemned.
White is the color of the regenerated, of the saved; black is the color of the
damned, the lost."[3] But the persistence of this moral imagery has converged
with nationalism, as Toni Morrison contends when she explains that in the
American tradition, "Whiteness alone is mute, meaningless, unfathomable,
pointless," needing blackness to speak meaningfully.[4] Morrison moves the
terms of the debate from a bipolar model to an interdependent model, in
which the process of building national and racial identity is based on simultaneous anxiety and desire. In this sense, the formation Morrison lays
before us for racial identification employs the same psycho-sexual elements
as gendered models of subjectivity.

   Othello explores the tragic relationship between gender and racial identity and because of this has achieved widespread recognition in American
culture, often based on very free interpretations of the original text. Becoming part of the narrative of American racial heritage, *Othello* grew popular upon the stages of early America, and it was performed in both impromptu
stage settings and elegant urban theaters.[5] Bastardized versions of *Othello*

appeared as comic entertainment in the American minstrel shows, translating the noble Moor into the tradition of Tambo and Bones.[6] *Othello* continues to appear on the American landscape in moments of political fervor and social definition; it was, for example, (mis)quoted at the Thomas-Hill hearings,[7] and more recently, it was exploited in the national media obsession with sports icon O. J. Simpson.[8] The rhetoric surrounding American racial obsession attempts to simplify the Othello myth into an image of the black sexualized beast threatening a white female victim, and frequently American versions use this image to demonize both white women and black men, in opposition to the white male psyche.[9] The erasure of Iago from the text seems to intensify in "low-brow" adaptations mass marketed to vast audiences. Two such adaptations, the 1947 Academy Award winning film *A Double Life* (dir. George Cukor) and the episode "Homicidal Ham" of the widely acclaimed television series *Cheers,*[10] erase Iago from the text entirely, internalizing blackness as a deviant aspect of the white male psyche. The elimination of Iago changes the terms of the production entirely because in these versions blackness signifies psychosis within the white man— rather a simpler version than the original text's suggestion that Othello's "blackness" resides in an external set of associations that Othello is seduced into accepting by his white confidant. The erasure of Iago is all the more striking in a play that has only thirteen speaking parts and in which traditionally the dramatic and critical focus has been on the relationship between Othello and Iago.[11]

In contrast, the American cultural insistence on perceiving blackness as a deviant masculine threat to the white female body, in effect, genders race. By examining theoretical models of masculine identity in crisis, we can begin to unravel and explore the cultural attraction to the image of a black man who sexually desires and punishes the white woman. In the aftermath of slavery and reconstruction, blackness becomes a fetishistic symbol of castration anxiety, aiding in the formation of a deeply ambivalent and fragmented white masculine American identity. The black male body was a tangible reminder of social, economic, and sexual power lost to the white male slave owners, a power that had often enforced itself through white male violence excused by the myth of the black man as rapist.

The two popular screen representations of *Othello* discussed here tell tales of a white masculine psyche in crisis, using both the black male and white female body to enact fantasies of fear and desire that eventually subside and are contained within patriarchal white dictates, revealing an American culture that is both titillated and appalled by black masculine eroticism. Thus, both the black male and white female bodies in these versions are mere toys for a central white male imagination. The name of Shakespeare adds a sense of cultural legitimacy to these fundamentally contemporary interpretations of blackness and femininity.[12]

Cultural "Spin": Rendering an American *Othello*

The text of the original *Othello* complicates the social ideology of race, positioning race in relation to the construction of self, society, and gender. Thus, the subject of the original text is the fragility of the self as a social construction, rather than the representation of an essential racial identity. Within American film, however, the exploration of racial boundaries is often limited to the psychological identity of the white male, making Othello's tale conform to nineteenth-century models of colonial consciousness.[13] *Othello*, elevated to a mythical tableau in American productions, has incorporated the social and economic uses of race into the psychological realm. Its continuous popularity arises in large part from its adaptability to modern culture by representing race not as a social reality, but as a psychological reflection of white male anxiety.

Contemporary American adaptations of *Othello* demonstrate the conflation of race and sex in the American white male psyche and employ race to represent conflicts of white male consciousness by projecting white taboo anxieties onto a black background. Although the disturbing potential of black sexual violence provoked by white femininity can be seen in Renaissance textual versions,[14] in American society Iago's role of luring Othello into spiritual blackness frequently becomes the *exclusive* domain of Desdemona. Traditionally Iago acts as the social-constructor, building the myth of race with all its tragic dimensions before the eyes of the audience, but in the two American adaptations discussed here the Iago tempter becomes an internalized version of Othello himself. Blackness represents the moral weakness of the white male protagonist, a weakness that is invoked by the spectacle of the white female body. *Othello* as depicted in *A Double Life* and *Cheers* eliminates Iago from the text and depicts the Desdemona figure as prompting the jealousy of the Othello figure. The story becomes that of the white man in metaphorical blackface who is forced to insanity by the female object itself, rather than the story of a black man seduced to jealousy by his fairer male companion, Iago. In this way, transgressive violent sexual desire is doubly displaced from the white male psyche onto the black sexualized beast and the white female object.

Nationality and Psychoanalysis: The Disintegrating Self in American Culture

Socially, economically, and politically the stage was already set for these twentieth-century visions of Othello as the immoral double of the white male protagonist. Colette Guillaumin maintains that the construction of race—like that of class and gender—was a reaction to bourgeois individualism, and race was redefined according to socially and economically appropriate power in the industrial era.[15] The network of associations surrounding blackness as race has expanded into what Toni Morrison terms "American Africanism," which includes the "denotative and connotative blackness that African peoples have come to signify" in American culture and literature.[16] As a means of representing who was empowered and who was not, blackness in Morrison's trope of Africanism becomes "inextricable from the definition of Americanness—from its origins on through its integrated or disintegrating twentieth-century self."[17]

American culture's fascination with the establishment of identity in relationship to race, defining the "authentic" white American against blackness and primitivism, has been well defined by Morrison, as she observes: "Americans choose to talk about themselves through and within a sometimes allegorical, sometimes metaphorical, but always choked representation of an Africanist presence."[18] Specifically, the disempowerment of American blackness positions white experience as empowered, but only in reference to the existence of the suffering black subject. Thus American culture needs the spectacle of black suffering to constitute white empowerment, and as both Frantz Fanon and Ralph Ellison have argued, the black male body becomes an article of cultural significance. Fanon and Ellison describe dominant culture as based upon a black/white dichotomy of racial power, established through a process of masking and unmasking. Consequently, the performance of blackness constitutes an American tradition.

Ellison in particular discusses the importance of masking to American racial identity, asserting that "Americans began their revolt from the English fatherland when they dumped the tea into the Boston Harbor, masked as Indians, and the mobility of the society created in this limitless space has encouraged the use of the mask for good and evil ever since."[19] But from the colonized perspective of Frantz Fanon, the racial mask becomes a self-limiting device in which the black man struggles to choose action over passivity, but finds himself identifying with the white mask rather than with his own black skin. Like Othello, he chooses identification with a collective white consciousness, rejecting his own blackness. Fanon enacts his own theory and reproduces many of the traditional terms that he seeks to critique, particularly in reference to femininity. For Fanon, the white woman continues to represent civilization, and the conquest of her body symbolizes the acquisition of subjectivity through dominance. Fanon himself is aware of the fundamental paradox of his psychoanalytic model of black subjectivity. Despairing the predicament of racial identity, he movingly remarks, "straddling Nothingness and Infinity, I began to weep."[20] But when he asks, does not the "fear of rape cry out for rape?" we realize how lost he truly is in his acceptance of dominant tropes of violent black masculinity and passive white femininity that are so prevalent in twentieth-century

American versions of the *Othello* myth.[21] Choosing gender identity over race, Fanon ultimately accepts masculine dominance over black solidarity. The finality of his rejection of cross-gender identification rings in his assertion regarding the woman of color, "I know nothing of her."[22]

Whereas Fanon raises the self-destructive possibilities of masking for the colonized subject of the Antilles,[23] Ellison's discussion of masking reveals its importance to American identity, making the father a figure of national importance mainly through his provocation of the son's rebellion. Ellison's equation of masking with rebellion against a father figure is a common motif in American film and is particularly associated with the assimilation of immigrants into the American identity through films such as *The Jazz Singer* (dir. Alan Crosland, 1927). Immigrants searching for an authentic claim to American experience used blackness to represent a native presence; thus, the immigrant needed to subjugate blackness in order to participate in the American tradition of colonization. As Morrison observes, "immigrant populations (and much immigrant literature) understood their 'Americanness' as an opposition to the resident black population."[24] Such constructions of identity from formulations of opposition have become central to American experience, and as Ellison confesses, "My cultural background, like that of most Americans, is dual."[25] Much like the oedipal formulation of gender identity, constructed racial and social identities define the American subject only through opposition to a subjected counterpart.

Although Morrison discusses these racial images primarily in terms of American *literature*, Michael Rogin posits that American *film* appropriates black race in much the same way:

> American film was born from the conjunction between southern defeat in the Civil War, black resubordination, and national reintegration; the rise of the multiethnic, industrial metropolis; and the emergence of mass entertainment, expropriated from its black roots, as the locus of Americanization.[26]

Thus, by the twentieth century, authentic American experience as reflected in American film was based upon alignment with established cultural dictates that linked economic production, social status, and whiteness, in contrast to blackness and its associated social and economic exclusion.

TWENTIETH-CENTURY *OTHELLO* ON SCREEN: THE *OTHELLO* WITHIN

Othello told in any temporal mode is a story of conflict between essential and represented identity, manifested in the crossing over of race. Recurrent allusions to white and black, fair and dark, throughout the play characterize blackness as base, sinful, and deceptive. The text moves Othello to be that which he least seems to be, but at the same time to be that which he is; that is to say, it moves him to be a murderer and a manifestation of the symbolic traits of the black man. But the traditional story is also a story of Iago's double identity, proof of his statement: "I am not what I am."[27] Reputation and the truth of identity are central to the plot and are referred to in pivotal speeches by Cassio (2.3.256–59), Iago (3.3.160–66), Lodovico (4.1.265–69), and Othello (5.2.347–65). *Othello* inverts the Renaissance stereotype of a Moor, with the white Iago acting as the deceptive villain. Iago himself emphasizes his link to Othello and the malleability of identity and appearance as he offers, "Were I the Moor, I would not be Iago. / In following him, I follow but myself" (1.1.58–59).

Iago's statement can be explained in part by Slavoj Žižek's analysis of the dissolution of boundaries between self and other. According to Žižek's analysis, in the struggle between the self and the Other, the outside Other becomes more than just a mask. It becomes an integral part of the self, a point of origin by which we define our own existence, either in conjunction with or in opposition to the Other. The process of masking and unmasking various identities becomes more than a game; it becomes an alternate reality. By pretending to be that which we define ourselves against, we become the thing itself: in "social-symbolic reality things ultimately *are* precisely what they *pretend* to be."[28] This exchange between the "real" and the "unreal" becomes a type of border crossing, and by extension of the metaphor, of racechange. As an outward, physically visible system of signification, the black/white racial border remains one of the primary social borders of American society, equaled only by the borders of gender.

Centered on the issue of male identity in relationship to race and gender, *Othello* textually incorporates the locus of American desire and identification. The actor playing Othello in the two American versions discussed here is a common man; his commonness is emphasized. He is the American viewer, the participant in American experience. When he confronts his latent "black" identity in Othello, he becomes a crosser of boundaries, a changer of race. The dissolution of such a potent axis of identification can have only one result, the madness that emerges when the barrier between "real" and "reality," self and Other, is eliminated.[29]

In a series of films ranging from 1931 to 1985, the American screen has repeatedly depicted *Othello* exclusively in terms of the degeneration of the white male psyche. These productions do not portray Othello as a "real" black man; instead they seek to employ the construction of race self-consciously as a means of discovering "true" white male identity. The problem of *Othello* shifts from black Othello's seduction into self-abasement by the white Iago, to a depiction of the white man's seduction by a black monster within, provoked by his desire for the white female body. These versions use as a frame an actor who, in playing Othello, becomes aware of his wife's threatening sexuality. As the dramatic frame extends to encompass the world surrounding the dramatic production, the woman outside the theater becomes a "real" threat. She begins to replace Iago as a figure of seduction into darkness. Cinematic versions of this tale seem to first emerge in *Carnival* (dir. Harley Knowles, 1921), a silent film produced by Alliance (Great Britain and Italy). It reappears in *Carnival: Venetian Nights* (dir. Herbert Wilcox, 1931) and *Men Are Not Gods* (dir. Walter Reisch, 1936).[30] Although these films were cooperative efforts among British and American actors, writers, and producers, I would argue that they represent a distinctly popular cinematic form of *Othello* that is broadly embraced by American culture precisely because it emphasizes the formation of white male identity via sexuality and race.

A DOUBLE LIFE

The popular Americanization of this technique clearly occurs in *A Double Life*, in which the husband and wife who are cast to play Othello and Desdemona are immigrants to America.[31] Othello, as presented in *A Double Life*, depicts the desire of the immigrant son to establish his American identity. The black interior self is linked to the immigrant identity and the rejected foreign father—the psychological Other. *A Double Life* supports Ellison's vision of American experience as a masked rebellion against the father of the old world, which establishes the social mobility of the son. The white man splits into two identities, one monstrous black and one civilized white. Particularly relevant to the immigrant experience, the authenticity of white male power can be established only in relationship to the disempowerment of the black male. The formulation of racial identity is accomplished by means of embracing or rejecting traits as dictated by dominant culture—a process that also forges an American identity from an immigrant identity. These two processes of identification in American society are inextricably linked in the film *A Double Life*.

   A Double Life linked popular film genres, stars, and sentiments of its era, culminating in an Academy Award for its popular leading man, Ronald Colman. It has been regarded as a *film noir*, a genre that Ian Cameron perceives as designed to "probe the darker areas of sexuality" and to explore a "crisis in masculinity."[32] However, *A Double Life* accommodates many genres, and it is difficult to categorize it as ultimately belonging to any one. As a melodrama, it represents the impact of external forces on the internal psyche: *A Double Life* externalizes the emotional/moral state through the metaphor of blackface.[33] Colman and Signe Hasso play immigrant actors (Tony and Brita) who, although divorced, still play opposite each other and maintain a close relationship. Brita has taught Tony how to take on a part and live it as though it were real.[34] This ability will be the source of his destruction; he has learned his lesson too well. In particular, Tony is haunted by his immigrant roots and, particularly, his Cockney father's ambitions for him. As he first contemplates playing Othello, he recalls his father's ambitions for him, imitating his accent as he exhorts his son to "get the best of it" for "the two of us." Tony contrasts his father's failed ambition, represented through his blue-collar life in which he dies a doorman, with Brita's successful shared ambition with Tony to become a theatrical star. Both Brita and Tony's father hold ambitions for him, but Brita understands the rules for achieving the American Dream of social mobility, whereas Tony's father dies frozen within the British class system. Tony's Othello role resists Brita's advice, and when Tony dons his blackface he is transformed into immigrant, alien, criminal. He is driven by social relationships between his ex-wife, his lover, and the American concepts of race and class. As Tony crosses social boundaries, he crosses psychological boundaries as well.

Moreover, *A Double Life* adapts the horror genre to make blackness a monstrous Other transforming the British gentleman into a crazed killer. As Kobena Mercer notes, "Women are invariably the victims of the acts of terror unleashed by . . . the monster as non-human Other . . . But as the predatory force against which the hero has to compete, the monster itself occupies a 'masculine' position in relation to the female victim."[35] The black man serves as monstrous Other in *A Double Life* since, like a werewolf or a vampire, he is a monster concealed within the white mask. Tony's monstrous Other is Othello, who threatens and takes female lives in order to sate his sexual and psychological appetites.

As the actors within *A Double Life* act out *Othello*, blackness becomes representative of the immigrant son's failure to reject his "darker" immigrant identity and assume an American identity. Tony is contrasted with Brita, who has assimilated American identity and continuously struggles against her casting in *Othello*. She begs Tony not to perform the part of Othello, saying, "It's been fun this past year, Tony. . . There were times when I even thought we could make it together again, but I know we couldn't if we got mixed up in an *Othello* sort of thing."[36] She knows that racial crossing will be the end of her relationship with Tony since he will take on the "blackness," both literal and figurative, of Othello. Brita perceives what Tony does not, that miscegenation is a powerful taboo in 1947, as it was in 1604. In fact, in 1947, the marriage between black and white is depicted as destructive not only to the black man but to the white man as well.[37] The mere empowerment of a black man by a white man is destructive; when coupled with desire for a white woman it is doubly so. Brita recognizes that in Tony's internalization of Othello, he will threaten not only his Americanization, but hers as well. She wants to stay within the definitions of white female star, not wearing the cloak of the interracially desiring and desired Desdemona.

Once Tony begins to perceive himself as a black man, he becomes obsessed with white female sexuality. After looking at his image in the reflection of a window and seeing an exotic Moor returning his gaze, Tony enters a back-street bar and finds a sexual surrogate for Brita. Pat Kroll,[38] the blonde waitress who serves him, becomes another representative of American experience. She comes from the Midwest and exemplifies the American ideal of the industrious blue-collar worker. Her female sexuality, however, makes this image potentially transgressive. Unlike Brita, she represents the "bad" actress, a failed version of the white male ideal of womanhood and the epitome of the lower-class fallen woman. Tony, a fallen man within himself, the blackface image still hanging over him, is attracted to and repelled by her, just as he was by the Othello character. He is at the extreme pole of his existence, reveling in the very Otherness against which he has risen to power as an American icon. When Tony and Othello have merged, he says, "I've reached the nightmare stage." The complete annihilation of socially constructed barriers is a dream, a nightmare, and a simultaneous reality.

After Tony internalizes black Othello, he elevates white female sexuality to the status of Žižek's "sublime object." The sublime object is an ordinary object elevated to the status of the unattainable object of desire and, according to Žižek, "the power of fascination exerted by a sublime image always announces a lethal dimension."[39] By masking himself in Othello, Tony loses Brita while simultaneously elevating her status of desirability. Thus, he seeks a sexual surrogate, which he finds in the quintessential blonde American waitress. The images of American experience and female sexuality are conflated. Tony, as immigrant, desires American authenticity; Tony, as black man, desires dominance over the white female body. The black man is presented as an interior, sexualized form of the immigrant. By agreeing to play Othello, Tony takes on a "false" identity, the identity against which authentic American experience is determined. Thus, he rejects his status as having achieved "true" American experience, that of upper-class celebrity, and instead embraces a figure of exclusion from that American experience. The irony is that, by pursuing the blonde American icon, Tony's American dream becomes a nightmare—he mentally transforms Pat into an American seductress, but because his desire also represents racial transgression, his interior "black beast" draws them to their destruction.

The film employs mirror scenes to represent the pivotal psychological moments of inner conflict in Tony, and the mirror image is used to depict Tony's attraction to and eventual internalization of Othello. R. Dixon Smith refers to these scenes as "demonic reflections of the second soul" and further notes that "Swallowed whole by Othello the actor finally succumbs, and the mirror image devours what is left of Tony John."[40] Again, the image of blackness is conflated with the monstrous cannibalistic force threatening to consume white identity.

A Double Life shows the performance of only the final scenes of *Othello*. Taken out of the context of the noble Moor, these scenes demarcate the white actor as lured into becoming a racially distinct Other, paradoxically contained within his own mind. Cinematically, these scenes are powerfully delivered, with the help of Milton Krasner's cinematography. Odd perspectives and sounds surround the scene of Tony/Othello's climactic, murderous insanity. The last act of *Othello* actually spans several scenes in *A Double Life*, as Tony kills the Desdemona-Brita surrogate, Pat Kroll, and then returns to the theater and his on-stage role of Othello before killing himself. The action that provokes Tony's murderous, dark insanity is Brita's refusal to remarry him. Immediately, he blames her refusal on the attentions of their theatrical publicist, Bill Friend. Retreating from Tony's jealous rage, Brita slams the door to her bedroom and sends his face into a dark shadow. At this point, Tony enters into a dialogue with himself, partly phrased in his own words, partly in the speech of Othello. He leaves Brita's house in a murderous stupor and wanders toward the neighborhood of Pat Kroll. The names Brita, Pat, and Desdemona become garbled and overlapping in his mind, and he uses them interchangeably.

Although many of the characters in the original *Othello* are paralleled in Tony's life (Bill is a Cassio character), there is no Iago equivalent. Instead, Tony's jealousy is always represented by metaphorical blackface: tawny makeup, dark shadows, his reflected psychotic stare from mirror images. When Tony knocks on Pat's door, she repeatedly inquires, "Who is it?" to which he can only reply: "Me, me." Tony is unable to provide a single name for his identity in this state; he is both Tony and Othello. Once inside Pat's apartment, Tony vacillates between speaking as Othello and as Tony. Another mirror moment figures prominently in this murder scene. As Tony's murderous rage sets in, he begins to interrogate Pat about other lovers. He walks forward to a mirror, turns and loosens his tie, blindly regarding the image of a wide-eyed maniac in his formerly composed, gentlemanly visage. As his rage increases, the noise of an approaching train grows louder and Tony repeats the name of his imagined rival, Bill, with greater intensity as the train grows nearer. As the noise subsides, Bill's name dies on his lips, dropping to a murmur. Tony's contorted countenance is reduced back to a state of disoriented, harmless confusion. Building on the early scenes in which Tony imagines his image in blackface, this mirror scene shows the completed connection between blackness, the murderous Other, and the psychological interior of the white man.

As Tony/Othello paces about Pat's apartment, she continues unknow-
ingly in Desdemona's part. The complicity of the white female victim is an
essential component of twentieth-century adaptations of the *Othello* myth
since it implicates the woman in her own murder, thus eliminating the need
for Iago. Finally, getting into her bed, Pat asks, "You wanna put out the
light?" This verbal cue provokes the emergence of murderous Othello, and
Tony responds: "Put out the light, Then put out the light," as he flicks the
light off and on by its chain. He recites Othello's murder speech, but concludes with "Seen Bill lately?" Although Pat responds, "Who?" Tony/
Othello continues with his part, and from this point on he hears Desdemona's
words whenever Pat speaks. He strangles her with a kiss, saying, "Nay, if
you strive—" and lowers her onto her bed. The overt sexuality of Tony's
murder makes the link between the female object and the dangers of race
change evident in this production and recalls Fanon's fascination with the
white woman's alleged plea for rape in her fear of it. Tony murders Pat
because she plays a part for him; she represents not herself, but the figure
of Desdemona as interpreted through psychoanalytic and social constructions of woman—the embodiment of whiteness and civilization.

Women in *A Double Life* act as interchangeable symbols. The cut after
Tony's murder of Pat is to Brita lying in her bed, caressing her neck thought-
fully and anxiously. Then the cinematic gaze returns to the dead face of Pat
Kroll seen through the bars of her bed. Race is also explicitly metaphorical, symbolizing insanity, murder, and sexual transgression. Tony's own
interpretation of Othello's murderous act creates a trademark "Kiss of death"
that he uses both in the stage production and in the murder of Pat Kroll.
Desdemona/Pat is not only physically stifled but is sexually stifled as well.
Thus, the twin taboo of miscegenation that simultaneously subordinates
black male and white female sexuality is tangibly represented in the death
kiss of Tony's Othello.

Tony/Othello's next death scene is on the stage, in blackface, within the
production of *Othello*. The movement toward his tragedy is shrouded in images of movement from whiteness to blackness. Trapped by the police, Tony/
Othello speaks the line, "Soft you; a word or two before you go" to the backstage police, not to the on-stage characters. At the mention of "one who lov'd
not wisely but too well," Tony moves to Brita, lying on the bed as the murdered
Desdemona, and kisses her. His mental instability increases throughout the
speech, and by the conclusion it is evident that he has become both Othello
and insane. As he stabs himself, the camera frames Brita lying on the bed with
him standing behind her, the field of the stage visible to the left, backstage
visible to the right. When he stabs himself, he falls from on-stage light into off-
stage darkness, saying "I kiss'd thee 'ere I kill'd thee" to Brita from behind her
bed. Tony's death critiques the dangers of performance, particularly performances that border on erasing the "real" by threatening stable identity.[41]

In the tradition of metatheater, *A Double Life* contemplates theater as a microcosm of the world, focusing its dramatic inquisition inward. In the case of *Othello*, this inquiry helps to illuminate the relationship between race within the drama of the theater, and within the society that engendered the dramatic associations of race. Specifically, in American culture of the 1940s, obsessed with distinguishing between the "true" American and the immigrant, blackness is a visible referent to the alien Other, as well as the interior Other. In *A Double Life*, Othello breaks free from the mimetic confines of the theater and becomes a manifest reality, the self rather than the signifying other. As in the cinematic dream sequence, the "real" is suspended and a different "reality" is imposed. Thus, the dream and reality are presented as interchangeable versions of the self.[42] In an actual manifestation of the images of the American cinematic dream sequence, Tony becomes the oppositions that define him. Both Tony and Othello are mutually dependent aspects of his identity. Tony himself repeatedly references the dream-state existence of his psychic blackness, and when Othello and Tony have become interchangeable in his mind, he groans, "I've reached the nightmare stage." The complete annihilation of socially constructed barriers is a dream, a nightmare, and a simultaneous reality. The Americanized immigrant is presented as being, at heart, the black foreigner. Tony has become a transgressive and threatening Other opposing the cultural system of belief. He has failed to follow the rules of immigrant Americanization: define the self against the antiself; claim authentic white male experience as your own and define it against that of the black man. Tony passes into the "enemy terrain" of blackness and is punished with the dissolution of his sense of self.

TECUMSEH AND THE MADMAN: *OTHELLO* IN THE REAGAN-ERA SITUATION COMEDY

In 1983 this version of *Othello* reappears in abbreviated form in the television comedy *Cheers*. Adapted to fit the needs of the home viewer of the 1980s, this version intensifies the psycho-sexual conflict and replaces the overt references to the interracial relationship with more subtle signifiers. *Cheers* eliminates blackface but relies heavily upon racist referents to invoke Othello's blackness. In fact, this version surrounds the performance with tangible, external symbols of violent, primitive blackness. The Othello-figure is a white ex-convict, Andy. Andy is convinced by his Desdemona figure, Diane, to play the role of Othello in order to restore his sense of self-esteem through acting and reject his identity as a violent criminal. In an immediate connection to *A Double Life*, Diane, like Pat, is a blonde waitress who is duped into bearing the burden of Andy's psychosis. Diane perceives Othello as a status figure in American theater but fails to recognize the danger his portrayal will represent to Andy's sense of identity and therefore to her own body. In fact, this episode implicitly blames Diane for instigating the *Othello* performance and for failing to return Andy to incarceration.

The initial conflict concerns the establishment of identity: is Andy a dangerous murderer or a childlike innocent? Andy occupies contradictory poles of sexuality, being violently transgressive, yet childlike—traits that primitivism traditionally associates with black masculinity. As Morrison observes, blackness within primitivism can be both "evil *and* protective, rebellious *and* forgiving, fearful *and* desirable."[43] Andy longs for a prepubescent or presexual state, either in the form of confinement from the world of heterosexual discourse or in the artificial realm of adolescent acting. Diane becomes his means of sexual salvation, his sublime object. She represents a rite of passage for Andy, who in turn represents the divided sexual consciousness of the heterosexual American male. When the ex-convict Andy first enters Cheers, he wields an unloaded gun in the hope that he will be returned to prison. Diane offers to be his source of redemption, inverting her previous interpretation of his textual meaning and defending him to the patriarch of the comic series, Sam:

> *Diane.* Sam, I can save this man's life.
> *Sam.* A minute ago you thought this guy was Jack the Ripper, now you're gonna go out browsing with him?
> *Diane.* Now I know him. Sam, look at him. Does he look like a dangerous person?
> [*Andy plays childishly with the shade on the window, pulling it up and down as if to study its mechanics.*][44]

Despite Sam's equation of Andy with a specific punisher of sexual women, Jack the Ripper, Diane chooses to interpret Andy as a presexual child. She chooses *Othello* as the text that they will perform, thus becoming an agent of her own potential destruction. Again, we see the Desdemona figure embodying Fanon's suggestion that the white women's fear of rape indicates desire for rape. Diane is presented as the provocateur of Andy's madness as well as an outlet for it. This misogynistic undertone is evident even in the title and subheading of the *Cheers* episode as printed in the NBC press release: "Diane's in Danger but It's All in Fun."[45]

Miscegenation, too taboo to present overtly as family entertainment to the middle-class viewers of the Reagan era, is alluded to rather than directly represented. Eliminating blackface, the television show instead surrounds the performance of Desdemona/Diane's death scene with racial images. Immediately prior to the performance of the deathbed scene, the audience sits in the bar cheering on a television prizefight between a black man and a white man. In an enactment of modern social construction, the audience of a television show invoking a battle along the lines of black/white male identity views the audience of a television show invoking a tangible physical battle between black and white men. Diane enters and, clicking off the television, announces that it is nearly time for her performance with Andy. She superimposes her version of the black/white dichotomy over that of the television within the television show, thus reducing the frame of reference back to its singular state.

Diane's shrill maternal voice guides this adaptation of *Othello*, just as the Cockney interior voice of the absent father motivates Tony's transformation in *A Double Life*. Thus the 1980s version emphasizes gender anxiety over anxiety about upward class mobility. Throughout the episode, Diane is represented as the maternal/sexual figure that drives white male consciousness to the brink of insanity. Andy is a conflation of Othello and Anthony Perkins's character in *Psycho*, as he reveals to Sam that what drove him to kill in his first crime:

Andy. . . . shrill voices that used to sound like my . . . my Mommy.
Diane. [*Voice from off-stage*] Come along Andrew!
[*Said in a shrill, maternal tone . . . Andy flinches and Sam laughs nervously.*][46]

This moment of psychosis becomes the signifier of "blackness" in the *Cheers* portrayal of Othello. It is marked by actual physical changes in Andy—a widening of the eyes, opening of the mouth, and general depiction of the stereotype of mental instability that recalls racial stereotypes from minstrel performance as well as Colman's performance in *A Double Life*. Psychological change is equated with racechange in this comic *Othello* produced for mass consumption. *Cheers* presents a 1980s version of the minstrel show, exploring social, sexual, and racial boundaries through comic entertainment. With blackface proscribed as a social taboo, blackness instead becomes an allusion within a frame of primitivist references to sexuality and madness.

Andy's race change occurs, predictably, when he reenters the room after changing into his Othello costume. As he enters, he sees Diane kiss Sam; they embrace longingly and plan a sexual liaison following her performance. Again, Andy's facial expression dons its form of blackface, the psychotic leer. The kiss, replacing the symbolic handkerchief of the original *Othello*, triggers insanity in the white male consciousness. Diane is aware of her position as sexual capital, capable of symbolizing punishable transgression. Sensing Andy's murderous intentions, she attempts to clarify her feelings for both Sam and Andy, depicting Andy as a platonic, nonsexual friend. Just as in *A Double Life*, rejection by the female sublime object fragments the male ego, and Andy immediately begins talking in Othello's speech, portraying his inner intentions as the superficial adaptations of the actor.

> *Andy.* [*With great intensity*] Yet she must die
>   Else she betray more men.
> *Diane.* Wonderful! [*Audience laughs. Diane exits.*]
> *Andy.* Put out the light, and then *put out the light.*[47]

Following this exclamation, Andy exits the room with a scream of rage, summoned for his performance. As Diane introduces the scene to the audience, she becomes increasingly aware of the presence of the transformed Andy/Othello at her side. Yet she continues with her scripted part. Unlike her predecessor Desdemona, however, Diane repeatedly bursts from the frame of script, responding to Andy/Othello's recitation "Yet I'll not shed her blood, nor scar that whiter skin of hers than snow" by leaping from her stage-bed, and saying, "There, good. It's agreed, no blood, no scarring, and that's the gist of our scene."

The audience (Sam, in particular) is dissatisfied, however, and Diane is forced back into the script of Desdemona. As she sits on the bed, a statue of Tecumseh looms over her right shoulder, another allusion to the sexuality linked with the nonwhite Other. Tecumseh acts as the background for the entire scene, a constant referent to primitivism. As Diane fights against Andy on her deathbed, the drama professor whom Diane has summoned to witness the performance—the spectator of legitimacy and white male hegemony—turns to a dark-skinned woman next to him and says, "I love it! A Desdemona that fights back!" The murder scene is surrounded by racial and primitivist referents although blackness itself is not overtly presented. Instead, blackness is the element surrounding male whiteness: the prize-fight over the stage, Tecumseh behind the bed, a dark woman spectator, the madness surrounding Andy's sanity.

The episode is framed by these racial referents, yet Andy's race change is exclusively psychological. The "black" man in this version is, as in several previous versions, fair of complexion. It is his psychological state that is "black," retaining the moral associations with race that existed even in the original Renaissance text. However, it is Desdemona alone, not Iago, in these modern American versions who prompts the psychological race change. Thus, blackness and femininity are dually demonized in these modern American versions and are used as mutually oppressive tools of social construction. The woman is complicit in her own destruction, and blackness is the agent that must be exorcised in order for a stable white identity to exist.

In an effort to adapt the *Othello* myth for consumption by popular culture, these productions characterize their contemporary society in a manner that the direct textual representation would not necessarily reflect. However, the *Othello* myth continues to employ race and gender to enact anxieties of white male consciousness, using both as symbolic capital to advance the ideology of predominant society and depicting the transgression of racial and sexual boundaries as a debilitative state of self-destruction. *Othello* itself is a dynamic text that provokes questions concerning the construction of race in relationship to sexual and social identity, but the elimination of Iago changes the problem of *Othello* from the vulnerability of self-construction to outside forces to a problem of internal psychic fragmentation.

Although textual aspects of *Othello* are continually adapted to fit various cultures and mediums, the twentieth-century translation of the tragic Moor as a tale of the fragmented American male ego keeps reappearing. As Stanley Wells notes, the "translation of Shakespeare to a different medium requires, and justifies, free treatment of the text."[48] But these versions of *Othello* corrupt the text for the explicit purpose of retaining the tale of *Othello* as a problem of white male identity, of the oedipal quest for successful psychic colonization, and the lingering threat of the colonized Other within. Thus, the American popular culture version of *Othello* corrupts the text in order to exploit a deeply resonant relationship with contemporary viewers. In 1947, the sexual and psychological associations of blackness were employed to encourage the rejection of an immigrant identity in return for assimilation into the white American identity; in 1983, the Othello myth retold employs both primitivism and threatening femininity to reflect the sexual and psychic anxieties of white masculinity.

Othello has become a symbolic referent to the aspects of white male consciousness that American society perceives as dark, foreign, and primitive—Tecumseh and the madman.[49] As such, he is both powerfully attractive and repellent to American popular culture, which thrives on the exploration and enforcement of boundaries of identification. The attraction of the *Othello* myth, however, has some horrifying and tangible implications. By playing white female sexuality off against black masculinity and invoking the specter of noble tragedy, we are left with the very real possibility of culturally misreading violent texts. Returning to one recent example of the American obsession with the Othello myth, in one of the quotations that opens this essay, Ellis Cose wonders that in the O. J. Simpson case "Iago is nowhere to be found."[50] On the contrary, American culture acts as its own Iago, murmuring images of black murderous sexuality and bestiality in all our Othellos' ears and then gasping in titillated wonder when they enact our racial fantasies. The tragedy of interpreting cases such as Simpson's in terms of this *Othello* myth is twofold: that our Othellos may be listening to racist cultural whispers, and that we are allowing interracial slaughter the status of entertainment.[51]

NOTES

1. Toni Morrison, *Playing in the Dark: Whiteness and the Literary Imagination* (New York: Vintage, 1993), ix.

2. For example, the threat of the unjustly lynched and castrated black body appears in popular texts such as Harper Lee's *To Kill a Mockingbird* (New York: Warner Books, 1960); Leroi Jones's *Dutchman* (New York: Morrow Quill, 1964); and James Baldwin's *Blues for Mister Charlie* (New York: Dial, 1964), and more recently Stephen King's *The Green Mile: Coffey on the Mile* (New York: Signet, 1996). The visual appeal of these stories resulted in the successful adaptation of most of these works into broad-release films.

3. Anthony Barthelemy, *Black Face: Maligned Race* (Baton Rouge and London: Louisiana State University Press, 1987), 3.

4. Morrison, 59.

5. Ray Browne discusses five basic vaudevillian treatments of Shakespeare in Negro minstrelsy of the nineteenth century in "Shakespeare in American Vaudeville and Negro Minstrelsy," *American Quarterly* 12 (1990): 374–91. According to Browne, "*Othello* had at least one vaudeville and one minstrel version," both depicting Othello as an eccentric comic figure (380). Two popular skits were "Dars-de-Money, a Travesty of Othello," and "Bones Plays O'Feller" (384).

6. Joyce MacDonald explores the adaptation of Shakespeare in the minstrel tradition, as well as on the British stage, in her essay, "Acting Black: *Othello, Othello* Burlesques and the Performance of Blackness," *Theatre Journal* 46 (1994): 231–49. Kris Collins also discusses the tradition of whitewashing *Othello* in nineteenth-century performance in "Whitewashing the Black-a-Moor: *Othello*, Negro Minstrelsy and Parodies of Blackness," *Journal of American Culture* 19, no. 3 (1996): 87–102.

7. See Linda Charnes, *Notorious Identity: Materializing the Subject in Shakespeare* (Cambridge: Harvard University Press, 1993) for a discussion of the function of this misquotation as deconstructive bardolatry used to establish the continuing cultural appeal of the Iago/Othello/Desdemona relationship (156).

8. For two explicit comparisons of Simpson to Othello see Ellis Cose, "Caught between Two Worlds: Why Simpson couldn't overcome the barriers of race," *Newsweek*, 11 July 1994, 28, and "Letters to the Editor," *The Washington Post*, 4 July 1994, A18.

9. Although it is not the domain of this article, I have argued elsewhere that the traditional celebration of whiteness embodied as femininity and blackness as masculinity serves to obscure the troubling specter of black femininity. For this argument, see Marguerite H. Rippy, "Exhuming Dorothy Dandridge: The Black Sex Goddess and Classic Hollywood Cinema," *Cineaction* 44 (1997): 20–31. In brief, the black female body disturbs American consciousness by serving as witness to the actual sexual crimes of the white man within the slavery system, thus vexing the systems of gender identification that associate violence with the black male body and the victimization with the white female body. This traditional system of gender/race identity defines black masculinity and white femininity as mutually exclusive, while erasing black femininity entirely. This is only one system of repression and displacement since, as Jacqueline Bobo argues, black women, when visible, are frequently reduced to static types that attempt either to place blame for sexual crime upon their own desire or to render them free of desire. See Bobo, "Black Women in Fiction and Nonfiction: Images of Power and Powerlessness," *Wide Angle* 13 (1991): 72–73.

10. The episode "Homicidal Ham," first aired on NBC on Thursday, 27 October 1983.

11. The program for the 1997 "photo negative" production of *Othello* that cast fair-skinned Patrick Stewart as Othello with a majority black supporting cast gives a concise listing of the traditional stature of the Othello/Iago diad for actors and critics. See "On

Stage Othello," in *Shakespeare Theater Playbill for Othello*, ed. Lindsay Eagle (Silver Spring, Md.: Theatre and Concert Magazines, 1997), 20–21. The title of "photo negative" seems to come from director Jude Kelly, quoted in Henry H. Chase, "Race," review for *Othello*, by Jude Kelly as performed by the Shakespeare Theatre, Washington, D.C., *American Visions* 12 (1997–98): 10.

12.   The use of Shakespeare's *Othello* to legitimate these interpretations is described by Linda Charnes as a contemporary American use of Shakespeare as "symbolic capital" (155); Charles Haywood similarly regards the historical use of Shakespeare as a sign of "culture, status and prestige" in nineteenth-century American consciousness in his essay "Negro Minstrelsy and Shakespearean Burlesque," in *Folklore and Society* (Harboro, Pa.: Folklore Association, 1966), 85.

13.   This attitude meant that black actors like Paul Robeson were prevented from playing Othello in America although he became enormously popular in this role in theaters abroad. American audiences preferred their Othellos in blackface as evidenced by the successful cinematic performances of Sir Laurence Olivier and Orson Welles. (Welles also stepped onto the stage as a blackface Macbeth in the 1936 Indianapolis performance of his Caribbean "Voodoo" version of *Macbeth.*) Asked why he darkened himself beyond the complexion of the original lead, African American actor Jack Carter, Welles confessed, "I had to prove that I belonged." Quoted in Barbara Leaming, *Orson Welles: A Biography*, 2nd ed. (New York: Limelight, 1995), 109.

14.   Karen Newman explores the link between femininity, blackness, and the monstrous in "'And wash the Ethiop white': Femininity and the Monstrous in *Othello*," in *Shakespeare Reproduced* (London and New York: Methuen, 1987), 151–52.

15.   "The Idea of Race and its Elevation to Autonomous, Scientific, and Legal Status," in *Sociological Theories: Race and Colonialism* (Paris: Wesco, 1980), 47–49.

16.   Morrison, 6.

17.   Morrison, 65.

18.   Morrison, 17.

19.   Ralph Ellison, *Shadow and Act* (New York: Random House, 1964), 54.

20.   Frantz Fanon, *Black Skin, White Masks* (New York: Grove Press, 1967), 140.

21.   Fanon, 156.

22.   Fanon, 180.

23.   Fanon's message troubles dominant racial and colonial ideologies on many levels but I would argue retains traditional oppressive gender mechanisms. Homi Bhabha further discusses the postcolonial implications of masking in his discussion of the fundamental ambivalence, yet menacing potential, of the colonized mimicking the colonizer in his essay "Of Mimicry and Man," in *The Location of Culture* (London and New York: Routledge, 1994), 85–93.

24.   Morrison, 47.

25.   Ellison, 58.

26.   Michael Rogin, "Blackface, White Noise: The Jewish Jazz Singer Finds His Voice," *Critical Inquiry* 18 (1992): 419.

27.   William Shakespeare, *Othello,* in *The Complete Works of Shakespeare*, ed. David Bevington, updated 4th ed. (New York: Longman, 1997), 1.1.66.

28.   Slavoj Žižek, *Looking Awry: An Introduction to Jacques Lacan through Popular Culture* (Cambridge: MIT Press, 1991), 74.

29.   Žižek, 20.

30.   For a more complete listing of cinematic adaptations of *Othello*, see Kenneth Rothwell and Annabelle Melzer, *Shakespeare on Screen: An International Filmography and Videography* (New York: Neal-Schuman, 1990), 208–27.

31.   The topic of immigrant assimilation in relation to race was powerful in 1947 as

revealed by the winner of the Academy Award for Best Picture that year, *A Gentleman's Agreement*, directed by Elia Kazan and starring Gregory Peck. This controversial film deals with American antisemitism and, like *A Double Life*, involves the "passing" of the white male protagonist. In this case, Gregory Peck pretends to be Jewish for the sake of journalistic integrity.

32.   Ian Cameron, ed., *The Book of Film Noir* (New York: Continuum, 1992), 8.

33.   Christine Gledhill defines emblematic melodrama as leading "not outward to society but inward to where social and ideological pressures impact on the psychic" in her collection *Stardom: Industry of Desire* (London and New York: Routledge, 1991), 209.

34.   This aspect of the film critiques "method acting," a technique introduced by the Group Theatre and still a recent development in 1947.

35.   Kobena Mercer, "Monster Metaphors: Notes on Michael Jackson's *Thriller*," in *Stardom: Industry of Desire*, 310.

36.   *A Double Life*, directed by George Cukor, 1 hr. 43 min., Universal International/Kanin Productions, 1947, videocassette.

37.   The social import of this debate is represented in a major challenge to the validity of antimiscegenation laws that emerged in the 1948 California case of *Perez v. Lippold*, which attempted to claim interracial marriage as a constitutional right under the rubric of religious freedom.

38.   Shelley Winters plays Kroll in this early performance on screen.

39.   Žižek, 83.

40.   R. Dixon Smith, *Ronald Coleman, Gentleman of the Cinema: A Biography and Filmography* (London: McFarland, 1991), 272. Also note that the double name "Tony John" is another example of the main character's dual consciousness.

41.   As Joyce MacDonald points out, the transgressive power of performing *Othello* resides in "its public contradiction of the supposedly rigid and absolute construction of ideologies of racial difference" (237).

42.   Žižek, 16–17.

43.   Morrison, 59.

44.   "Homicidal Ham," episode of *Cheers*, directed by James Burrows, 30 min., NBC Television, 27 October 1983.

45.   Both the press release and the original tape of "Homicidal Ham" are available for research at the Library of Congress in Washington, D.C.

46.   "Homicidal Ham."

47.   "Homicidal Ham."

48.   Stanley Wells, "Television Shakespeare," *Shakespeare Quarterly* 33 (1982): 266.

49.   The tradition of white Othello in American performance reappeared in the nation's capital during the Shakespeare Theatre's "photo-negative" production of *Othello* in 1997. Although the performance failed to capture the power of the original text by pitting visual imagery against the contradictory spoken lines, it seems an appropriately "national" Shakespeare. By playing Othello as "white" and Desdemona as "black," this performance captured many of the nuances of white-Othello-in-crisis that are discussed in this essay.

50.   Cose, 28.

51.   Even years removed from the contrasting criminal and civil trials of Simpson, he remains a source of cultural curiosity. His next venue appears to be the Internet, where he promises to appear to discuss his case candidly with curious "fans."

Works Cited

Baldwin, James. *Blues for Mister Charlie*. New York: Dial, 1964.

Barthelemy, Anthony. *Black Face: Maligned Race*. Baton Rouge and London: Louisiana State University Press, 1987.

Bhabha, Homi. "Of Mimicry and Man." In *The Location of Culture*. London and New York: Routledge, 1994.

Bobo, Jacqueline. "Black Women in Fiction and Nonfiction: Images of Power and Powerlessness." *Wide Angle* 13 (1991): 72–81.

Browne, Ray. "Shakespeare in American Vaudeville and Negro Minstrelsy." *American Quarterly* 12 (1990): 374–91.

Cameron, Ian, ed. *The Book of Film Noir*. New York: Continuum, 1992.

Charnes, Linda. Epilogue to *Notorious Identity: Materializing the Subject in Shakespeare*. Cambridge: Harvard University Press, 1993.

Chase, Henry H. "Race" Review of *Othello*, by Jude Kelly. The Shakespeare Theatre, Washington, D.C. *American Visions* 12 (1997–98): 10.

Collins, Kris. "White-Washing the Black-a-Moor: *Othello*, Negro Minstrelsy, and Parodies of Blackness." *Journal of American Culture* 19, no. 3 (1996): 87–102.

Cose, Ellis. "Caught between Two Worlds: Why Simpson couldn't overcome the barriers of race." *Newsweek*, 11 July 1994, 28.

Ellison, Ralph. *Shadow and Act*. New York: Random House, 1964.

Fanon, Frantz. *Black Skin, White Masks*. Translated by Charles Lam Markmann. New York: Grove Press, 1967.

Faulkner, William. *Intruder in the Dust*. 1948. Reprint, New York: Vintage, 1991.

———. *Light in August*. 1932. Reprint, New York: Vintage, 1990.

Gledhill, Christine, ed. *Stardom: Industry of Desire*. London and New York: Routledge, 1991.

Guillaumin, Colette. "The Idea of Race and Its Elevation to Autonomous, Scientific, and Legal Status." In *Sociological Theories: Race and Colonialism*, 37–65. Paris: Wesco, 1980.

Haywood, Charles. "Negro Minstrelsy and Shakespearean Burlesque." In *Folklore and Society*. Harboro, Pa.: Folklore Association, 1966.

Jones, Leroi (Amiri Baraka). *Dutchman and the Slave*. New York: Morrow Quill, 1964.

King, Stephen. *The Green Mile: Coffey on the Mile*. New York: Signet, 1996.

Leaming, Barbara. *Orson Welles: A Biography*. 2nd edition. New York: Limelight, 1995.

Lee, Harper. *To Kill a Mockingbird*. New York: Warner Books, 1960.

"Letters to the Editor." *The Washington Post*, 4 July 1994, A18.

MacDonald, Joyce Green. "Acting Black: *Othello*, *Othello* Burlesques, and the Performance of Blackness." *Theatre Journal* 46 (1994): 231–49.

Mercer, Kobina. "Monster Metaphors: Notes on Michael Jackson's *Thriller*." In *Stardom: Industry of Desire*. Edited by Christine Gledhill. London and New York: Routledge, 1991.

Morrison, Toni. *Playing in the Dark: Whiteness and the Literary Imagination*. New York: Vintage, 1993.

Newman, Karen. "'And wash the Ethiop white': Femininity and the Monstrous in *Othello*." In *Shakespeare Reproduced*. Edited by Jean E. Howard and Marion F. O'Connor. London and New York: Methuen, 1987.

"On Stage *Othello*." *Shakespeare Theater Playbill for Othello*. Edited by Lindsay Eagle, 20–21. Silver Spring, Md.: Theatre and Concert Magazines, 1997.

Rippy, Marguerite H. "Exhuming Dorothy Dandridge: The Black Sex Goddess and Classic Hollywood Cinema." *Cineaction* 44 (1997): 20–31.

Rogin, Michael. "Blackface, White Noise: The Jewish Jazz Singer Finds His Voice." *Critical Inquiry* 18 (1992): 417–37.

Rothwell, Kenneth S., and Annabelle Melzer. *Shakespeare on Screen: An International Filmography and Videography*. New York: Neal-Schuman, 1990.

Shakespeare, William. *Othello*. In *The Complete Works of Shakespeare*. Edited by David Bevington. Updated 4th edition. New York: Longman, 1997.

Smith, R. Dixon. *Ronald Colman, Gentleman of the Cinema: A Biography and Filmography*. London: McFarland, 1991.

Wells, Stanley. "Television Shakespeare." *Shakespeare Quarterly* 33 (1982): 261–77.

Žižek, Slavoj. *Looking Awry: An Introduction to Jacques Lacan through Popular Culture*. Cambridge: MIT Press, 1991.

FILMS CITED

A Double Life. Directed by George Cukor. 1hr. 43 min. Universal International/ Kanin Productions, 1947. Videocassette.

A Gentleman's Agreement. Directed by Elia Kazan. 1 hr. 58 min. Twentieth Century Fox, 1947. Videocassette.

"Homicidal Ham." Episode of *Cheers*. Directed by James Burrows. 30 min. NBC Television, 27 October 1983.

"How very like the home life of our own dear queen": Ian McKellen's *Richard III*

LISA HOPKINS

Towards the close of the credits in Ian McKellen's film version of *Richard III* (dir. Richard Loncraine, 1995)[1] there appears the disclaimer, "[t]he events and characters in this motion picture are fictitious. Any similarity to persons, living or dead, or to actual firms is purely coincidental."[2] To some extent, this remark is clearly prompted by McKellen's awareness of interest groups like the Richard III Society, which have been vigilant in seeking to protect the historical Richard's good name in the face of what they see as Shakespeare's mischievous adherence to fictitious Tudor propaganda. Some Ricardians, particularly in the United States, called for the film to be banned or boycotted, although McKellen in his introduction to the published screenplay is careful to consider the possibility of the historical Richard's innocence and shows himself rather noticeably well-informed about some of the most recent claims on the subject.[3] However, the choice of the phrase "actual firms" clearly widens the potential applicability of the disclaimer well beyond reference to Richard III himself (who is already accounted for in the category of persons "living or dead"). Slyly, covertly, it points straight to the real heart of the film's concerns with history, for "the firm" is the present queen's term for the British royal family. It is the Windsors, not the Plantagenets, whom this film represents, and to whom the ironic disclaimer applies.

The understated, coded nature of the disclaimer's message is typical of the tactics used throughout the film as a whole in its delicate task of referring to the history of the current royal family: after all, as the prominent emphasis of McKellen's delivery reminds us, "We are the queen's subjects, and *must* obey." The queen's preference for the term "firm" is no state secret—it is regularly referred to in articles in the English newspapers—but it is information casually disseminated and not easily documented or

47

verified, since it is part of a common cultural currency of information and anecdote.[4] As such, the phrase lies squarely within the range of discourse habitually deployed for an ironic in-joke or topical allusion; its use draws the viewer in and invites a sense of shared positioning and response. I suspect, however, that this is likely to be its effect only on the *British* viewer, for as well as operating as a knowing reference, "firm" must surely work also as a shibboleth, excluding from comprehension those who have not been regularly exposed to the language of the British press.

While not deliberately or overtly marginalizing an American audience, this specialized use of the term is certainly not based on what are likely to be their own experiences or expectations (it might indeed prove a red herring by leading them to think more of corporate America), and this is, moreover, an effect reinforced by the fact that the film offers other pleasures available only to a British audience and not to an American one, such as that of spotting the London locations and recognizing the deadly accuracy with which McKellen has captured the strangulated vowel sounds of the English upper classes (epitomized in the British joke that says that the queen believes a crèche to be a car accident in Kensington High Street). For those who pick up on the clue provided by the word "firm," however, it will provide an important indication of the film's sustained interest in America and Americanization, in the British royal family in its own right and as emblematic of British culture and history, and in the intersection of the two, the historical paradigm of which, the marriage of the Duke of Windsor to Wallis Simpson, is brilliantly revisited in the film through its and our awareness of the imperatives underlying the casting of Annette Bening.

Though this single credit is only a tiny detail of the film, and indeed one perhaps unlikely to be seen by a majority of the audience, it is nevertheless symptomatic of some key aspects of McKellen's approach to the project of transferring Richard Eyre's Royal National Theatre production to the screen. Its mischievous, tongue-in-cheek allusiveness typifies McKellen's tone throughout his comments on the published screenplay, and so does its adoption of a resolutely British perspective and approach. Given the embattled position of the British film industry and the constant vulnerability of British screen presence to the superior wealth and clout of Hollywood, the occasional asperity of McKellen's comments on American culture is perhaps unsurprising, though here too understatedness may sometimes conceal pointedness, as when he comments on the use of the phrase "pitchers have ears" by Annette Bening's Queen Elizabeth: "Today's English audience will misleadingly hear the nonsensical 'pictures have ears.' Americans, like Queen Elizabeth, will understand Shakespeare better. . . . No-one and nothing can be trusted, not even a jug on the tea-table" (152). In context, it is, of course, quite clear that the "pitcher" referred to is the young Duke of York, and the proverb is well enough known for it to be highly unlikely for a British audience to misunderstand it. Does McKellen's feigned tribute to an American culture which, in fact, he subtly codes as paranoid refer to some private joke arising during filming, perhaps concerning Annette Bening's pronunciation or comprehension of the script?

Similar barbs, with similar veiling, consistently characterize McKellen's references to American culture. He piously hopes that the film's use of Battersea Power Station "will encourage Londoners to care more for one of our most distinctive landmarks. It could house an exciting 'Richard III Ride' like at Disneyland or Universal Studios!" (266). He also enjoys himself vastly on the subject of British perceptions of Americans as very prudish when he comments on the portrait of himself in the original stage production:

> From a quick Polaroid, I was painted naked, the left arm wholly restored and held aloft, in the manner of the Third Reich's monumental symbols of manhood. Richard Eyre believed that the penis (although a copy of my own) was ill-proportioned and had it slightly painted over. For the USA, the portrait was again exhibited but modestly clad in a full suit of armor. (182)

McKellen's prose, like Gibbon's, offers nothing but "springs and mantraps" here. Firstly, he vibrantly notes that the largeness of his penis defies credibility, so that it had to be painted over to seem credible. Then he wields his pen to explain that American notions of modest clothing require the presence of a full suit of armor. Just as his penis is too much for Americans to take, so his pen is deployed to put them down, while British readers are covertly invited to join in the joke. Given that the two little princes are half American and given cowboy hats by their feather-headdress-wearing Uncle Rivers, there is thus a particularly acerbic irony as McKellen's off-screen persona coalesces with his on-screen one to order their execution.

This is a conjunction of attitudes found elsewhere in the film as well—Richard's rejection of Lady Anne, for instance, parallels McKellen's own declared homosexuality—and may well lead audiences who associate Richard with McKellen to regard him less harshly than they might have otherwise done. Indeed, our first sight of him switches from registering him as a frightening and incomprehensible presence to not only seeing the face beneath the mask but also to hearing his breathing echoing all around us, as if it were our own and we were inside his head. And to the extent that we identify with Richard and collude in the intimacy of his camp asides to the camera, so we are invited into sharing the distaste and wariness with which he treats all things American.

The reason for the anti-American animus may well be thought to lie at least in part in McKellen's acute awareness of the harsh realities of commercial filmmaking. Although it tells a story from the past, the film flaunts its understanding of the present: the first thing we see is technology, in the shape of the ticker-tape machine, and soon afterwards comes the playful self-consciousness of the overtly artificial cut from public to private space when Richard, during his opening soliloquy, is whisked from ballroom to toilet by cinematic magic. This awareness of film's technical potential is matched by a firm grasp of its material circumstances, as illustrated by McKellen's observation that the distributors insisted that at least two of the cast had to be "internationally famous" (28). Since "internationally famous" effectively means "American," this recalls such infelicities as the insistence on a Hollywood presence in films like Kenneth Branagh's *Much Ado about Nothing*, where, though Denzel Washington's Prince was justly praised, Michael Keaton's Dogberry received reviews which were at best highly mixed, and Keanu Reeves's Don John has never, to my knowledge, prompted a favorable word. It was presumably McKellen's acute awareness of these economic realities that inspired him to the transcendentally catty move of asking Meryl Streep, after telling her that Queen Elizabeth would be played as an American heiress, if she could do an American accent (15).

McKellen's question to Streep was doubly mischievous because the film's Queen Elizabeth (eventually played by Annette Bening) is primarily identifiable not as a member of any generic category of American heiress but as a very specific American woman, Wallis Simpson, which is where the film's interest in the British royal family intersects with its resolutely anti-American aesthetic and agenda. McKellen himself actually comes quite close to admitting this: "[i]n the play, Queen Elizabeth's Woodville Family are reviled by Richard as provincial outsiders to the metropolitan power-center. A 30s equivalent was to make them American: witness the British Establishment's outcry in 1936, when King Edward VIII wanted Wallis Simpson to be his queen" (54). The sentence has the neat effect of deflecting any suggestion of anti-American feeling onto the shoulders of "the British Establishment," and certainly McKellen himself is generous in his tributes to the adaptability and capability of both Annette Bening (who played a similar man-catching figure in *The American President* [dir. Rob Reiner, 1995]) and Robert Downey Jr., who plays Earl Rivers (McKellen notes bitingly that his "title might be a credible first name" [54], implying that Americans may imagine that he has actually been christened Earl). In fact, the casting of both is a stroke of sheer genius since it serves so many purposes at once, fulfilling the need for internationally recognizable stars, allowing the actors to play to their natural strengths rather than trying to elide the difference between their accents and others', and, through the Mrs. Simpson associations, strengthening the specificity of the allusions to the House of Windsor.

Although McKellen himself makes this connection only once, and that not explicitly, the film is in fact very firmly rooted in the year of the Abdication Crisis, 1936.[5] The designer for *Richard III* notes that the costumes were "very specific to 1936" (44), and the narrative as a whole is saturated with references to the events and personnel most closely concerned with the transition from the reign of Edward VIII to that of George VI. Though McKellen in the screenplay describes Maggie Smith's Duchess of York as "tiara to toe, an Edwardian matriarch" (53), he is again being disingenuous, for she too is readily identifiable in dress and bearing as a specific member of the royal family, Queen Mary, mother of both Edward VIII and George VI. When, in the film, Edward IV dies short of breath in the Brighton pavilion, he recalls both George IV, who built it, and the painful death from lung cancer of George VI, Edward VIII's successor. When McKellen's Richard hands Queen Elizabeth a glass of gin, this surely alludes to the famous fondness for gin of the present Queen Mother, George VI's wife, whom the abdication made queen.[6] Our sense of echoes in nomenclature between the real and the fictional Queen Elizabeth here is reinforced when McKellen transforms the "Lady Grey" of the original to "Elizabeth the Queen, Clarence, it's she" (67).

The daughter of George VI and Queen Elizabeth, the present Queen Elizabeth II, presents an equally obvious analogue for the film's Princess Elizabeth, whose role McKellen's screenplay greatly enhanced. Indeed, Lynda Boose and Richard Burt suggest that "shortly after Great Britain solemnly celebrated the fifty-year anniversary of the end of World War II, *Richard III* replayed that history by reinscribing it into the cycle of dark days that had eventually led to the Tudor triumph, British mythology now promising an Elizabeth (II) for an Elizabeth (I)."[7] The Victory Ball, during which the young Princess Elizabeth visibly falls for Henry Richmond, was originally planned to take place on a replica royal yacht, until that proved too expensive (56); the queen is well known to have met and fallen in love with Prince Philip when he too was in the navy as a young Lt. Philip Mountbatten. McKellen later says that he put his Richmond in the navy because of the line "Richmond is on the seas" (258), but the relevance of the parallel can hardly have eluded him. Moreover, given that he is adapting a play that includes no seaside locations and closes with a battle in the virtual center of England,[8] McKellen displays a surprisingly sustained interest in the navy. In an early draft, King Henry VI was to have been in naval uniform, visiting a family mausoleum obviously evocative of Frogmore or Windsor (20). Moreover, the Prince of Wales appears wearing the uniform of "a junior Admiral of the Fleet" (157) and smoking Senior Service cigarettes (150; the navy, by virtue of being the first established, is the senior service).

It is perhaps not coincidental that the British royal family has a long tradition of service with the navy, which was, after all, founded by Henry VIII: George VI served on a destroyer during the Battle of Jutland, and the present queen's second son, the Duke of York, fought in the Falklands and is making a career in the navy. In McKellen's *Richard III*, the "goodies"— or at least the winners—all serve in either the navy or the air force: Lord Stanley is the air vice-marshal, and McKellen notes that "the upright Stanley, although he never wears the black uniform, is the only person to fool Richard throughout. . . . [I]t is Stanley's Air Force which is decisive" (258). (If Richmond is Prince Philip, Stanley may well be seen as Lord Mountbatten, and it is thus politically decorous to associate him strongly with the air, to avoid any recall of the debacle involving Mountbatten's father, who, because of his German connections, was seriously slighted by the admiralty.) By contrast, members of the army, who do wear the black uniform, are consistently suspect. Richard is their commander-in-chief, Tyrell is in charge of the regimental mascot, and it is one of Tyrell's fellow NCOs (noncommissioned officers) who assists in the murder of Clarence. We see, too, the poor slum dwellings of the army men, very different from those we are invited to posit for the film's air and naval officers. The film thus reveals a society that is not only distinctively rooted in British institutions but that also reveals those institutions as endemically at odds with each other, structured by rigid and unyielding class stratifications.

The reason for *Richard III*'s insistent parallels with the British royal family as it was constituted at the time of the Abdication Crisis is initially presented by McKellen as a fairly casual decision:

> As with all the other Shakespeare I've most enjoyed doing, Richard Eyre's *Richard III* would be staged in a modern context. The clinching moment was when one of us asked: "How should the Prince of Wales be brought back to London before being sent to the Tower?" One of us said: "Don't the royals always arrive in London by rail?" (12)

Here, what is important is apparently just "a modern context," rather than any specific set of parallels; any correspondences with the actual royal family are virtually a design concept, growing out of the wish to use a train. McKellen, though, elaborates on some additional motivations:

> Nor could we expect our audience to imagine *Richard III* happening in present-day England. . . . The historical events of the play had occurred just a couple of generations before the first audience saw them dramatized. The comparable period for us would be the 1930s, close enough for no-one to think we were identifying the plot of the play with actual events. . . . Also, the 30s were appropriately a decade of tyranny throughout Europe, the most recent time when a dictatorship like Richard III's might have overtaken the United Kingdom. (12–13)

The idea of using the historical period of the film to parallel Shakespeare's

own chronological relationship to the events he dramatizes was a very as-
tute one. The gap is not in fact very closely analogous—just over a century
separated Shakespeare's play from the Battle of Bosworth, as opposed to
the "'tis sixty years since" of the film, and some of those alluded to in the
adaptation are still alive, calling for more circumspection in their treatment
than Shakespeare was obliged to use. Nevertheless, it could well be argued
that the film's fictionalizations and displacements do indeed correspond
very closely to similar elements of Shakespeare's cavalier approach to the
dramatization of history.

For all this, though, one can hardly suppose that the choice of the thirties
lies merely in their suitable "pastness." McKellen himself notes the possible overlap with things that might really have occurred in British history.
As the papers buzz with rumors of Edward VIII's alleged treachery, we
hardly need his discreet reminder that "The fascistic references are a reminder that an English dictatorship (even by a Royal claimant) is credible
within the 1930s setting" (216). But though he does concede here the applicability of the Edward VIII parallel, he also immediately deflects it by
the reminder of a much more widespread and more general interest in fascism in the 1930s, and this is of course strongly developed throughout the
film. McKellen notes the stage Hastings' resemblance to Neville Chamberlain (170) and refers to Buckingham's "Himmler glasses and his Goering
smile" (164).

He also observes of the scene in which Richard and his entourage view
footage of his coronation that "Hitler enjoyed watching newsreel of his
public appearances in the company of his inner circle. He was also partial
to sticky chocolates. I discovered this when playing the Führer in the drama/
documentary *Countdown to War*" (214; once again the note of identification between Richard and McKellen himself is sounded, and once again
the audience too may perhaps be at least to some extent drawn in, since it is
impossible not to register the genuine pleasure which Richard, for the first
time, is feeling in this scene). Indeed, when the stage production toured,
resemblances with dictators from Ceaucescu to Saddam Hussein were found
by audiences, and McKellen comments that "audiences across the world
took the point and revealed a paradox: the more specific a production, the
more general its relevance. Although our story was obviously an English
one, audiences took the message personally wherever we toured" (13).

Nevertheless, despite these diversionary signals, McKellen's Richard is
no Hitler; he is not even, despite that black uniform, significantly like that
nearest British counterpart, Mosley. McKellen notes that in the film he
dropped the full-arm, obviously fascist salute, which his Richard had used
in the original stage production, because he "did not want to specifically
identify Richard with fascism" (206). That reluctance is not surprising, for
whatever other parallels may be perceived, this is a story which is indeed

"obviously an English one." Moreover, for all McKellen's declared resolution not to parody current affairs, the play's links with the British royal family travel well beyond its configuration in the thirties. As McKellen notes, "'Now' is the first word spoken" (18), and "now" comes very close indeed to "then" when McKellen in the screenplay slyly observes that the young Prince of Wales has probably been away at Eton (150).

In the play, of course, the young prince has been at Ludlow, and even within the context of the film we might not necessarily think of Eton, since no member of the royal family attended it in the thirties, or indeed at any other time—until quite recently, when much press attention was focused on Prince William's recent enrollment there. (He has been followed by Prince Harry.) And if we think of Prince William in connection with Eton, we are surely also reminded of the notorious disintegration of his parents' marriage when the middle-aged Richard ignores the sexual attractions of his young and beautiful wife,[9] or when internecine family warfare takes place around a dining table, since consumption and refusal of food played so large a part in the turbulent personal life of Princess Diana. Slight though they may be, these veiled allusions do work to suggest that the turbulent family history of the Windsors is ongoing.

The history of the 1930s is thus linked with the 1990s in ways that do indeed make Shakespeare still our contemporary. In a subtle way, the use of the 1930s even enables the note of personal identification to be sounded once again, for when the film's opening words prove to be not Shakespeare but Marlowe we may well remember not only Shakespeare's relationship to his predecessor but another use of Marlowe, Derek Jarman's 1991 film version of *Edward II*, his swansong before his death from AIDS, where, as in *Richard III*, the enemies are church and army, who are opposed not only to homosexuality but to the arts in general (a viewpoint McKellen would surely share as much as he does Jarman's sexuality), where the pearl-bedecked Tilda Swinton oscillates between imaging Princess Diana and embodying the queen, and where Edward's death is ironically heralded with the words that announced that of George VI, "The king's life is moving peacefully to a close." Moreover, in a film that thus delicately alludes to such numerous histories, the use of the Brighton pavilion extends the chain of historical reference still further, with its clear evocation of George IV (we may also remember that the film's Clarence, Nigel Hawthorne, is fresh from an acclaimed performance as another Hanoverian in *The Madness of King George* [dir. Nicholas Hytner, 1994]).

This strong awareness of the past and its ties with the present does indeed correlate very closely with Shakespeare's own interest in reworking a moment of history that had had ongoing repercussions for his own century's politics. Peter Holland astutely terms the film "a precise cinematic analogy to the Shakespearean history play: a drama that can never offer anything more than a deliberate and self-conscious construction of history, a history that is always aware of the complicities involved in its pretence of being history."[10] But it also builds an arc between our moment and Shakespeare's, reminding us of the very strong elements of continuity that, even across changes of dynasty, still characterize the habitual configurations of the British royal family. Conservatism in use of Christian names, in particular, leads to some very striking echoes in nomenclature between the thirties and the nineties, and indeed Shakespeare himself draws attention in *Richard III* to the extent to which this is an enduring feature of the royal family in the notoriously convoluted lines of Queen Margaret:

I had an Edward, till a Richard killed him;
I had a Harry, till a Richard killed him:
Thou hadst an Edward, till a Richard killed him;
Thou hadst a Richard, till a Richard killed him.[11]

Unsurprisingly, given their complexity, McKellen chose to omit these lines from his screenplay, though he was concerned about the effect of omitting Margaret (17). He was, however, acutely aware of the proliferation of similar names within both the royal family and the *dramatis personae* (on set, the younger prince was rechristened James to avoid confusion).[12] Thus, the film's insistent use of the name "Queen Elizabeth" may be seen as encoding a reference not only to the original Queen Elizabeth Woodville, but to Queen Elizabeth the Queen Mother, and perhaps also to Queen Elizabeth I; Queen Elizabeth's daughter, Princess Elizabeth, may signify not only Elizabeth of York but Elizabeth II, similarly named after her mother, who was indeed Princess Elizabeth of York at the time of the Abdication Crisis. Edward IV's name similarly echoes Edward VIII's,[13] completing a set of parallels that do indeed bring "now" close to "then."

These verbal links provide more than piquancy: they also suggest a substantive link between the royal family's present and its past (in which, after all, its authority and prestige are rooted). Such a suggestion is obliquely reinforced by the casting of Tim McInnerny as Catesby, for McInnerny is enduringly famous as Lord Percy Percy in Rowan Atkinson's four *Blackadder* series, which precisely follow various incarnations of the same individuals at different periods of royal history. Notably, the first series deals with the immediate aftermath of the reign of Richard III, portrayed by the celebrated comic Peter Cook as a physically whole, perfectly competent king who is accidentally killed while *winning* the Battle of Bosworth by his idiotic great-nephew, Atkinson's Edmund Blackadder. (Henry Tudor has meanwhile escaped to fight another day after three witches have failed to intercept him and prophesy greatness to him: they misidentify Blackadder as him instead.) Cook's Richard III is succeeded by his nephew,

Brian Blessed's "little-known" Richard IV, until Blackadder's inept machinations lead to the entire court being accidentally poisoned.

When Atkinson returned for a second series, it was set at the court of Miranda Richardson's dizzy Elizabeth I, with Atkinson himself as Lord Edmund Blackadder; in later series he appeared as Regency nobleman to Hugh Laurie's splendidly vacuous Prince Regent (the builder of the Brighton pavilion) before bowing out as the First World War shirker Captain Blackadder. In all of these, Percy Percy is his faithful sidekick, and Tim McInnerny's Catesby will thus be immediately recognizable as a part of this earlier retelling of "history," which has so many correspondences with the periods signaled by the film's own costumes and set.

This is, then, a film that systematically and deliberately presents the story of Richard III not as some isolated phenomenon of a long-gone fifteenth century, but as an episode that could in fact have formed part of much more recent history. As H. R. Coursen notes, Edward VIII "would have been king again had Operation Sea Lion succeeded."[14] The assertion properly belongs perhaps to the realm of opinion rather than fact, but it is nevertheless widely believed and perhaps contributes to the continuing fascination with the Duke and Duchess of Windsor.[15] Had it happened, what would the result have been? Would it have been George VI and his family who, in turn, found themselves asked to step down, and perhaps exiled? Since the Windsors had no children, Princess Elizabeth would still have been the heir, and the duke would in any case have been unlikely to have her and Princess Margaret smothered in the Tower. However, while the members of the House of Windsor, unlike those of the House of Plantagenet, have proved able to refrain from murdering each other, the duke's alleged wish to return and displace his brother certainly suggests unhappiness and a continuing interest in politics as well as in love. It invites speculation about the relationship between the brothers as well as about the duke's emotional state. In short, it raises the whole question—still so prominent in the British press—of the family life of the British royals and of what is alleged to be the severe emotional damage that each generation persists in inflicting on the next.

This history of intergenerational conflicts is a process often first traced to the notorious father-son feuds of the Hanoverians, so sharply depicted in Alan Bennett's *The Madness of George III*,[16] and the use of the Brighton pavilion reminds us very clearly of that Hanoverian legacy. In more recent years, there has been much publicity about the alleged emotional coldness with which both the queen and the duke of Edinburgh are said to have treated Prince Charles; however, he and his siblings have in turn come under the spotlight as parents as their marriages fail, their former spouses suffer or die, and their children are subjected to the resultant fights, separations, and publicity. The collective memory has also not forgotten that Princess Margaret was forbidden to marry Group Captain Peter Townsend because he had been previously divorced, leading to yet another conflict of love and duty so shortly after the Abdication Crisis, which had centered on that very issue. Lovelessness and subsequent failed relationships have indeed been prominent in the recent history of the British royal family.

Lovelessness and dysfunctional family relationships are also issues of clear concern in McKellen's screenplay. McKellen's Richard is an accomplished, devious manipulator, who has nothing but contempt for those like Anne, Clarence, and Queen Elizabeth, who fail (or, in the final case, appear to fail) to see through him. His only companionate relationships appear to be with Buckingham, whom he executes, and with Tyrell, whom, in a shockingly abrupt *coup de théâtre* in the closing moments of the film, he shoots in the face after the latter has suggested flight. Even with his last companion gone, however, Richard continues to offer an apparent emotional impregnability. In the end, he preempts Richmond's decision to shoot him by voluntarily stepping out into space, a last willed act that continues to assert his capacity to control events. As he falls, Al Jolson's voice sings "I'm sitting on top of the world," as in the Jimmy Cagney film *White Heat*— "Made it, Ma—on top of the world." It is not clear whether McKellen had originally known that this would happen, but he obviously relishes what he terms the "double irony" of the way that the song can, albeit in very different ways, apply to both Richard and Richmond (286). The song, however, suggests not only triumph. It also reminds us of the one person who, in this film, has been able to penetrate Richard's emotional defenses: his mother.[17]

McKellen's notes leave us in no doubt that Richard's relationship with his mother was crucial to his conception of the character. Though obviously in pain from his physical handicap (he is several times seen massaging his arm), Richard has managed to surmount his disability and demonstrates extraordinary dexterity and independence (as in the stage production, McKellen is spectacularly adept at one-handed maneuvers). He has risen to the highest military rank, and he persuades a beautiful woman to marry him under the most unpromising of circumstances. But nothing that he does can win over his mother. After Edward's death, he says to her, "Madam, Mother, I do humbly crave your blessing"; when she rebuffs him, he is visibly hurt, and both Catesby and Hastings—neither depicted elsewhere as a particularly sensitive soul—tactfully retreat, thus showing more consideration for Richard's feelings in this scene than does his mother.

Moreover, the Duchess of York's obvious coldness is further pointed up by the strong contrast between her own mothering practices and those of her daughter-in-law, Queen Elizabeth, who plays with her children, lets them stay up late to join in family activities, and presides over a household full of playthings. The fact that the Duchess of York is so clearly garbed as Queen Mary lends, in turn, sharp contemporary point to her characteriza-

tion. Queen Mary was indeed perceived as a chilly mother, supplementing
the iciness of her husband, George V; the persistent stammer of their younger
son, later George VI, is sometimes attributed to the emotional bleakness of
his upbringing, whereas the more open affection of his wife, Queen Elizabeth (the present Queen Mother), is widely credited with helping him overcome it. Certainly Queen Mary is said to have left her elder son, King
Edward VIII, in no doubt about her displeasure at his decision to abdicate.
Perhaps the most enduring image of her is at the funeral of George VI,
when she, Queen Elizabeth the Queen Mother, and the new Queen Elizabeth II all appeared dressed and veiled in black—an image perhaps subtly
matched by the film's scene of the Duchess of York taking leave of Queen
Elizabeth and her daughter Princess Elizabeth. Finally, the film also offers
another silent, though potent, connection to the idea of bad parenting:
McKellen notes that his makeup was done by Daniel Parker, who had just
been nominated for an Oscar for his work on *Mary Shelley's Frankenstein*
[dir. Kenneth Branagh, 1994] (28)—another deformed "child" abandoned
by its "parent," as well as an obvious point of reference for *Richard III*—
given *Frankenstein's* status as Kenneth Branagh's next career move after
Henry V (1989) and *Much Ado about Nothing* (1993).

If Richard's character can be at least partly attributed to his affection-
starved upbringing, and if that upbringing is in turn so clearly equated with
that historically afforded by the actual royal family, then the film offers a
stark suggestion: its Richard III is no aberrant monster, but an all too typical scion of recognizable British royalty—at virtually any time from the
fifteenth century to the late twentieth. His usurpation might well be said to
differ from that of his brother, Edward IV, merely in style rather than in
substance (the film's designer comments on precisely such differences in
visual style in the two courts [44]), presenting Richard, again, as the norm
rather than the exception.

Moreover, one might well wonder how easily distinguishable Richard's
coup is from the alleged plans of Edward VIII to effect his own restoration.
In the great scene of ghostly visitations towards the end of *Richard III*, and
in general characterization throughout, Shakespeare is consistently at pains
to differentiate Richard from Richmond as sharply as the similarities of
their names will allow; by contrast, McKellen, in his notes on the final
scene of the screenplay, comments that "Richmond's grin is unsettling"
(286), hinting at some such effect as the famous last moments of Polanski's
Macbeth (1971), with their clear indication of future treachery to be expected from Donalbain. Shakespeare might have drawn a clear line between Plantagenets and Tudors, but McKellen consistently blurs the
distinctions between Plantagenets and Windsors to suggest that this film,
which so defiantly advertises its Englishness, takes a very sharp scalpel
indeed to its anatomization of English royal identities. At the same time,

however, it treats its subject matter through veils of irony and suggestiveness that make it closely parallel to the circumspection of Shakespeare's own politicized handling of the history play.

NOTES

1. Although Loncraine was the director, it was McKellen who provided the continuity with the original stage production, and McKellen who, in his introduction to the screenplay, explains the reasons behind many of the adaptation's decisions.

2. Ian McKellen, *William Shakespeare's Richard III* (London: Doubleday, 1996), 300. All further quotations from the screenplay will be taken from this edition and reference will be given in the body of the text.

3. He refers, although without naming him, to the theories of Mr. Jack Leslau, who posits the survival of both princes well into the Tudor period (McKellen, 9–10).

4. A quick straw poll of the twelve people in the building this morning, with the question, "Do you know how the Queen refers to the royal family?" produced six people who said "the firm" and six people who did not know. Interestingly, five of those who knew were women; all of those who didn't were men. When I pointed this out, the consensus view was that women are generally more interested in the royal family.

5. On the 1930s setting, see also James N. Loehlin, "'Top of the world, ma': *Richard III* and Cinematic Convention," in *Shakespeare, the Movie: Popularizing the Plays on Film, TV, and Video*, ed. Lynda E. Boose and Richard Burt (London and New York: Routledge, 1997), 68–69.

6. All twelve of the people in the building—even the men—were able to answer "gin" to the question "What is the Queen Mother's favorite drink?"

7. Lynda E. Boose and Richard Burt, "Totally Clueless? Shakespeare Goes Hollywood in the 1990s," in *Shakespeare, the Movie*, 15.

8. Even McKellen's Battle of Battersea does not include a naval element though the trip to Brighton does introduce a coastal location into the film.

9. McKellen himself compares Lady Anne's decision to remarry to that of Jacqueline Kennedy Onassis (72). The shot of her shooting up (213) also recalls Bertolucci's film *The Last Emperor*, in which Elizabeth, estranged wife of Emperor Henry Pu Yi (an interesting coincidence of names) becomes a drug addict because of his sexual neglect of her. Suggestively, a scene later deleted showed Lady Anne's first appearance with a Ming vase in shot (49), and the music when Lady Anne is first seen has a faintly Oriental flavor. See Edward Behr, *The Last Emperor* (London: Macdonald & Co., 1987), 176 and 216, on the possible relationship between Empress Elizabeth's addiction and Pu Yi's bisexuality; McKellen is famous as the first self-proclaimed homosexual to be knighted by the queen. Samuel Crowl also notes a similarity between the film and Bertolucci's oeuvre ("*Richard III*," *Shakespeare Bulletin* 14:2 [Spring 1996]: 38).

10. Peter Holland, 'Hand in Hand to Hell,' *Times Literary Supplement*, 10 May 1996, 19.

11. William Shakespeare, *Richard III*, ed. E. A. J. Honigmann (Harmondsworth: Penguin, 1968), 4.4.40–43.

12. The one name that does *not* echo through the film is George. All mention of Clarence's initial being G is omitted, and by analogy with Earl Rivers, one might imagine the duke's Christian name to be Clarence. Only the young son of Stanley (whose vulnerability McKellen initially wished to stress by having him suffer from Down's Syndrome) is openly named George. Conceivably, the name is omitted from the cast of the royal family

out respect for George VI. McKellen is reported to be on friendly terms with the present Queen Mother, George VI's widow.

13.   A recent British television documentary made by the queen's youngest son, Prince Edward, played a similar game: centering on Edward VIII, it was entitled *Edward on Edward*. Another very close echo, but one not present in the film, is between Richard of Gloucester and the current Duke of Gloucester, also named Richard (the first time this coincidence has occurred). Though the present duke is patron of the Richard III Society, there are no other parallels between him and his namesake, at least not so far as that namesake is depicted by Shakespeare.

14.   H. R. Coursen, *Shakespeare in Production: Whose History?* (Athens: Ohio University Press, 1996), 137.

15.   In spring 1996, about the time the film was launched, the British papers were full of headlines like 'Was Wallis Simpson a man?' as they reported the suggestion that she might have been a genetic male who suffered from androgen insensitivity. It certainly provided a new angle on the celebrated romance.

16.   It was widely reported in Britain that Hollywood had insisted on changing Alan Bennett's title from *The Madness of George III* to *The Madness of King George* lest audiences be confused into thinking the film must be a sequel to *The Madness of George I* and *The Madness of George II*. McKellen, however, remarked in a *Guardian* interview (19 April 1996) that this story was untrue.

17.   See also Loehlin, 74–75.

WORKS CITED

Behr, Edward. *The Last Emperor*. London: Macdonald & Co., 1987.

Boose, Lynda E., and Richard Burt. "Totally Clueless? Shakespeare Goes Hollywood in the 1990s." In *Shakespeare, the Movie: Popularizing the Plays on Film TV, and Video*. Edited by Lynda E. Boose and Richard Burt, 8–22. London and New York: Routledge, 1997.

Coursen, H. R. *Shakespeare in Production: Whose History?* Athens: Ohio University Press, 1996.

Crowl, Samuel. "*Richard III*." *Shakespeare Bulletin* 14, no. 2 (1996): 38.

Holland, Peter. "Hand in Hand to Hell." *Times Literary Supplement,* 10 May 1996, 19.

Loehlin, James N. "'Top of the world, ma': *Richard III* and Cinematic Convention." In *Shakespeare, the Movie: Popularizing the Plays on Film, TV, and Video*. Edited by Lynda E. Boose and Richard Burt, 67–79. London and New York: Routledge, 1997.

McKellen, Ian. *William Shakespeare's Richard III*. London: Doubleday, 1996.

Shakespeare, William. *Richard III*. Edited by E. A. J. Honigmann. Harmondsworth: Penguin, 1968.

FILMS CITED

Blackadder: The Television Series. Directed by Mandie Fletcher and Martin Shardlow. 4-season series. BBC Television, 1983–89.

The Last Emperor. Directed by Bernardo Bertolucci. 2 hr. 40 min. AAA, 1987. Videocassette.

Macbeth. Directed by Roman Polanski. 2 hr. 20 min. Playboy Productions, 1971. Videocassette.

The Madness of King George. Directed by Nicholas Hynter. 1 hr. 50 min. Samuel Goldwyn, 1994. Videocassette.

Mary Shelley's Frankenstein. Directed by Kenneth Branagh. 2 hr. 3 min. Tristar, 1994. Videocassette.

Richard III. Directed by Richard Loncraine. 1 hr. 44 min. United Artists, 1995. Videocassette.

White Heat. Directed by Raoul Walsh. 1 hr. 54 min. Warner Bros.,1949. Videocassette.

(Un)Doing the Book "without Verona walls": A View from the Receiving End of Baz Luhrmann's *William Shakespeare's Romeo + Juliet*

Alfredo Michel Modenessi

"Two loves I have . . ."
— Para Mónica y Sarah

" . . . I wonder who
Will be the last, the very last, to seek
This place for what it was . . ."
—Philip Larkin, *Church Going*

A DARK SCREEN. A FRAME WITHIN A FRAME MOVES TOWARD US. IT IS ANOTHER screen, a TV screen inside the cinema screen. The film we are about to see is framed by the TV experience—the experience of popular arts and media. An anchorwoman delivers the opening sonnet of William Shakespeare's *Romeo and Juliet* in the received monotone of the Evening News, offering us an unlikely segue into Tonight's Special Report on the recent turmoil in Verona Beach. When she is almost finished, we plunge wildly through the TV screen until we stop at the face of a statue of Christ; thunderous music fills the air as white lettering splashes across the screen, which now reads: "In Fair Verona." The camera pulls back to a wide shot of a busy urban landscape presided over by the gigantic statue. Piece-by-piece a circus of urban chaos unfolds in a schizotimic clicking of images until we return to the solemn face of Christ, which is suddenly transformed into a photograph on the front page of a tabloid as a male voice-over recites the Prologue to *Romeo and Juliet* anew. Thus, in the midst of a rough visual ride we have experienced two far from "bookish" renderings of the Prologue to our story; but in spite of our own eyes, we have entered a "book" entitled *William Shakespeare's Romeo + Juliet*, a film by Baz Luhrmann (1996).

It is not long before we see a collection of cinematic images that resemble the unfolding of another kind of book: a comic book. At a gas station, a car stops; violently, emphatically, its front plate invades our framed view. What follows is a drastically cut and filmed reelaboration of act 1, scene 1, from Shakespeare's "precious book of love,"[1] which we experience less as a continuous sequence of filmed action than as the stark juxtaposition of rapidly scanned frames displaying one aspect after another of the participants and their doings.[2] One of these pictures is a close-up of Abra's face, an unmistakably Latin American young man clad in the obligatory black vest, carrying a large gun in a chest holster. The camera has settled on Abra,[3] his gun, and his metal-biting teeth showing the engraved word "SIN" only after a series of tense, schizoidal cuts and flashes of faces resembling drawn—not filmed—expressions, have added momentum to this "comic book" effect.

Later, an extreme close-up discreetly frames the chin, mouth, and nose of another young Latin American, Tybalt, who lights up a dark cigarette to whistling music, evocative of a spaghetti-western leitmotif. A shot, strategically filmed in slow motion, closes in on the metal heels of his boots, framed within an almost blank aural atmosphere, where the only sounds we can hear are those of a match falling and the boots crunching it. Thus emphasized, the combination of images and sounds emanating from the screen generate comic book onomatopoeia: SWISHH, CRRRUNCHH! And then The Brawl begins, underscored by more spaghetti-western music and choreographed through a mix of formulaic moves from classic action films and comic strips. The entire sequence, by far the best in this film, is a disruptive interpretation of a popular play in a popular medium, as well as a comment on popular media. In choosing to dwell on the "bookishness" of the materials with which he is working, Luhrmann has created—at least from the receiving end—yet another kind of book: a postmodern "book."[4]

Another version of this "book" may help to clarify how Luhrmann's postmodern rendering of "bookishness" works. Once more, we begin by confronting a frame within a frame—this time, a dark computer screen. The sound of a door opening is followed by a flash of red light that dissipates, like a comic book flash, into the still, dark background as a voice says, "SHHH, somebody is coming." Two shots ring out: BANG! BANG! On the screen now appears a drawing of a gun pointing at us, held by a pastel-colored hand with partially superimposed lettering reading "Circumstance." Then, vaguely visible under slowly roaming lights, the coats of arms of the Capulets and the Montagues emerge as another voice—the same male voice from the film—delivers the opening lines of the Prologue. We have now entered the "book" entitled *William Shakespeare's Romeo + Juliet: An Interactive Trip to Verona Beach*, a CD-ROM production by Fox Interactive and Circumstance Design, made in collaboration with the film's team at the time of shooting. As music and images begin to saturate the screen, we may leaf (click and drag) through the "pages" of this "Interactive Trip." Yet the "book" it constitutes—pages, texts, images, frames and framing devices, and so forth—remains a "book," howsoever ("comic-ly") bracketed.

Luhrmann's film is a radical example of the apparent historical depletion of Shakespeare's books,[5] thereby inviting conversation about the interaction of book and cinema within the conditions of reception in our frame-and-screen-wise postmodern world. Practically no review I have read, nor any colleague with whom I have discussed the film, has failed to label Luhrmann's version of *Romeo and Juliet* "postmodern." Every readily recognizable feature of this now comfortably numb category may be invoked while examining the movie: furious juxtaposition; re- and de-contextualization; rejection of representation; seemingly random self- and cross-reference and allusion; media- and genre-jumbling; undermining of plot and character (and of their conventions in general: conflict, motivation); and, of course, the quintessential denial of totalizing and totalized meaning. In short, the postmodern text is all about the disruption and/or depletion of the conventional concept of the Work of Art and, by extension, the literary Work, that is, the sovereign Book.

The productivity of any Shakespearean text far outdoes its possibilities of particular performance, thereby necessitating selectivity and interpretive commitment from directors. The conventional representation of Shakespeare's *Romeo and Juliet* has consistently foregrounded the "lamentable tragedy" of a frustrated affair, at best entailing a great emotional shock and frequently conveying a sort of universal lesson: "Thou shalt look before thou leapest." Like most early modern texts, however, *Romeo and Juliet* hosts many alternative narratives open to actualization and controversy, whether critical or artistic. One of the merits of Luhrmann's directorial approach is its flashing, pop-cultural translation of several interesting features of the play that are often ignored, repressed, or only subtly brought to life in modern productions: for example, Mercutio as Drag Queen; Juliet somewhat freed from fatal helplessness and here and there accorded a status closer, say, to Alice Arden's; Lady Capulet and Tybalt as incestuous lovers worthy of talk show sensationalism; Friar Lawrence as a cross between redeemed ex-con and recovering drug addict; an ending that does not yell reconciliation, contrition, or redemption; and so on. But as the recent history of stage and screen adaptation suggests, once provocative features such as these surface, they tend to fall flat, generating either naive attempts at socially charged irony (as in the last scene of Michael Bogdanov's 1987 RSC production)[6] or ultimately harmless, though funny, films like Lloyd Kaufman's *Tromeo and Juliet* (1996), a case of depletion by laxative.

I do not intend either to question or validate the assessment of Luhrmann's movie as a performance rendered in a postmodern style. My approach presumes "postmodern" as a label assumed by Luhrmann's film with regard to form, which therefore does not demand or welcome elucidation. Yet, from a critical standpoint, if postmodernism has indeed rejected "the idea that the . . . work of art would disclose or reveal the deeper meaning of life," thereby accelerating "the demise of traditional categories, genres and canons,"[7] then the question is: does Luhrmann's postmodern version of *Romeo and Juliet* "soar above a common bound"? (1.4.18); that is, does it reach beyond conventional interpretations of the Book and mere homage to the Bard?

Assuming also that "An important part of the postmodern movement has been the questioning of legitimizing authority with a concomitant surge in writing from the previously marginalized sectors of society,"[8] a postmodern filmic performance of Shakespeare's *Romeo and Juliet* might be expected to actualize a critical perspective,[9] a dissident reading promoting a response opposed to the kind that keeps the play sunk "Under love's heavy burden" (1.4.22) as an endearing but inevitably reiterative icon of "lamentable chance" (5.3.146). On the one hand, such a film would be expected to differ from its predecessors while pointedly alluding to them. Doubtless, Luhrmann's movie does so, its immediate source being Zeffirelli's 1968 version.[10] On the other hand, however, such a film would also be expected to differ critically more than merely being different, more than simply eliciting similar responses through different means. How far from the commonplace response is *William Shakespeare's Romeo + Juliet*? In what follows, I will try to explore these questions, focusing on some aspects of Luhrmann's work that are indeed provocative from the receiving end, but that remain either merely sketched out or actually quiet and unquestioning in the background of an otherwise brilliant display of postmodernistic dexterity and quick flashes of dissidence.[11] Luhrmann's film fluctuates between splendid thrusts of disruption of received authority and an ultimately time-pleasing reiteration of the Book "as is," that is, as it has been historically and ideologically fixed. As we shall see, *William Shakespeare's Romeo + Juliet* ultimately delivers a fable of young love caught well *within* "Verona walls" (3.3.17).

☆ ☆ ☆

My initial response to Baz Luhrmann's *William Shakespeare's Romeo + Juliet* was an example of unrepentant professional bias. The first things that came to my mind were: (1) this film poses some interesting problems in subtitling that went unnoticed among its translators for the Spanish-speaking market; and (2) this film raises provocative difficulties for compilers of Shakespearean filmographies. At first glance, Luhrmann's picture might be added to Graham Holderness and Christopher McCullough's "Selective Filmography," which is defined as a "reference list of 'complete', straightforward versions of Shakespeare's plays in film, television and videotape form."[12] Indeed, the film does roughly comply with the authors' explanation that "'complete'" means "a full though possibly abridged version of the play's action," as opposed to "an uncut version of the received texts,"[13] a criterion that protects their list from considerable shrinking.

By the same token, however, the term "straightforward" presents us with a nagging ambiguity, which is reinforced by the fact that Greenaway's *Prospero's Books* (1991) is pointedly *not* included in the filmography, although Derek Jarman's version of *The Tempest* (1979) is. While Holderness and McCullough's list "specifically excludes free adaptations,"[14] it is worth noting that Greenaway's picture, despite its apparent liberties, contains a version of the text which is not as radically cut as, say, Zeffirelli's *Hamlet* (1990), nor does it fail to offer "a full though possibly abridged version of the play's action."[15] And what about the exception the authors make for including films like Kurosawa's *Throne of Blood* (1957) which, they explain, is accorded such status because it has been "placed at the center of critical debate"?[16] Does this mean that roughly three years after its release, *Prospero's Books* had not yet caused enough of a stir within the ranks of the Shakespearean establishment? While this may be the case, there is no denying the controversiality of Greenaway's film, which remains rich in implications for the reassessment of much Shakespearean film criticism, as Douglas Lanier brilliantly demonstrates.[17]

Just as Greenaway's film has caused uneasiness with regard to classification, so might Luhrmann's movie, despite both the quick "postmodern" label and its self-definition as *William Shakespeare's Romeo +[&] Juliet*.[18] The first problem derives from this very fact: the film goes by the name of Baz Luhrmann's *William Shakespeare's Romeo + Juliet* instead of *Baz Luhrmann's Adaptation of Shakespeare's Romeo and Juliet*, or something to this effect. Of course, this choice could be explained away by the logic of a review in *The Economist*: after a quick but devastating comment on *Tromeo and Juliet*, the anonymous reviewer concludes that since Kaufman's film was so unmercifully bad, "to avoid confusion, Baz Luhrmann (perhaps inspired by *Bram Stoker's Dracula*) chose to call the rival film he had directed *William Shakespeare's Romeo and Juliet*."[19] But even if this were the actual reason behind such a title, that would not prevent it from adding an interesting twist to the authorial controversies the film invites from the receiving end.

Despite the modifiers "complete" and "straightforward," a system of classification like Holderness and McCullough's depends on the fundamental criterion that the items on their list are "versions of Shakespeare's plays in film, television and videotape form." The phrasing of this classificatory scheme stresses the authorial weight of Shakespeare and, at best, remains neutral with regard to the status of the filmmaker. Filmmakers exercise authorial prerogatives, however, as Douglas Lanier observes of *Prospero's Books*: "Greenaway recasts *The Tempest* within a filmic vocabulary that constantly acknowledges its competition with Shakespearean textuality while remaining faithful . . . to the play's received text."[20] Greenaway's title is, of course, only one of the many sources that point to his authorial approach, but it is also a crucial one, as Lanier's discussion suggests.[21] In the case of Luhrmann's movie, however, the capacity of the title to signify authorial control is rendered ambiguous by the accumulation of possessive marks. "Shakespeare" appears here as a writer, but as a writer who is also part of the text, of the fiction's name, which both claims and disclaims authorship for/from Shakespeare and Luhrmann.

The problem is further complicated by the fact that many of Shakespeare's plays do not bear titles in a modern sense, and therefore those that are provided titles encourage speculation about authorial issues from the giving as well as from the receiving end. Such plays have traditionally been named after the play's principal characters by a combination of figures other than the author. These "titles" are thus more descriptive than literary, but remain ambivalent, for they lack the clear marks of early modern title-pages, as in "The Most Lamentable Tragedy of Romeo and Juliet, as it hath been sundry times acted . . ." and tend to include categories that become debatable in view of historical processes of reception. It is true that Luhrmann's title seems to avoid an automatic association of the play with the Aristotelian category of tragedy, for instance, suggesting a remove from conventional readings. Still, after two-thirds of alluringly unconventional performance, the film offers a simple—at times overdone—dénouement in the purest "tragedy of circumstance" style.[22]

While Greenaway's countertitle of *Prospero's Books* makes the game of name and book even more relevant to his overt "competition with Shakespeare's textuality," Luhrmann's choice of title may also be approached as one of many disruptive moves that inform his film. Luhrmann appears to adopt a strategy opposite of Greenaway's, and yet, in his "Note" to the published screenplay, he plays a similar palimpsestic hand, albeit in a covert fashion:

> I've always wanted to do *Romeo and Juliet*. Shakespeare's plays touched everyone, from the street sweeper to the Queen of England. He was a rambunctious, sexy, violent, entertaining storyteller. We're trying to make this movie rambunctious, sexy, violent, and entertaining the way Shakespeare might have if he had been a filmmaker. . . . Everything that's in the movie is

drawn from Shakespeare's play. Violence, murder, lust, love, poison, drugs that mimic death, it's all there.[23]

The authorial game is played to the point of making us wonder whether Luhrmann's "we" functions as a synecdoche for the collaborative authorship of filmmaking or the Royal We of kingly authority. While the former offers a more likely explanation for Luhrmann's ambiguous use of "we," the idea of the "collaborative" begs the additional question: Luhrmann & Co., Luhrmann and Shakespeare, or Shakespeare and Luhrmann? Granted, *William Shakespeare's Romeo + Juliet* is not unlike other productions that diverge from the conventional delivery, performance, or representation of the Shakespearean text; but it is unlike such predecessors in that the latter have been released and received as products of "avant-garde" artists pointedly assuming a dissident position—most of the time in the form of "adaptations"—while Luhrmann's movie is an avowedly industrial product essaying a radical formal approach that does not ultimately escape the constraints of what constitutes a "complete version" with a specific target: the teen moviegoers.[24] However, the assimilation of Shakespeare's name to the film's title makes it hard to sustain the idea that this "complete version" is not also a "depleted" one. And, in acknowledging its source, Luhrmann's *William Shakespeare's Romeo + Juliet* also invites us to ponder a more fundamental authorial dilemma: how can any adaptation, even a "complete" one, avoid being a palimpsest?

Judging from the title and the "Note," Luhrmann makes no claim that his film is an adaptation, a term which, in Ace G. Pilkington's view, "put[s] film-makers at risk."[25] Moreover, he does not characterize the film in a way that invites us to label it "an obvious re-writing," the kind of product over which "few critics worry,"[26] since such films are not concerned with issues of fidelity and authenticity in the first place. Accordingly, despite his offhand approach to identifying what stuff his movie is made of, Luhrmann seems to define his film in precisely the terms he expresses above: he has recreated Shakespeare's Book as Shakespeare would have "had he been a filmmaker." In other words, the Australian director has opted for a radical approach to what may be "done" to/with a Shakespearean text for the production of a movie while suggesting that his work is "authentically" Shakespeare's—a clever commercial move, among other things. Deliberately or not, the longer and certainly bolder history of adaptation, cutting, reassigning, and rewriting for the stage (translations included) has interacted with Luhrmann's imagination in order to convince him that the "certain text" (4.1.21) of *Romeo and Juliet*—at least the violence, murder, lust, love, passion, drugs, etc.—is indeed "all there."[27]

In the long run, is there anyone who thinks that Shakespeare's "precious book of love" would be viable as a stage or screen product without some serious editing, pruning, rewriting, adapting, or even ax-play? Put differently, is there any way to perform a play like *Romeo and Juliet* without some degree of authorial trespassing? The play itself is long and at times redundant or, at least, of uneven quality (e.g., 2.4, 3.2, 4.5, etc.). To my knowledge, *Romeo and Juliet* has never really made it to the scholars' top shelf; despite its status as a favorite object of performance, it has sparked relatively less interest as an object of study.[28] Perhaps one explanation for this has to do with the fact that *Romeo and Juliet* is closer to depletion as text than it is to depletion as film. Being a fixture in Western tradition, its basic anecdote is well known to everybody—even to those who have never read it, nor ever will. The story of two adolescents who die because their parents' strife makes their love impossible is thus apparently "complete" in the minds of all prior to any specific act of performance/reception. In fact, I do not think it too daring to say that today *Romeo and Juliet* is, for most people, Zeffirelli's *Romeo and Juliet*, and that Luhrmann's version may be expected to replace the "Italian" version soon enough, at least in the minds of Generation X and Y. In terms of reception, then, the text is curiously depleted before and after performance of any kind—except, maybe, a radically dissident one. Is Luhrmann's one such performance?

Although the relevant issues are many—and I believe they are better approached by reading Luhrmann's film as a palimpsest of Zeffirelli's— we may begin to tackle this question by considering some of the implications of Luhrmann's authorial—even actual—trespass in his choice of setting for *William Shakespeare's Romeo + Juliet*.

☆ ☆ ☆

At first sight, it seems safe to assume that, beyond a simple relocation of the play's "original" setting, Luhrmann opted for the creation of a postmodern dystopia within which to frame the lovers' plight. Indeed, the world of Luhrmann's movie defies definition as a mere translation of an "original" setting into a "contemporary" one, or even as an adaptation of whatever is encompassed within "fair Verona walls" to a postmodern, transcultural frame. Although such principles do underlie the film, it takes place in "(un) 'fair Verona' Beach," a setting that is not so much "another" or a "new" place and time but rather a (dys)place in a (dys)time. And there is another twist to this already complicated mapping. Verona Beach is built upon signs easily recognizable as originating on *either* side of the U.S.-Mexico border, but *most* of them are rooted in the Mexican landscape and religious iconography. Moreover, in Verona Beach such signs are rendered unspecific by their combination, magnification, and reiteration through an equally eclectic disruption of style as unifying device. Thus, *William Shakespeare's Romeo + Juliet* occurs in a twilight area where conventional notions of adaptation are complicated by conflicts between poetic drama and cinema, underscored by the disruptive aesthetics of comic books and of pop and rock music and videoclips. Luhrmann's film is a chronicle of tension between artistic concepts, artistic vehicles, and the artists themselves. In this context, the film's setting presents us with not only "fair Verona" turned dystopia, but a testimony—as much flawed as fascinating—of the unstable critical point at which we meet the Bard (not)here and (not)now, in a dystopia of reception.

The variety of definitions of "Verona Beach" to which Luhrmann's film gives rise testifies to this problem of reception. The CD-ROM version of *William Shakespeare's Romeo + Juliet* defines Verona Beach as a "mythical city similar to Los Angeles or other contemporary cities in the world." David Gates somewhat debatably suggests that "while it evokes Rio, Mexico City, L.A. and Miami, it's absolutely Elizabethan."[29] An abstract from Samuel Crowl's 1997 Shakespeare Association of America seminar on "Kenneth Branagh and His Contemporaries" dubs Verona Beach an "imaginary South American Verona, a place of magical realism,"[30] overplaying a widespread but fragile card pertaining to Latin American literature. The editors of the recent collection *Shakespeare, the Movie* call the setting of *William Shakespeare's Romeo + Juliet* "a Cuban American community."[31] And finally, the anonymous review in *The Economist* talks of "an imaginary American resort,"[32] betraying a frankly European confusion.

All of these "definitions" of Verona Beach play right into Luhrmann's dystopic hand, for we are probably not meant to identify this place as anything other than a shimmering no-place, although H. R. Coursen wrote an entry in anticipation of the film's release where he did mention that the film was "set in Mexico," adding that the picture might "incorporate a cross-cultural, instead of merely a cross-town, love affair. We will wait to see."[33] He simply waited in vain: the "cross-cultural" is beyond the compass of Luhrmann's non"interactive trip" to Mexico. Counteracting the efforts of directors like Zeffirelli, who strove to showcase the "Italian" element in the play, Luhrmann un-documents his setting by underplaying its fiction. In so doing, *William Shakespeare's Romeo + Juliet* reduces its Mexican landscape to a trope for the postmodern city.

There are reasons for this, of course. Postmodern criticism has identified the architecture of the modern city—purportedly a paradigm of good living turned hostile, meaningless maze—as a token of the failure of the modern world to achieve its ideal of "progress." According to this narrative, the modern world tried to create places for perfect living, whose projects bore optimistic names such as *Broadacre City, Prospective City, Turmstadt,*

Weltraumstadt, Cité Totale, Ville Solaire, Ciudad Jardín, Villa del Mañana,
etc.; what emerged instead was the *New Babylon*.[34] In Luhrmann's film we
see several aspects of this failure of modernity in a quasi-comic book narrative from the top of Christ's statue down to the schizoidal rhythms of the
city below. The statue at the top of the church, that of the Sacred Heart of
Mary, allegorizes this failure, its seemingly inexhaustible empathy rendered
indifferently angular, absurdly unmoved in the midst of chaos. The use of
helicopter shots to frame the statue makes the elevation of the Lady still
more noticeable and, more importantly, the distance proportionately larger
between her imploring patrons and her stony embrace. Her open arms, like
the openness of many vistas of the city, seem more to mock than to man-
date its inhabitants' freedom of action. And the same may be said, in general, of the statue of Christ, nicely digitalized on top of the monument to
the Independence of Mexico. The presence of helicopters alone reiterates
what nineties moviegoers—as well as many urban dwellers—know all too
well: that a chopper's scan-light locates and isolates people, rendering them
small and helpless within a vast and indifferent urban landscape.

Luhrmann's film also relies on the suffocating recurrence of horrid billboards and dilapidated sites to create a sense of irredeemable urban decay.[35] The Babylon in Luhrmann's film aims at the (un)doing of City, as if
Erewhon reverted to *Nowhere/now-here*. Out there, buildings are destroyed
beyond purpose and recognition; or, as is the case with Luhrmann's Mantua,
there lies a wasteland where trailer houses make the prospect of permanence hopeless and, perhaps, unwanted. Here Luhrmann's fiction smacks
of a comment on our mixed culture: this place "South of the border" (all
souths and borders being relative) *has* failed to achieve the modern world's
ideal of "progress"—not entirely to the disapproval of some of us who
inhabit Verona Beach. Unfortunately, such a comment remains a flashing
spot in the midst of a gigantic videoclip, the kind of work that compels
little, if any, "talk (that is, memory) of . . . sad things" (5.3.306). Herein,
perhaps, this movie becomes more MTV than postmodern, more a new
way to illustrate the old Bard than a provocative way to question illustra-
tion; it wants a more intense dialogue with its context.

☆ ☆ ☆

Unsurprisingly little has been made of the fact that "Verona Beach," the
mysteriously unlocatable home of the infamous Capulet and Montague feud,
is quite specifically, if accidentally, Mexican. The choice of Mexico City
and other parts of my country—namely, the town of Boca del Río, now
inside the port of Veracruz on the coast of the Gulf of Mexico—for the
shooting of *William Shakespeare's Romeo + Juliet* adds another problem-

atic layer to the already complex "textuality" of Luhrmann's film. The first issue to consider is that Mexico was not the site originally planned for shooting; it became an alternative to Miami or Los Angeles because of budget constraints. Perhaps this explains the mixture of fascination and disregard, rendered formally through patterns of saturation and depletion, with which Luhrmann approaches this locational (and cultural) intertext. If Zeffirelli sought to situate his *Romeo and Juliet* firmly in a "Shakespearean Italy," Luhrmann imagines a time and place caught between here-after and no-where, unidentified and unidentifiable, yet capable of misleading the viewer into thinking it some place "South of the border." Indeed, there is much of our urban, small town, church, and home imagery in this film, but Luhrmann's rendering often foregrounds otherness and foreignness even to a native Mexican. Such imagery is used in both random and highly derivative combinations—a consequence, perhaps, of the desire to create a rarefied atmosphere capable of exercising a certain fascination over the viewer, without specifying its Mexican source—as well as some *un*desirable associations that it may conjure. For to do so would be to acknowledge yet another "text" competing for the authority of and authorization by *William Shakespeare's Romeo + Juliet.*

In keeping with Luhrmann's postmodern maneuvers of disruption and depletion through visual and aural saturation, the Mexican element is present in the film as an overelaborate display of signs that inundate our perspective and ultimately actualize nonsignifiers, vehicles for un-documentation. In the gas station sequence, for instance, Tybalt delivers the Book's meaningfully ironic line "Turn . . . and look upon thy death" (1.1.64) as he opens his jacket to reveal his guns. But what he more emphatically reveals is a splendid vest bearing the image of the Sacred Heart of Christ almost *wearing* the guns; such is the bizarre, pastiche image of "death" that confronts Benvolio and the unwary viewer. While Shakespeare's text suggests here an Elizabethan approach to Death (capital "D"), Luhrmann's emphasis on Death as an object of aesthetic fascination provokes a fragmented mode of reception: religiosity and shock suddenly combine to inspire worship of admirable comic book artwork. The end result is a veritable montage of: (a) Mexican religious iconography; (b) an unspecified context of actual and irrational violence (an L.A.-cum-Miami street-gang blend, perhaps); and (c) an overdramatized, even parodic gesture of gun-worshipping by Tybalt as he falls on his knees to kiss the gun before demonstrating his deadly kitsch Tarantino-meets-Rodríguez marksmanship. The hardcore Catholic image of the Sacred Heart of Christ—though legitimately Mexican while Spanish and Italian in origin—therefore becomes a saturated icon offering a quick formal thrust of authorial disruption. Although it might be more profitably approached in cross-cultural terms, Luhrmann's camera clearly has no time to linger over such details. Hence, it may be worth doing so here, where we can pause to consider how the provocatively uncertain text of Mexican culture is brought to bear on the "certain text" of Shakespeare's play.

Because Mexican culture has emerged historically as a site of contestation between and "border-crossing" among multiple cultures and subcultures, it would seem to offer a rich ideological backdrop for Luhrmann's rendering of the internecine conflict between the Capulets and Montagues. Instead, the visual details contained in the above scene render these politicized conflicts in purely spectacular terms, as competing artistic and cultural influences vie to monopolize the viewer's attention. Tybalt's waistcoat, for instance, is actually the handmade product of a fine Mexican designer, but it may be better examined as a combination of basic Mexican religious iconography with a powerfully Chicano fashion sense. The same may be said of the low-rider interpretation of the Capulet Boys' car, as well as of their clothing, tattoos, hairstyles, eyewear, and footgear. Chicano style points to the affirmation of cultural identity through the preservation—by a sort of mythologizing magnification—of our popular traditions and extravagance. This kind of affirmation is very clearly made through works such as Diane Gamboa's serigraph "Little Gold Man" (1990),[36] a splendid depiction of Chicano attitudes, wardrobe, hairstyles, tattoos, icons, and colors that might even be cited as indirect visual sources for Luhrmann's pictures of life in Verona Beach. In this context, then, Tybalt's boots may thus be overframed by a fetishistic camera, but they are not in the least respect overdone: they exemplify the best (which is to say the worst) version of kitsch in the Mexico-U.S. border style. These signs, merely on display in Luhrmann's film, could have been taken to a stimulating critical level had they been explored in the context of this intriguing area of cultural clash and redefinition. However, these potentially intertextual complements to the fictional conflict *Romeo and Juliet* dramatizes get lost in the shuffle of Luhrmann's relentless privileging of production values over text and context. Demonstrating a sort of paranoia with regard to "totalization," the profusion of multireferential icons in Luhrmann's film serves, formally, a postmodern purpose: meaning—intertextual and intercultural—becomes engulfed and obliterated in the obsessive reiteration of signs. Still, it does not seem to accomplish any sort of "questioning of legitimizing authority," much less activate "a concomitant surge in writing from the previously marginalized sectors of society."

To illustrate this want, consider the interest that Luhrmann's camera shows in the Catholic imagery that pervades and characterizes this marginalized place called Verona Beach. The director seems to be looking for a way to establish a visual atmosphere of passionate devotion mixed with irrational violence, but he succeeds only insofar as form is concerned. The published script and the CD version emphasize that Verona Beach is a place where a modern world of free trade and globalization and an old but alive world of feudal structures merge and collide; a place where people speak "Elizabethan English with an American accent" (CD version), and profess the Catholic faith with a sixteenth- and seventeenth-century passion; where they carry the most sophisticated guns, dance to cheesy pop music, and get high on "Queen Mab" ecstasy pills. However, these people are merely pasted against bizarrely picturesque Third World landscapes—nothing like clean, well-lighted, and comfortable Suburbia, but neither like dark and terrifying Inner City, *barrios*, or slums, or truly lawless territories. With the exception of Mercutio's drag queen act and the opening and gas station sequences, Luhrmann's exaggerated, comic book portraits fail to achieve an effectively critical level of postmodern undoing of stereotypes in the way that, say, Robert Rodríguez's *El Mariachi* (1992) succeeds. Thus, what seems to begin as an interesting take on how living conditions in Verona Beach reflect intra- and intersocial, ethnic, and cultural conflicts, ends up being very close in spirit to the oldest stereotypes of a land inhabited by big sombreroed, *mucho-macho bandidos* and misguided blond kids.[37]

Despite their ingenuous overdramatization, the signs in Verona Beach do somehow characterize the surface of the social tension, economic distress, and insecurity that pervade my country and other Latin American nations. Yet, Luhrmann's deft gun-teen-men are rather naïve if judged against the realities of worlds where the social contract is increasingly losing ground to lawlessness,[38] especially due to an artificial modernization of economic structures that in fact has made our economies even more vulnerable to the volubility of capital and its far-reaching consequences—among which the growth of economic, social, and educational gaps is not least. Granted, we are allowed a Grand Guignol glimpse at the corruption and decay of social and religious institutions, but no effort is made to dwell on causes; although the film sketches out, and the CD version explicitly mentions, the rivalry of Montagues and Capulets as a feud between two big corporations,[39] the issue is never pursued beyond the commonplace. Thus, if the Book offers a variety of cues for the actualization and exploration of problems underlying its narrative of "lamentable tragedy," the film rests at ease foregrounding some of them as a frame with a hole in the middle, like the movie-house of Sycamore Grove, or the screen where we have seen the picture, when at the end the TV pulls back until it disappears. The role of religion and the religious institution is a case in point.

If we return to the rich opening sequence of the film, or take a look at the decoration of Juliet's chamber, we may locate added layers of undetected cultural significance in the Mexican interpretation of dramatic Catholic imagery, which is the result of a long and complex dialogue of our indigenous roots with Counter-Reformation art. The images of saints and the suffering countenances and pierced hearts of Christ and Mary that pervade Luhrmann's film (which are just as characteristically and eclectically displayed in Chicano art)[40] were among the artistic interests of Francisco Albert, the Spanish-Mexican sculptor who made the monumental statue of the Sacred Heart of Mary that looms over the film from the top of the church.[41] Moving from the exteriors of Verona Beach to its ornate interiors, we find a variety of visual allusions to our religious tradition of *Día de muertos* (All Saints). This rich cultural event is reelaborated in the decoration of the church interior as "Capel's monument" (5.1.18) with the strictly fin-de-siècle touch of the neon light crosses, a somewhat recent addition to our religious paraphernalia. The flower carpet therein is also a fine artisan tradition linked to religious fervor that extends from Spain to, among other places, Mexico, Guatemala, and El Salvador. The decoration of actual tombs during *Día de muertos* provide examples of more conventional displays of artistry characteristic of this celebration, which also has complex pre-Hispanic connotations beyond the grasp of the film.[42]

H. R. Coursen has pointed out, in conversation, that the statue of Christ shows how in Luhrmann's film "religion is under repair." Indeed, one cannot help noticing the scaffolding. Hence, at first sight, it would be attractive to read in Luhrmann's use of the church as "Capel's monument" a subversion of "Church" as "Tomb."[43] But, as suggested above, the decoration of the place (though once more taken to an extreme) clearly corresponds to the altars we set up for *Día de muertos*, an occasion when our dead are expected to come back and remind us of their permanence by leaving some trace of their visit, often, by eating some of the food that is offered at the altars. It is, therefore, a complex celebration of life *and* death, a ritual literally on the borderline. One begins to wonder whether Luhrmann was actually aware of any such things. My guess is that he and his production designer, Catherine Martin, were fascinated by the visual contents of this tradition, and imagined the outstanding atmosphere of the death scene mainly as a wonderful display of *their* understanding of how the Catholic mind works in a place where religiousness and violence meet. In other words, this vision of "Capel's monument" serves more as the destination of yet another of Romeo's "trips" than as an intertext subverting the Book's received textuality or as an eruption of the setting's complex ideological fabric in the conventional narrative. Luhrmann's Juliet is thus not placed inside a hell on earth (or underground, both conventional readings, of course) nor inside a critical environment, but only in a fascinatingly "alien" funeral parlor, while his Miami-dressed Romeo remains a sort of tourist lost in the wilderness of a semisacrificial site, in turn lost in its own spectacular profusion.

Other examples of Mexican culture culled from the film relate more closely to our imagery and customs as modified by our interaction with foreign traditions capable of greater—say, colonial—reach. At the ball, for example, the skeleton disguise for Abra is a token of our adaptation of foreign, mainly American, customs that operate as universally accepted excuses for commercial transaction. It is a curious combination of a Halloween piece with features of one of our own icons of Death, drawn from the historical tradition of the Mexicans' humorous disregard for death and one of its conspicuous correlatives, the naked skull. Originally intended to appear as "a demon" in the screenplay,[44] Abra wears the full body disguise of the skeleton with a Mexico-U.S.-border cowboy hat and boots, as well as skull-like makeup, once more alluding to our traditions concerning the commemoration of *Día de muertos*.[45] Abra's costume also evokes the work of the superb engraver José Guadalupe Posada, whose characters presented as *calaveras* (naked skulls) or *calacas* (skeletons) have been reinterpreted continually since the beginning of the twentieth century—either directly by people who participate in such celebrations wearing masks of death, or by other artists, as the Chicano Dolores Guerrero-Cruz in her serigraph "The Bride" (1985),[46] where the face of the wife-to-be is that of a naked skull. The substitution of the screenplay's Abra "the demon" by the film's Abra *la calaca* o *la huesuda* (literally, "the bony one": a feminine icon of Death, a gendered concept in our language and culture) in an overtly male *norteño* outfit reveals the extent to which the film's location enhanced the already kitsch imagination of the filmmaker—with the (mostly unacknowledged) help of his creative Mexican crew. At the same time, however, such images also suggest how much of their power vanishes into the air of Luhrmann's wandering lens.

·Mexico's nightlife/"lowlife" does not escape this totalistic but far from "totalizing" representation in *William Shakespeare's Romeo + Juliet*. As if inspired by Romeo and Juliet's own preference for "night," Luhrmann offers us a "garish"[47] rendering of the Mexican (and ultimately Latin American) subculture of *antros* (roughly, "joints" or cheap nightclubs) showcased in the film's depictions of carnivalesque revelry. Following the frenzied street processional to the ball, for example, we encounter a Tybalt whose disguise is uncannily evocative of the outfit of the devil who dances with a stripper in a still from *Tívoli*, a 1974 film about a popular mid-twentieth-century vaudeville theater in Mexico City.[48] The provincial Gulf Coast streets, billiards, fairs, and *cantinas* glimpsed at in Luhrmann's film may be traced back to the numerous 1940–1960 films of *rumberas* (female dancers of Afro-Caribbean music) or to more stylized, expressionistic, and often grotesque visions, such as José Clemente Orozco's portraits of the clientele of such places, or else to the recent and derivative work of Loren Elder, an artist from the U.S.-Mexico border.[49] Since these rich images only play the role of makeup artists for the film, once again a cluster of provocative icons is left hanging in the breeze of an underplayed transcultural card.

Amid this flurry of fashionable cultural signs, then—which include a drug-lord-looking Capulet who speaks with a distinctly Latin accent and a Nurse who bears a more than passing resemblance to a Mexican "Nana" turned illegal alien—it is not surprising that Verona Beach should ultimately strike us as a no-land inhabited by a no-people.[50] Similarly, the most distinctive feature in Luhrmann's vision of Sycamore Grove offers a correlative for what the film performs with respect to its Mexican materials and to the Book that originates it: the movie-house in this "Forest of Lovesickness" is ruined, depleted, and disrupted. So, too, our cultural element is wildly displayed, but unsolicitous of the serious critical consideration it warrants, in spite of the film's use of a Mexican location and, by extension, its peoples. Perhaps the Mexican iconography employed by Luhrmann dovetails with purposes of ironic mythologizing; but if so, it demands a series of metacinematic cross-cultural operations beyond the scope of the film. In the absence of these moves, the film presents us with a mise en scène replete with an almost "coffee-table-bookish" inventory of cultural elements that are, in turn, depleted of ideological significance.

☆☆☆

The main problem raised by Luhrmann's own reading of Shakespeare's "precious book of love" is, perhaps ironically, precisely a problem of readability, or, more specifically, of reception. In Luhrmann's film, the viewer is assaulted with signs but is as helpless to decode them as Shakespeare's fated protagonists, who fail to read the warning written in their own crossed stars. However, the sense of helplessness that emerges from the receiving end of *William Shakespeare's Romeo + Juliet* cannot be completely explained away by Luhrmann's schizoidal juxtaposition of postmodern film and the early modern playtext, for a lethal inevitability has inhered in this story long before it was a "book" by William Shakespeare. It is a story that, in spite of centuries of popular retellings, never relinquishes its death drive toward the inevitable silencing of its protagonists, even as their awareness of this narrative machinery increasingly dawns on them. Like the impatient motion of Luhrmann's camera, which hungrily canvasses and converts its location to a tantalizing enigma, so too, the story of Romeo and Juliet refuses to pause for its protagonists to read, alter, or undo the tragic writing on the wall. In the case of Luhrmann's production, this tragedy redoubles and implicates the viewer in its activity, although it disables the spectator to decipher the multivalent texture of Mexican culture written not merely on the walls of Verona Beach's colorful interiors, but also in its statues, carpets, costumes, and carnivals. What Luhrmann's film emphasizes and "acts out," then, is the notion that *Romeo and Juliet* is above all a tragedy of (mis)reading.

Like *Prospero's Books*, Luhrmann's movie seems preoccupied with acts of writing, reading, and interpretation. Unlike Greenaway's film, which is richer in filmic imagination, more critically provocative, and free from the constraints that Luhrmann's visual appetite paradoxically exerts upon the final product, *William Shakespeare's Romeo + Juliet* underscores the irony of a play that repeatedly tricks its protagonists into performing a predetermined script for which few acting tips are provided, but where improvisation is impossible. Act 1 of the film, for instance, presents us with a conspicuously "bookish" Romeo who, in a corner of the proscenium of the abandoned movie-house, reads the strangely detached verses that we will soon notice are in his own handwriting. Similarly, from the published script we learn that while Romeo's initial encounter with Juliet was to culminate in their shared gaze through the fish-tank, it was also to begin with Romeo spotting Juliet as "a beautiful girl in an angel costume perched on an ornate chair *reading* a slim leather-bound book."[51] The final act of this reading tragedy occurs, paradoxically, even before Romeo learns of Juliet's mock-death from Balthasar: Romeo reads his deceiving dream of reunion with Juliet as he writes it, literally punctuating a climax that will never materialize. As if operating by a "will" of its own, the book writes itself from its depleted state to imprison anew these lovers who play themselves without rehearsal, and we are left wondering if the Book will ever tolerate a critically different incarnation, let alone a dissident one.[52]

Luhrmann's Romeo + Juliet reenact the "precious book of love" as a sort of previewed palimpsest of the depleted Book, if only for "the two-hours' traffic of our stage" (Pro. 12). For it must be remembered that, for many expected ticket-buyers, the most important thing is precisely this: that films usually take about two hours before you can *really* go somewhere and *really* do something. But neither R + J nor the spectators were pre-scribed as players. Once they start to play it, the Book takes over the depleted imagination, remaining, after all, "this" and no other "precious book."[53] Had Luhrmann actually made a statement with this film, instead of repeating one with a stylishly different accent, we might have seen a version of *Romeo and Juliet* allowing moments of critical reception to interrupt the whirl and hum of production. Despite its overt claims to differ from earlier versions—stated *in* the film *as* film, especially with respect to Zeffirelli's movie—*William Shakespeare's Romeo + Juliet* remains faithful to the conventional expectations inscribed in its title, playing "by the book" and constituting "a certain text" in a seemingly endless line of reiteration. Its strengths surface mainly in terms of method, but the film stays well within "a common bound" where greater critical drive is desired. Its unchecked fascination with the culture from which it draws so much and yet so little, and its lack of critical stand, speak of rich potential but ulti-mately poor execution.

If *William Shakespeare's Romeo + Juliet* does nothing else, then, it pro-vides an example of the stylishly postmodern work's inability to critically undermine the grand mechanism of received authority that informs its sources—both Shakespeare's Book and the burden of canonization that fashions it all the way to Zeffirelli's version—a failure, in effect, to create anything other than a *répétition différente* of previous, "precious book[s] of love," replete with MTV fun and games, great but fleeting moments revealing a compelling yet fickle artistic intuition, and (perhaps unwarily) a bit of cultural colonialism or, at least, the usual look of the curious tour-ist. Perhaps because of this, the film's yet-provocative force resides more in its periphery and blank spots, where the depletion of text foregrounds the depletion of critical reception in a place much closer to us than the dilapidated haunts of Sycamore Grove: our own postmodern frame-and-screen-wise movie-house.

NOTES

With special thanks to Courtney Lehmann, Alicia Rosenblueth, Lisa S. Starks, and H. R. Coursen.

1. William Shakespeare, *Romeo and Juliet*, New Arden Shakespeare, ed. Brian Gib-bons (London and New York: Methuen, 1980), 1.3.87. All subsequent references to Shakespeare's play will refer to this edition and be noted parenthetically in the text.

2. For a description of the various ways in which narrative materials are organized in comic books, see Scott McCloud, *Understanding Comics: The Invisible Art* (Cambridge, Mass.: Tundra, 1993). Particularly in the gas station segment, Luhrmann seems to subscribe the "aspect-aspect" style favored by Japanese comic book artists.

3. Unlike Shakespeare's characters, Luhrmann's Abra(m) belongs to Capulet's party, while Gregory and Sampson are "Montague Boys": the Montagues, not the Capulets, start the quarrel. This reversal of the original roles seems to promise critical disruption and parody from the outset of the film; however, it is one of several provocative issues brightly intro-duced but practically unexplored.

4. Not necessarily the "kind of glorified comic book" denounced by Kenneth Rothwell in "Representing *King Lear* on Screen: From Metatheatre to Metacinema," in *Shakespeare and the Moving Image: The Plays on Film and Television*, ed. Anthony Davies and Stanley Wells (Cambridge: Cambridge University Press, 1994), 217.

5. In referring to Shakespeare's "books" I am following Douglas Lanier's discussion of the term in his "Drowning the Book: Prospero's Books and the Textual Shakespeare," in *Shakespeare, Theory, and Performance*, ed. James C. Bulman (London: Routledge, 1996), 187–89.

6. Bogdanov set the play in contemporary Verona and split the last scene in two, the second part showing the inauguration of the golden statues by a busy Prince, who delivered the closing lines as hypocritical political speech. Capulet and Montague were made to em-brace in the prescribed fashion of the photo-op.

7. María Elena De Valdés, "Questioning Paradigms of Social Reality through Postmodern Intertextuality," *Poligrafías* 1 (1996): 227.

8. De Valdés, 227.

9. The terms "expected" and "perspective" are meant to evoke the German *Erwartungshorizon*. See Robert Jauss, *Literaturgeschichte als Provokation* (Frankfurt: Suhrkamp Verlag, 1970).

10. The present paper develops and enlarges upon ideas initiated in an earlier article, in which I address this issue along other lines. See Alfredo Michel Modenessi, "(Un)Doing the Book 'by the book,'" *Poligrafías* 2 (1997): 191–227. A presentation based on this paper was delivered at the "Shakespeare on Film: The Centenary Conference" in Benalmádena, Spain, September 1999, entitled "The Bard Goes Dystopic: Baz Luhrmann's Pictures of (Un)'fair Verona.'"

11. Luhrmann's style intimates his experience as a videoclip maker. The MTV culture of high-speed imagery testifies to the picture's targeting of an audience accustomed to short-lived, fragmentary visual experiences and occasionally reach beyond this. Perhaps the best correlative for this method of quick substitution of pleasurable moments is the fact that the MTV Movie Awards include categories such as "Best Kiss" and the like.

12. Graham Holderness and Christopher McCullough, "Shakespeare on the Screen: A Selective Filmography," in *Shakespeare and the Moving Image*, 18.

13. Holderness and McCullough, 19 n. 1.

14. Holderness and McCullough, 18.

15. Holderness and McCullough, 19 n. 2.

16. Holderness and McCullough, 19 n. 2.

17. Lanier's discussion does warrant his conclusion that "By problematizing (though certainly not escaping from) the hegemony that Shakespearean textualism continues to hold over our critical imaginations, even in an age of electronic reproduction, Greenaway points performance criticism toward a double challenge: a fuller account of the relation of performance criticism to recording technologies, and the shaping of a practice more attentive to the mundane specificities of the media that render performance capable of study" (204–5).

18. The signs "+[&]" seek to indicate what should be assumed everywhere else: that the title is written thus in (almost) all textual materials pertaining to the film, i.e., with a small "&" inside the cross. The cross, in turn, is a conspicuous feature on the ring that the "star-crossed" lovers exchange at, yes, "crucial" points. The title of the film transfers to text a cinematic item, materialized as an icon, an essential part of the textual and metatextual fabric in and around the film. In the Mexican posters, the title read "Romeo +[y] Julieta de William Shakespeare."

19. "The Inaccessible Bard," *The Economist*, 15 February 1997, 81.

20. Lanier, 194.

21. "Greenaway adopts several strategies in the film for addressing the burden of the Shakespearean book. First, he puts before us Prospero's act of reciting and writing down what will eventually become the text of *The Tempest*, showing us not a finished Shakespearean book but the imaginative process by which that book is produced" (Lanier 195). The title is, then, central to Greenaway's purpose. So, when Lanier concludes that "*Prospero's Books* confronts directly the issue of the Shakespearean medium, raising anew the crucial question of what forms the Shakespearean book and the cultural capital it represents can take in a post-literate age" (204), the name speaks out the point.

22. The "suspenseful" treatment of the death scene, with Juliet awakening to see Romeo drink the poison, is a blatant example. The elimination of the Friar from this part, which could otherwise be construed as an interesting authorial transgression, seems merely subservient to effect.

23. Baz Luhrmann, "A Note," in *William Shakespeare's Romeo & Juliet: The Contemporary Film, the Classic Play*, screenplay by Craig Pearce and Baz Luhrmann (New York: Bantam, 1996), no pagination given. The unstable title involves problems of industrial in-

consistency. Almost everywhere in the printed material pertaining to "the contemporary film" (credits, posters, press kit, Internet pages, CD-ROM, etc.) the title reads as indicated above: *William Shakespeare's Romeo +[&] Juliet*. Yet, in this edition of the screenplay the title sometimes reads "William Shakespeare's *Romeo & Juliet*" and, more often, simply "*Romeo & Juliet*." In Luhrmann's "Note," however, it reads as quoted: "*Romeo and Juliet*." In the same edition, the title page of "the classic play" reads "*Romeo and Juliet* by William Shakespeare."

24. An example of this is that the CD-ROM version of *R+J* may be construed as a sort of surrogate for the "action-figures" that nowadays are a standard part of intensive marketing strategies for movies aimed at younger consumers. The "pages" of the *R+J* CD-ROM feature an attractive combination of stills from the film; audio- and videoclips; animation; the text of both play and screenplay; explanations of several items that the film treats as icons for worship by future generations (the ring, the necklace, the guns, the cars, etc.). Also, it serves as a kind of modified substitute for "study-aids" (such as *Cliffs Notes*): one of the "pages" offers a summary of who's who and what's what in the play/film. Moreover, already in January 1997 Luhrmann's movie had "gross box-office takings of $65m worldwide" ("The Inaccessible Bard," *The Economist*, 15 February 1997, 81), while the first volume of the soundtrack reached the top of the charts in February 1997.

25. Ace G. Pilkington, "Zeffirelli's Shakespeare," in *Shakespeare and the Moving Image*, 164.

26. Pilkington, 164.

27. What is missing is a lot of text, as some observant (though colloquial) scholar might put it. Pilkington's calculations show that Zeffirelli's film includes only about 35 percent of a standard text (165). Does Luhrmann's pruning outdo the former scissor-hands champion?

28. For instance, in the 1993 *World Shakespeare Bibliography* the number of entries on *Hamlet* more than doubles the amount of entries on *Romeo and Juliet*: 525 vs. 237 (a difference of 288, or a ratio of 2.25 to 1, approximately). But the proportion decreases radically when considering the number of entries referring to performances of various sorts: 213 for *Hamlet*, 155 for *Romeo and Juliet* (a difference of only 58, or a ratio of 1.3 to 1). The significant fact, then, is that there are many more entries on texts about *Hamlet* (312) than on performances of it (213, a 1.5 to 1 ratio); whereas in the case of *Romeo and Juliet* it is exactly the opposite: 82 texts about it, and 155 performance items (nearly a 1:2 ratio).

29. David Gates, "The Bard is Hot," *Newsweek*, 23 December 1996, 46.

30. Patricia Lennox, "Baz Luhrmann's *William Shakespeare's Romeo + Juliet*" (paper presented at the annual meeting of the Shakespeare Association of America, Washington, D.C., April 1997), 1.

31. Lynda E. Boose and Richard Burt, introduction to *Shakespeare, the Movie: Popularizing the Plays on Film, TV, and Video*, ed. Lynda E. Boose and Richard Burt (London and New York: Routledge, 1997), 18. This may be due to several factors: that "Verona Beach" is reminiscent of "exotic" American name combinations such as "Venice Beach"; that the film is also influenced by the style of the TV series *Miami Vice*; and that the fashion sense of the Montague Boys is partly "Floridian." The Gulf Coast of Mexico does have many things in common with Cuba and the rest of the Caribbean islands, but the film's setting remains predominantly Mexican.

32. "The Inaccessible Bard," 81.

33. H. R. Coursen, "Shakespeare and Film," *Shakespeare and the Classroom* 4, no. 2 (1996): 22, 23.

34. See Tilo Schabert, "La cosmología de la arquitectura de las ciudades," *Diógenes* 156 (1991): 23–24.

35. Mexico City is infamous for the number of billboards that clutter its gray skies.

36. A reproduction of this silkscreen print may be found in the catalogue of the exhibition *Chicano Expressions: Serigraphs from the Collection of Self Help Graphics*, ed. Tomás Benítez (Los Angeles and Mexico: USIS, 1993), 31.

37. My own informal survey shows an interesting discrepancy between Mexican teenagers roughly closer to and farther from scenarios of actual use of weapons and violence. In general, the former—belonging mostly to the lower and lower-middle classes—found much of the relevant material in the film ridiculous or silly, or at best, amusing or worthy of parody; while the latter—especially boys, mostly from upper and upper-middle classes—received it as satisfying action-movie stuff and in many cases found the Montague Boys attractive as role models.

38. While the unrestricted possession and use of guns in Verona Beach may be intended to relate to the situation in some parts of the U.S., when viewed against the film's predominant cultural setting, it cannot help suggesting an unwitting reiteration of the commonplace that in Mexico and other Latin American countries guns are as common and available as in the "Wild West." In *El Mariachi*, Rodríguez's at once naive and far-fetched approach to the violence along the Mexico-U.S. geographical and cultural borders manages to undermine the stereotype by taking it all the way to parodic detachment. Luhrmann's fantasy of violence does not even begin to address the conditions of living either in an incipient democracy caught between misery, corruption, crime, and its own inadequacies to offer protection or under an openly brutal military regime. His problem is not lack of realism, nor excess of estrangement, but that he simply and quietly remains in between.

39. Or, given the ostentatious display of private security, the free possession and use of weapons, and the nouveau-riche atmosphere at Capulet's mansion and ball, it may be read as a feud between legitimate firms serving as fronts for illegal operations.

40. See for example, Yreina Cervantes's serigraph "The Long Road" (1985), also reproduced in *Chicano Expressions*, 18. In it all sorts of ex-votos (miniature images traditionally offered at altars)—among which the Sacred Heart stands out—combine with masks, candles, the figure of the Virgen de Guadalupe (Mexico's supreme deity), a stylized picture of a guerrilla woman holding a rifle, and an unmistakably Aztec representation of a jaguar, all presided over by a feminine figure in flames, with open arms, whose bleeding and burning heart shows an Aztec icon at the core.

41. The Church of the Sacred Heart of Mary stands in the middle of an area known as Colonia del Valle (late forties through early sixties). The architecture of this area is Mexican interpretation of French and American modernism, with Colonial pastiche. The church was inaugurated in 1954, although the project started in 1950, the same year in which Albert finished the statue. The zone was used to advantage by Luhrmann. The gas station, for example, stands at a corner from which one can easily see the Virgin. The church, now severed from its neighborhood by an absurd half-freeway/half-street, is widely regarded as an icon of ugliness, a sort of monstrous though practical landmark: it can be seen from a long distance and rapidly identified for quick traffic reference. For want of a better one, among its notable features is the fact that it is made entirely of concrete. All this has led to the funny loss of its identity as the Church of the Sacred Heart of Mary; most of us now refer to it as "The Church of Concrete," or, more interestingly, we call the statue "Our Lady of Traffic." A potentially provocative but ignored fact about the statue is that, in its original form, its heart and complexion were black and were later transformed into their present state.

42. A fundamental discussion of this tradition and its implications may be found in Octavio Paz, "Todos Santos, día de muertos," in *El Laberinto de la Soledad* (Mexico: Fondo de Cultura Económica, 1950).

43. Likewise, one feels tempted to—but cannot really—see in these wild allusions to All Saints a reminder that Juliet's birthday at the end of July may imply her conception around Halloween. See François Laroque, *Shakespeare et la fête: Essai d'archeologie du spectacle dans l'Anglaterre élisabéthaine* (Paris: Presses Universitaires de France, 1988).

44. Pearce and Luhrmann, 50.

45. The other "man-Death" with Tybalt is identified as "Petruchio" in the screenplay and credits. Although more memorable as the name of a character (likewise from Verona) in *The Taming of the Shrew*, since it is also mentioned by the Nurse in 1.5.130, this may or may not be one of the many cross-references to Shakespeare's plays in the movie (e.g., Abra's "Double, double, toil and trouble" at the gas station; a billboard announcing some product advertised by "Don Próspero," etc.). After a while, Luhrmann's fashionable playfulness gets a bit boring.

46. Reproduced in *Chicano Expressions*, 21.

47. "Give me my Romeo; and when I shall die / Take him and cut him out in little stars, / And he will make the face of heaven so fine / That all the world will be in love with night, / And pay no worship to the garish sun" (3.2.21–25).

48. A still of this figure from the film may be found in *Eros* 1 (July 1975): 67. A reproduction is included in Modenessi, 212.

49. A reproduction of an untitled, near-expressionistic, and revealing engraving by Elder—the interior of a cantina where a devil shares a drink with some prostitutes and a grotesque mariachi—may be found in *Biombo negro* 1, no. 7 (1994): 13. A reproduction is included in Modenessi, 213.

50. The Nurse's room, significantly, is an accurate rendering of a Mexican lower-middle class, one-room apartment, very close to the interpretation of such interiors by Chicano artists; for instance, see Patssi Valdéz's serigraph "The Dressing Table" (1988), in *Chicano Expressions*, 25.

51. Pearce and Luhrmann, 47 (emphasis added).

52. Less than dissident with regard to Shakespeare's Book, Kaufman's film is an amusing reelaboration of what could be called the Ur-*Romeo and Juliet*. For an extensive reading of the dissident potential of Luhrmann's film, see Courtney Lehmann, "Strictly Shakespeare? Dead Letters, Ghostly Fathers, and the Cultural Pathology of Authorship in Baz Luhrmann's *William Shakespeare's Romeo | Juliet, Shakespeare Quarterly* 52 (forthcoming).

53. Unsurprisingly, *R+J* was chosen "Picture of the Year" by *The Face Magazine*. Tokens of its praise: "Defining data: teen rebellion . . . design excess . . . true romance . . . mind-blowing pop spectacle. . . . If *Romeo & Juliet* is the best film released in 1997. . . that's to no small degree because it is a TOTAL FILM. . . . It is bold-strokes—the twin towers of the . . . business empires bestriding the statue of Jesus—and tiny details: the red hearts on the Queen Mab pills, the silver heel of Tybalt's boot." Bit by bit, however, the note gets to the point, likewise unsurprisingly: "Luhrmann & Co. have made the bravest choice of all: boy meets girl, they fall in love, they die. [. . .] there is, finally, a rare truth and beauty" (Charles Gant, "Film of the Year: *Romeo & Juliet*," *The Face Magazine,* 12 January 1998, 77–78). Alas, the "certain text" again.

WORKS CITED

Benítez, Tomás, ed. Catalogue of the exhibition *Chicano Expressions: Serigraphs from the Collection of Self Help Graphics*. Los Angeles and Mexico: USIS, 1993.

Boose, Lynda E., and Richard Burt, eds. *Shakespeare, the Movie: Popularizing the Plays on Film, TV, and Video*. London and New York: Routledge, 1997.

Coursen, H. R.. "Shakespeare and Film." *Shakespeare and the Classroom* 4, no.2 (1996): 22–23.

Davies, Anthony, and Stanley Wells, eds. *Shakespeare and the Moving Image: The Plays on Film and Television*. Cambridge: Cambridge University Press, 1994.

De Valdés, María Elena. "Questioning Paradigms of Social Reality through Postmodern Intertextuality." *Poligrafías* 1 (1996): 227–39.

Gant, Charles. "Film of the Year: *Romeo & Juliet.*" *The Face Magazine,* 12 January 1998, 77–78.

Gates, David. "The Bard Is Hot." *Newsweek,* 23 December 1996, 44–47.

Holderness, Graham, and Christopher McCullough. "Shakespeare on the Screen: A Selective Filmography." In *Shakespeare and the Moving Image: The Plays on Film and Television.* Edited by Anthony Davies and Stanley Wells. Cambridge: Cambridge University Press, 1994.

"The Inaccessible Bard." *The Economist,* 15 February 1997, 81.

Jauss, Robert. *Literaturgeschichte als Provokation.* Frankfurt: Suhrkamp Verlag, 1970.

Lanier, Douglas. "Drowning the Book: Prospero's Books and the Textual Shakespeare." In *Shakespeare, Theory, and Performance.* Edited by James C. Bulman, London: Routledge, 1996.

Laroque, François. *Shakespeare et la fête: Essai d'archeologie du spectacle dans l'Anglaterre élisabéthaine.* Paris: Presses Universitaires de France, 1988.

Lehmann, Courtney. "Strictly Shakespeare? Dead Letters, Ghostly Fathers, and the Cultural Pathology of Authorship in Baz Luhrmann's *William Shakespeare's Romeo + Juliet.*" *Shakespeare Quarterly* 52. Forthcoming.

Lennox, Patricia. "Baz Luhrmann's *William Shakespeare's Romeo + Juliet.*" Paper presented at the annual meeting of the Shakespeare Association of America, Washington, D.C., April 1997.

Luhrmann, Baz. "A Note." In *William Shakespeare's Romeo & Juliet: The Contemporary Film, the Classic Play.* Screenplay by Craig Pearce and Baz Luhrmann. New York: Bantam, 1996.

McCloud, Scott. *Understanding Comics: The Invisible Art.* Cambridge, Mass.: Tundra Publishing, 1993.

Modenessi, Alfredo Michel. "(Un)Doing the Book 'by the book'" *Poligrafías* 2 (1997): 191–227.

Paz, Octavio. "Todos Santos, día de muertos." In *El Laberinto de la Soledad.* Mexico: Fondo de Cultura Económica, 1950.

Pearce, Craig, and Baz Luhrmann. Screenplay. *William Shakespeare's Romeo & Juliet: The Contemporary Film, the Classic Play.* New York: Bantam, 1996.

Pilkington, Ace G. "Zeffirelli's Shakespeare." In *Shakespeare and the Moving Image: The Plays on Film and Television.* Edited by Anthony Davies and Stanley Wells. Cambridge: Cambridge University Press, 1994.

Rothwell, Kenneth S. "Representing *King Lear* on Screen: From Metatheatre to Metacinema." In *Shakespeare and the Moving Image: The Plays on Film and Television.* Edited by Anthony Davies and Stanley Wells. Cambridge: Cambridge University Press, 1994.

Schabert, Tilo. "La cosmología de la arquitectura de las ciudades." *Diógenes* 156 (1991): 3–35.

FILMS CITED

El Mariachi. Directed by Robert Rodríguez. 1 hr. 21 min. Columbia Pictures/Los Hooligans Productions, 1992. Videocassette.

Prospero's Books. Directed by Peter Greenaway. 2 hr. 7 min. Channel Four/Allarts/Caméra One/et. al., 1991. Laserdisc.

Romeo and Juliet. Directed by Franco Zeffirelli. 2 hrs. 18 min. BHE Films/Dino de Laurentis Cinematografica, 1968. Videocassette.

Tívoli. Directed by Alberto Isaac. 1 hr. 7 min. Conacine/DASA Films, 1974. 16 mm.

William Shakespeare's Romeo + Juliet. Directed by Baz Luhrmann. 2 hr. Twentieth Century Fox/Bazmark Films, 1996. Videocassette.

Part II
Reframing Romance:
Sex, Love, and Subjectivity

Cutting up Characters: The Erotic Politics of Trevor Nunn's *Twelfth Night*

Laurie Osborne

AFTER CONTRASTING TRADITIONALIST READINGS OF CONTINUOUS, INTERIORIZED Shakespearean characters and poststructuralist analyses of their fragmentation and discontinuity, Alan Sinfield concludes that "some Shakespearean *dramatis personae* are written so as to suggest, not just an intermittent, gestural, and problematic subjecti[vity], but a continuous or developing interiority or consciousness; and we should seek a way of talking about this that does not slide back into character criticism or essentialist humanism."[1] Sinfield pursues this new way of talking about character, or rather "character effects," by noting the history of responses to particular figures; he argues that a character such as Macbeth, for example, "is not a mysterious natural essence. Rather he is situated at the intersection of discourses and historical forces that are competing, we might say, to fill up his subjectivity."[2] Recent Shakespearean films speak directly both to critical concerns with discontinuity or inexplicable characterizations in Shakespearean plays and to readings of "a continuous or developing interiority or consciousness." To put it another way, these films help us see how we also produce "coherent characters" from discontinuous fragments.

Specifically, the radical use of crosscutting and intercutting in such recent works as Trevor Nunn's *Twelfth Night* (1996) and Al Pacino's *Looking for Richard* (1996) reveal how film editing produces cinematic fragments that paradoxically "fill up" the subjectivity of early modern characters. Although this essay concentrates primarily on Nunn's *Twelfth Night*, *Looking for Richard* is perhaps most blatant in using cutting and fragments to create continuity in character. The film presents only brief scenes of *Richard III* in its quest to explore whether Richard is relevant today. For example, the crucial and critically vexed scene of Richard's wooing of Anne is spliced into a series of crosscut scenes in which the actors worry, first, about the scene itself and whether it can work and, second, about which actress is best suited for the part.

89

By juxtaposing the crosscut scenes discussing the play with act 1, scene 2, Pacino suggests that looking for Richard requires looking for Anne. Although critics have not necessarily been kind to Winona Ryder as the choice for this very difficult scene, the action itself takes on a compelling continuity in contrast to the intercut scenes that precede and follow it. Set against the talking heads of scholars discussing Anne's dilemma and the earnest round robin of actors debating the scene's purposes, this scene, like many chosen by Pacino for inclusion here, seems at first to play continuously. However, Pacino uses startling cutaway shots to himself—outdoors, out of costume, and without Anne—to maintain attention definitively on Richard. Three interruptions mark the scene. Her spitting at him cuts away to his fierce declaration, "I'll have her."[3] At her announcement of contempt, Pacino inserts a brief of image of himself, smiling, in the same visual context as the declaration—a swift reminder that he *will* have her. Her capitulation and rejoicing "to see you are become so penitent" (2.2.220) yields immediately to the alternate setting and Pacino's bark of laughter.

These cutaways are all the more effective as emphasis on Richard's coherence of purpose because of the startling shift from the darkened, seemingly interior and somber lushness of the "performance" to the bright daylight, exterior shots of just Pacino, unkempt with his characteristic backwards baseball cap, leaning on what looks like a contemporary metal sculpture. In a scene that is labeled "Lady Anne" and that presents such a provocative reversal in Anne's responses, Pacino uses cutaways to underscore Richard's single-minded focus and coherence. Moreover, like so many of the play's characters, Anne does not need continuity beyond this scene within the structure of Pacino's film because the quest here is for Richard's character, itself a monster of discontinuity, broken into by actors, critics, and crucial scenes. Even Kevin Spacey's Buckingham or Alec Baldwin's Clarence, who appear more than once, may command our interest but do not survive the obsessive attention to Richard himself as a character.

In *Twelfth Night*, Trevor Nunn also uses extensive film editing and rearrangements to elaborate character. Because of his cinematic choices, *Twelfth Night* has provoked radically contradictory reviews that often extend their critique to filming Shakespeare generally. Stanley Kauffmann laments the film as a disaster and concludes that "the film medium is like an x-ray that enlarges the flaws in plays," in his assessment, the flaw of Malvolio's treatment.[4] At the opposite extreme, John Podhoretz suggests that "Trevor Nunn's *Twelfth Night* is a glorious piece of work, and one that brings to mind a heretical question: Is it perhaps the case that the cinema is the ideal medium for Shakespeare?"[5] My answer to that question is that cinema is certainly the ideal medium for Shakespeare in the twentieth century, largely because film both creates and reinscribes our ideologically based expectations about character.

Other critics of Shakespearean film have made comparable claims, often using the structures of stage criticism to justify film's suitability for the plays. In *Shakespeare, Cinema, and Society*, John Collick effectively demonstrates that early film developed out of Victorian stage display in ways that persisted even until the BBC Shakespeare plays.[6] Peter Donaldson places the great film auteurs implicitly in the crucial interpretive place that actor/ directors have held since the late eighteenth century.[7] Critics from Barbara Hodgdon to Douglas Lanier look to the valuable and provocative interpretations that individual films, like individual stagings, have brought to the text.[8] My argument here follows these in several features: it draws upon the continuity from the play's stage traditions as they are reworked in the film, it analyzes Nunn's approach as an auteur's vision, and it concentrates on the cinematic potential for Shakespearean performance, which this film in particular realizes.

My discussion actually runs closest to Lorne Buchman's analysis of how film techniques relate to and rewrite Shakespearean dramaturgy. In particular, I share Buchman's interest in how spectators interact with the temporal display allowed (or disabled) by film; however, I do not agree that difficulties in analyzing time in Shakespearean film arise because "Shakespeare's own temporal structure is so close to that of the film medium itself."[9] In fact, what I find most intriguing about the current trend of restoring the text in films like Nunn's *Twelfth Night* and Kenneth Branagh's *Hamlet* (1996) is the implicit affirmation that fuller texts require very aggressive film editing—less cutting of the text requires more elaborate cutting in the film. In Nunn's *Twelfth Night*, twentieth-century constructions of character emerge from within ideologies of romantic love and gender; moreover, these constructions thrive through film cuts rather than the textual cuts used in earlier centuries.

Since film editing most obviously influences the audience's sense of time, I find Franco Zeffirelli's description of that effect compelling: "You see, cinema creates a different chemistry, a different taste, and the attention of the audience moves so fast. Really, fantasy gallops in the audience in movies. They know all before the image is finished."[10] The speed Zeffirelli notes is everywhere in cinematic editing of late twentieth-century Shakespearean films, ranging from Baz Luhrmann's *William Shakespeare's Romeo + Juliet* (1996) to Branagh's *Hamlet*. From a postmodern perspective, these quick cuts—or "flash cuts," as Branagh calls them in his screenplay edition—offer the interplay of surfaces without depth.[11] However, as Buchman points out, the spectator's interaction with these disruptions of expectation, like that of Iser's readers interacting with the disruptive text, produces a dynamic sense of time in film.[12] And, I argue, this dynamic is produced in *Twelfth Night's* film editing to invoke depth of character for the twentieth-century spectator. The resultant "galloping fantasies" significantly extend and revise the stage practices that produced the "character effects" of earlier centuries. Nunn's cinematic solutions for apparent problems in the Shakespearean text on stage actually reveal the ideological imperatives of character construction in both the early modern and twentieth-century versions.

In his *Twelfth Night*, Nunn clearly draws upon changes made in performances since the late 1700s and often recuperates what typically was excised from the text. The film recasts in a modern idiom of crosscutting and the short take both the discontinuity of character produced by the twinning in the Renaissance text and the "character problems" that eighteenth- and nineteenth-century critics discovered within the play. As a result, far from agreeing with one of Nunn's detractors, who claims problems "can be laid at the feet of the director, who's hugely experienced in the theater but has his limitations when it comes to . . . the camera,"[13] I see Nunn's film growing from stage conventions into quite thorough cinematic practice.

His *Twelfth Night* continues traditional theatrical changes, for example, opening the play with Viola's landing (1.2) rather than Orsino's speech (1.1). However, that reversal is translated through film convention: Viola's landing functions as part of the opening credits, as Nunn points out, "before the work proper, which would still begin with one of the most famous opening lines in the canon, 'If music be the food of love, play on.'"[14] Moreover, Nunn also employs a cinematic flexibility of setting and sequence to enact extreme revisions of the scenes between Orsino and Viola. Thus, his construction of these characters both draws on current cinematic models for displaying "depth" of character and on the Renaissance strategy of creating character through onstage relationships, suggested in the variable early speech headings.[15] The interactions between Orsino and Viola are clearly key in the creation of both characters in the film; Nunn's several elaborations and elongations of that association actually emphasize the hierarchical connections between master and servant that underlie their mutual attraction in the Folio text. In this way, the Renaissance investment in the hierarchical nature of erotic involvement serves as the occasion for living up to twentieth-century assumptions that "true love," as opposed to lust, develops over time.[16]

Nunn not only draws out Viola's involvement with Orsino, but also he brings her into the play early. Viola appears in act 1, scene 1, as the hapless musician first called upon to play "that strain again" and then forestalled because "'tis not so sweet now as it was before" (1.1. 4, 8). However, her presence is silent, unlike earlier stage performances, including those of Charles Calvert and Henry Irving, who combined and condensed act 1, scenes 1 and 4; none that I know have registered Viola's *silent* presence in Orsino's first scene.[17] Moreover, Orsino connects with this musician specifically, first by walking over to stop his piano performance ("No more"

[1.2.7]) and second by addressing Cesario directly in close-up before the premature ending of the scene. Whereas the early modern text exploits the conventions of the patronage system and the favoritism obvious in Orsino's confiding in Cesario after just three days, Nunn chooses to show the early moments of Cesario's service in order to mark out Orsino's awareness of his page from the start of the film and to track the development of their intimacy.

In a move that recuperates the closeness displayed in the Folio text, Nunn also restores a large proportion of the lines typically cut from act 2, scene 4, where Orsino once again sends Cesario off to woo Olivia. From the early nineteenth century on, 2.4 has undergone radical cutting, including the omission of all of Feste's role in the scene as well as the excision of Orsino's discourse on men's wavering love and its causes.[18] Not only does Nunn retain Orsino's advice to Cesario about why "he" should choose a woman younger than himself, he also keeps the call for Feste to sing as well as the song itself. However, Nunn revises the scene just as radically as those early performances did: he intercuts act 2, scene 3, and act 2, scene 4, and disperses the remaining conversations between Orsino and Cesario throughout the film. The song that plays behind their initial conversation in 2.4 is the one that Feste sings to the below-stairs crowd in 2.3. And the song of the "fair cruel maid" is shifted well into act 3, the occasion for the near-kiss between Orsino and his page in the barn, which is the prelude to Orsino's perhaps overly vehement command: "once more, Cesario, / Get thee to yond same sovereign cruelty" (2.4.79–80). No other performance, not even John Dexter's inventively reordered 1968 television production, has so radically dispersed the various moments and moods of Cesario's second scene with Orsino. Nunn effectively keeps Viola and Orsino right before our eyes almost right up until the denouement.

These choices for *Twelfth Night* yield significant insight into characterization as reworked in cinematic productions of Shakespeare. In film, fragments paradoxically produce coherence and apparent depth of character within the sustained development of a relationship that critics since the eighteenth century have found both crucial and difficult. Samuel Johnson's early objections to Viola as an "excellent schemer" found their way into Francis Gentleman's commentary in Bell's 1774 edition of Shakespeare's plays: "Viola—It is very singular that a young lady, just escaped from a shipwreck, under apprehension for her brother, should so suddenly form a design upon the duke, whom she had never seen: But when Shakespeare wanted to push on his plot, he was not very ceremonious with probability."[19] By the mid-nineteenth century, Mrs. Elliott, whose praise for Viola is unstinting, finds Orsino problematic as the object of her affection: "It is earnestly to be hoped that Viola won as good a husband as she deserved. Orsino is no hero."[20] In the 1888 introduction to the *Henry Irving*

Shakespeare, Arthur Symons offers the following brutal assessment of the problems posed by Orsino and Viola together:

> The great defect of *Twelfth Night* as an acting comedy lies, no doubt, in the fact that the love interest never takes very much hold on our sympathies. Viola is a charming young woman and makes a pretty boy; but who can possibly sympathize with her in her ardent pursuit of such a lover as Orsino, a man whose elaborate sentimentality reminds one of those delicacies which cloy rather than delight the appetite, and whose plastic readiness to transfer his affections makes one suspect they were, after all, scarcely worth such trouble to win.[21]

The distaste that Symons displays for the crucial love between Viola and Orsino reveals the difficulties caused by nineteenth-century perception of Viola's character: idealizing her constancy throws Orsino's "weakness" into sharp relief. Orsino's apparent inconsistencies, especially in 2.4, were anathema in the nineteenth century because of the high value set on coherence and consistency in characters. The result was that Viola's relationship to Orsino became the radical flaw in the play.

Nunn takes a distinctively cinematic approach to the "problem," which he frames specifically in terms of theater: "the biggest problem of the play in stage performance is that Orsino, who dominates the early part of the work, drops out at the end of Act Two and doesn't return again until the last scene of Act Five."[22] Nunn reworks the relationship between Orsino and Viola through the distinctive temporal strategies of film and edits their scenes together in three ways: he films continuous scenic sequences across a series of settings; he crosscuts pairs of scenes, like 2.3 and 2.4, so that continuous action becomes discontinuous by virtue of apparently simultaneous interactions; and he literally divides up both of the scenes between Viola and Orsino and spreads them throughout the film. Nunn uses these several strategies to earn the emotional impact of Viola's most famous, self-revelatory speech about her imaginary sister and the poignancy of her voice-over declaration "Whoe'er I woo myself would be his wife" (1.4.42), which he has moved to the end of their penultimate meeting in the film. As a result, the fragments and combined scenes produce a coherence in their developing relationship that a twentieth-century audience both "reads" and helps to produce as the film progresses.

The first of the displaced moments from the theatrical text emphasizes Viola's "tending" to Orsino and underscores what Nunn argues are the crucial difficulties of Cesario's disguise: "It was important to me that Viola, converting herself into her brother, Sebastian (who she believes has drowned), should have to face considerable physical and temperamental challenges."[23] For example, Cesario's appearance in act 1, scene 1, follows directly from the emotional trauma of shearing her locks and the physical pain of confining her breasts in the disguise; the difficulties of playing the piano and passing as male in this scene, which seems to include all of Orsino's court, abruptly gives way to the emotional pain of remembering her brother's death when Orsino looks straight at her in praising Olivia— "She that hath a heart of that fine frame / To pay this debt of love but to a brother" (1.1.34–35). Her brief flashback to the scene of her drowning brother vividly invokes the parallels between Viola and Olivia's situations while beginning to reveal what Viola might find so appealing about Orsino— his speech makes it seem that he knows the book of *her* secret soul. This first scene marks Viola's literal repositioning in the text and initiates the almost subliminal expansion of their relationship.

Nunn's strategies reveal an investment in the relationship developing over time, especially in contrast to the concentrated interactions between Orsino and Viola in the Folio. Love, according to current assumptions evident in film, television, and even romance novels, both arises from and generates continuous interaction. Nunn's *Twelfth Night* displays and reproduces this ideology.[24] However, this film also, paradoxically, demonstrates that the impression of such "continuity" can only be achieved through the fragmentation and dispersal of scenes between the two.

When Nunn breaks Viola's encounters with Orsino into smaller, separate scenes, the time that will untangle Viola's dilemma becomes three months of service most convincingly, especially when scenes that run continuously are filmed in different locations and situations. For example, act 1, scene 4, plays continuously, but its temporal frame is visually extended. Orsino first interrupts Cesario's fencing lesson, "Who saw Cesario, ho?" (1.4.10) and then leads him out to the seaside to ask his help. Nunn's screenplay even registers an imagined length of time in this cut: "ORSINO is sitting by the sea, with the castle in the background, next to CESARIO, having told the whole story of his love for OLIVIA."[25] After Orsino teases him about his near-girlishness, inadvertently threatening both the false mustache above the lip "more smooth and rubious" (1.4.32) and her concealed breasts by grabbing the front of Cesario's jacket, Cesario punches him to get free and knocks Orsino over onto his injured arm. Nunn then cuts to Orsino, reclining as in the opening scene on his couch with his arm in a sling, as he reaches for Cesario's hand: "I know thy constellation is right apt / For this affair" (1.4.35–36). Although the scene's lines flow without interruption, the three complete scene changes and interaction of injury and forgiveness elongate the exchange. The abandonment of Orsino's sling by the middle of the film serves as a further subliminal reminder that, as Orsino puts it, "Three months this youth hath tended upon me" (5.1.97).

Beyond revisions in setting which nonetheless maintain textual continuity, Nunn also uses interwoven scenes to create "character effects" in Viola and Orsino. Although some critics have complained that "the film compulsively cross-cuts among the characters, rarely allowing a scene to build,"[26] in fact that film strategy accomplishes several things. First, like extending a single scene across several settings, the crosscutting stretches out the conversation between Orsino and Cesario. Second, the strategy of intercutting the two scenes, uses specific aspects of the text, for instance, Feste's song, to illuminate the content of the scenes as well as Nunn's interpretation. All in all, Nunn fleshes out the verbal and thematic connections between sequential scenes—a cinematic underscoring of the diptych/triptych structure that Mark Rose has discussed in Shakespearean scenic construction.[27] Nunn portrays as simultaneous the actions in two plots that explore the yearning singled out by some critics as the central insight of Nunn's production.

As Podhoretz's glowing review suggests, "two scenes are combined into an exquisitely edited expression of the way in which sister and duke and noblewoman pine for each other,"[28] but the intermingling of act 2, scenes 1 and 2, is actually even richer, given the backdrop of Feste's song. "Oh Mistress mine" is the song that the twins originally sing on the boat before the shipwreck. Whereas their voices combined jest with the line "that can sing both high and low" during the boat scene because they do sing both high and low, in the middle of the film that line marks a cut to Olivia half-sleeping as she hears the singing from the kitchen. The scene thus foreshadows the replacement of Sebastian's low voice for Viola's high one in her affair of the heart.

Nunn also uses songs to mark significant parallels linking 2.3 and 2.4. For example, when Andrew Aguecheek and Sir Toby ask for a song, the scene cuts immediately to Orsino's request for a song.[29] The account of this missing singer that Curio gives—"Feste the jester, my lord, a fool that the Lady Olivia's father took much delight in" (2.4.11–12)—cuts back to Feste's question to the revelers in the kitchen about what kind of song they would like. The song itself makes a vivid bridge between the two scenes, underscoring both the ambivalently voiced lover and the invocation of transitory youth in both scenes. For example, "high and low" not only functions as voice-over for Olivia but as the cue to cut back to Orsino's music room with the same tune playing in the background and his question to his page "How dost thou like this tune?" (2.4.20). Viola's "masterly" (2.4.22) response yields to Feste's verse "Every wise man's son doth know" (2.3.45). The "present laughter" (2.3.49) of the song then becomes Orsino's laughter at Cesario when perceiving that the youth's eye "hath stay'd upon some favour that it loves" (2.4.24). During their entire exchange, the music of Feste's song plays in the background, creating aural continuity between the interleaved scenes. When Orsino's comments on women as roses culminate in Cesario's lament, "alas, that they are so: / To die, even when they to perfection grow!" (2.4.40–41), the song's response in the cut back to the kitchen is that "what's to come is still unsure" (2.3.50). As Maria begins to sing with Feste, they arrive at the carpe diem motif in song, expressing her longing and the lament that "youth's a stuff will not endure" (2.3.53). That echo of Orsino's and Cesario's comments about women becomes a refrain repeated four times and a commentary on Maria's lost youth and palpable longing for Sir Toby in this production.

Nunn uses Feste's role rather than cutting it, as the nineteenth-century productions did, in order to emphasize part of what he thinks the play is about: "It's about mortality, the transience of youth, the transience of the happiness that we associate with youth."[30] Nonetheless, he has changed the song that Orsino requests at the beginning of act 2, scene 4, from "Come Way, Death" to "Oh, Mistress Mine," in effect doubling the number of scenes that use song and lyrics to elaborate Orsino's relationship with Cesario. The impression of unrequited longing created by "Oh, Mistress Mine" is reinforced by a very brief, final, silent cutaway first to Cesario looking at Orsino and then to Orsino looking at Cesario after the song closes. Even Andrew Aguecheek, whose face on film supplies us with powerful emotional cues when, for example, he says, "I was adored once" (2.3.181). These images, especially the silent close-up, implicitly *refute* Mark Rose's contention that "the presentation of character in Shakespeare is perhaps less like a modern film in which the figures are in constant motion than an album of snapshot stills to be contemplated in sequence, each photo showing the subject in a different light, a different stage of development."[31] Shakespearean filmmakers incorporate these visual parallels without sacrificing the "constant motion": the cut itself becomes the constant motion that engages the audience in comparing different views of a single character or comparing different characters entirely.

Although the entire sequence takes place continuously over the card table, the conversation is extended and builds audience involvement. The two scenes also become mutually interpretive. For example, the overt clues marking out Maria's painful longing for Sir Toby underscore the more subtle hints of Viola's apparently futile desire for Orsino—even though we have not yet heard about her love in the film. With this crosscutting, Nunn teaches his audience to expect and to "read" the brief scenes between Orsino and Viola with which he has seeded the rest of the film. Feste's song effectively situates the brief encounters between Orsino and Viola as evidence of desire functioning below everyday activities. Thus this scene prepares the audience still more thoroughly to perceive the "depth" of character in the yearning that underpins Viola's subsequent brief scenes with Orsino.

This strategy works especially well since Nunn creates a series of dislocated, composite scenes that flesh out and elaborate the closing conversations of act 2, scene 4. One pair of scenes interpolated into act 3 offers Viola the combination of "physical and temperamental challenges" I have already mentioned in the opening scene. Cesario's appearance, riding hard and jumping her horse with the Duke's court, leads directly to Orsino's calling for the "boy" to help him in the bath. Cesario's response to the physical difficulty of jumping the hedge ("cries of distress welling up in her") yields to "the most compromising position so far."[32] The actual summons is taken from 2.4—"Come hither, boy" (2.4.15)—but the speech Orsino gives from his bath continues his early meditation about how Olivia's love for her brother augurs well for her later love, while Cesario, at first embarrassed and then bemused, bathes his back:

> How will she love, when the rich golden shaft
> Hath kill'd the flock of all affections else
> That live in her. When liver, brain, and heart,
> These sovereign thrones, are all supplied and fill'd
> Her sweet perfections with one self king.
>
> (1.1.35–49)

This speech, completing the one interrupted in act 1, scene 1, applies as vividly to Viola as Olivia, as Nunn once again draws out the parallels implicit in the Shakespearean text and allows Viola to hear this meditation. The accompanying action, the lingering intimacy of Cesario sponging Orsino's back, shows Viola in just the position that Orsino is imagining for Olivia—having taken him as her "one self king."

What the Renaissance text implies in scenic parallels between act 1, scenes 1 and 2, Nunn's film interweaves explicitly for a twentieth-century audience. When Viola herself breaks off this moment, she reverts to act 2: "Sir, shall I to this lady?" (2.4.123). His response, though lacking the jewel he sends in the Folio text, follows directly: "Ay, that's the theme, / To her in haste; [Give her this jewel;] say, / My love can give no place, bide no delay" (2.4.123–25—bracketed material has been omitted). The physical challenge of riding like a man is juxtaposed here with the emotional challenge of acting the page to the man she loves and recalling the death of her brother. The two are spliced together in a scene that combines one speech from 1.1 with fragments from 2.4. Such brief sequences encourage an awareness of Viola's hopeless desire operating "beneath" her direct service to the Duke throughout the film, creating the sense of a coherent character through carefully dispersed fragments.

In a second reworked and relocated scene from 2.4, Nunn offers yet another location—the billiards room—and a useful separation of Orsino's contradictory representations of love. In this encounter, shifted still later in act 3 after Sebastian's meeting with Antonio in Illyria (normally 3.3), the film explicitly stages Orsino's advice to Cesario in the context of the two "men" playing billiards:

If ever thou shalt love, remember me;
For such as I am, all true lovers are,
He takes his shot and misses badly.
Unstaid and skittish in all motions else,
Save in the constant image of the creature
That is beloved.

                    (Nunn 74; 2.4.15–20)

In this context, Orsino's comment is a laughing excuse for his failed motion—he has missed his shot. Nunn thus displaces and recasts Orsino's claim of constancy well away from his account earlier in the film of wavering male affection that must choose a younger woman to "hold its bent" (2.4.37). The scene also offers Cesario the first chance to present her greater constancy; to her surprise, her motion is not skittish, and she makes her shot.

Moreover, this brief scene introduces the remainder of 2.4, which, like 1.4, emphasizes different moods by stretching the encounter across different settings. After Cesario successfully sinks his ball, Nunn cuts away to the two rushing down to the barn to solicit the song from Feste. The scene then resumes where it left off several sequences before with Orsino's request to the fool for "that old and antic song we heard last night" (2.4.3). The actual song from 2.4 that Feste sings provides the backdrop for the growing closeness of the two characters listening, as first Orsino crosses the room and places his arm behind Cesario and, next, in an over-the-shoulder shot, Nunn shows Cesario gradually leaning back as if to kiss Orsino. At Feste's final line of the song, the point of view cuts to a head-on two-shot of the pair, startled out of the intimate moment. Feste's reactions both during the song and immediately thereafter draw direct attention to the near-kiss—the measure of the intimacy the pair achieve by "act 3" of Nunn's film.

The scene continues directly from there, but only after Orsino and Cesario abruptly rush outside to stand by the sea. Shouting to be heard above the surf (much louder now than 'twas before), both Orsino and Cesario seem pushed beyond the "normal" friendly interaction of the game of billiards. In Orsino's case, the abrupt command, "Once more, Cesario" (2.4. 80) seems an almost desperate attempt to gain heterosexual equilibrium; moreover, Cesario both reveals and hides her love simultaneously in the story of her sister. Her speech serves both as a forceful defense for women "as true of heart as we" and a self-revelation that paradoxically seems to promise silence about "his" feelings for Orsino—"she never told her love" (2.4.107, 111). Through these sequences, Imogene Stubbs fully earns the poetry and poignancy of the "Patience on a monument" speech as she smiles at grief with a tear flowing down her cheek. Only after this scene, in fact the next morning when Cesario returns to Orsino still on the battlements, does Nunn produce Viola's telling comment from the end of 1.4: "Whoe'er I woo myself would be his wife" (1.4.42).[33] The filmed fragments of her scenes with

Orsino have effectively built up the conflict between her "interior" grief and love and her "exterior" participation in Orsino's household.

Thus Nunn elaborates the growing closeness between Orsino and his page by elongating the interactions of the playtext through filmic time. He claims to "alter the chronology so that the Viola/Orsino story could continue developing throughout, by being interleaved between Olivia scenes and Malvolio scenes, so that we never lose sight of the relationship about which we are required to be so joyously happy at the end."[34] This development actually builds the relationship in a variety of ways. Music room, seaside, riding country, bath, billiards room, battlements—all these varied settings demonstrate how thoroughly Cesario tends upon her lord. The dispersal of their concentrated time together illuminates Viola's life in Orsino's court while expanding Orsino's character and separating some of the startling, even incoherent reversals in his various speeches about love in 2.4. Most important, even continuous scenes, especially the crucial last one hundred lines of 2.4, spread across a variety of settings and an array of sounds—silence, song, surf—display the evolving relationship between Orsino and Cesario in visual and aural variations that justify the changes in tone and Orsino's sudden changes of attitude.

In fact, through film editing, Nunn resolves the inconstancy that leads Arthur Symons ultimately to dismiss Orsino as "a sentimental egoist." Symons's distaste for Orsino's character derives from the scene he describes as "Shakespeare's judgment on him," namely, Orsino's "shallow words on woman's incapacity for love (2.4), so contradictory with what he has said the moment before, an inconsistency so exquisitely characteristic; both said with the same lack of vital sincerity."[35] In the twentieth century such inconsistencies of character have been attributed to Shakespearean scene structure or even Renaissance ideology. Rose suggests that "a Shakespearean scene, when it is concerned with 'character,' will show us a figure in a given emotional posture, or assuming one, switching from joy to grief";[36] more recently, Sinfield argues that "when critics believe they find a continuous consciousness . . . [in Shakespearean characters], they are responding to cues planted in the text for the initial audiences."[37] In planting film cues for a twentieth-century audience, Nunn separates Orsino's inconsistent assertions across space and time; he disperses Orsino's emotional postures rather than radically cutting an already comparatively small role as the nineteenth-century performances did. In Nunn's version, Orsino's inconsistency in act 2, scene 4, becomes less striking because his conflicting comments occur in different locations, even at different times. Moreover, these interactions in the film's configuration register his complex responses to Cesario as their relationship develops.

The success of these techniques suggests that such fragmentation—or intimations of fragmentation in changing settings—functions as the twentieth-century technique for developing character. Whereas the lengthy sustained intimacy of 2.4 in the Folio marks out the mutual definition of the two principals in the Renaissance theatrical context, and the eighteenth- to nineteenth-century versions simply cut Orsino's role to promote character consistency and ameliorate his suitability as Viola's love object, in twentieth-century film we can have almost all of the complicated interaction between the two characters, but only if those varied interactions extend across the surface of the action and allow us to supply their imagined depths. In both the seventeenth-century play and the twentieth-century film, the conventions registering the mutual attraction of Orsino and Viola expose ideologies of erotic union. The playtext stages multiple emotional postures that show Orsino's influence over Viola, displaying erotic alliance as hierarchical at its core; the film deploys fragments to convey long-term, continuous interaction. As a result, each in different ways and at different times produces "character effects."

At the same time that the film editing of Orsino's and Cesario's relationship and characters exploits twentieth-century ideologies of romantic love, Nunn's treatment of the twins invokes ideologies of gender. As a result, he tests the limits of creating character complexity through cinematic fragments. Viola's abilities, developed through her tenure in Orsino's court, match her brother's, offering a version of gender equality in her mirroring of him. However, his appearances and their addition to Cesario's character and activities ultimately make Cesario an unreadably complicated figure, whose "depth" becomes obscurity when too many pieces of cinematic behavior are attributed to "him."

In the process, Nunn uses the same strategies of intercutting and expansion in elaborating the relationship between Olivia and Sebastian as he has between Viola and Orsino. However, the later crosscutting, which mingles 3.4 and 4.1 and again 4.2 and 4.3, more significantly exposes, in the first pair of scenes, the potential to confuse the twins and, in the second pair, the madness that seems to result. Cesario's resistent reactions to Olivia's household are, at first, mirrored explicitly in her brother's responses. Cesario's final plea that Olivia love Orsino leads into Feste's question of Sebastian: "Will you make me believe that I am not sent for you?" (4.1.1). However, Sebastian's response is limited to "Go to, go to, thou art a foolish fellow"(4.1.2) before Nunn returns to Cesario listening to Olivia, who declaims, "Come again tomorrow. [Fare thee well;] / A fiend like thee might bear my soul to hell" (3.4.218–19). Cesario's attempt to depart cuts to and echoes Sebastian trying to shake *Feste's* persistence: "Let me be clear of thee" (4.1.2–3). After Sebastian walks off, with Feste swaggering along behind, Nunn then cuts quickly back to 3.4 and a side shot of Cesario walking, collar up and in the same coat as her brother, just before she is stopped by Toby for the duel. In addition to establishing the twins' parallel reactions to Olivia's solicitations, this scenic juxtaposition invites our confusion of the two characters as well as Feste's.

This echoing effect develops further in the unexpected interruption of Cesario's duel at the end of act 4, scene 1, when the mistaking of the twins for each other becomes part of Viola's experience as well. When Antonio is dragged off, pleading for the money Sebastian has been holding for him, Nunn cuts to Sebastian denying that he knows Feste yet a third time: "I prithee, foolish Greek, depart from me, / There's money for thee, if you tarry longer, / I shall give worse payment" (4.1.18–20). Unfortunately, as he denies that he knows Feste, he performs the same sleight of hand that Cesario did earlier when giving money to the fool. In this context the switch of hands in the coin trick not only further convinces Feste that Sebastian is Cesario but also resonates thematically with the money that Antonio has given into the other twin's hand. In effect, the twins embody the coin trick. Viola's purse is almost empty but Sebastian's is full; the hand that appears to hold the money is empty, while the identical but opposite hand actually does have the coin. The comparable abilities of the twins as entertainers from before the shipwreck emerge here as the sign that they are a single person.

This doubling underscores the emergent and contested Western ideas about gender equality that prove almost as significant to Viola's character as is her relationship with Orsino. Of all the *Twelfth Night* films I have seen, this one best creates the twinning of brother and sister. Viola's "training" in Orsino's military court gives her rough equality to her brother that extends beyond dress. This Viola plays cards and billiards as well or better than a man; she rides and jumps obstacles successfully, even if she gives muffled cries of distress; "Cesario" even (for once) acquits himself well in the duel. Although Antonio still interrupts to fight on "Sebastian's" behalf, Viola is at that point putting her fencing tuition into practice and fighting well against Aguecheek. This Viola is not only "as true of heart" as a man; she is also as competent as a man in several pursuits that face her during her adoption of male attire. Like the coin trick, which convinces Feste that the twins are the same person, Viola's skills as well as Sebastian's arrival make their ultimate confusion for each other unavoidable. By encouraging the audience to share the bemusement of the doubling, Nunn adds layers to Viola's character, playing upon twentieth-century gender ideologies as well as romantic ideologies in his construction of her plausibility as a character.

As Nunn very carefully places Sebastian in a world going mad even before Olivia lays claim to him, the film produces the Illyrians as the audience to the twins as a single character. The wholly unexpected assault by Aguecheek becomes the penultimate oddity in a series of strange encounters that Sebastian experiences. His question, "Are all the people mad?" (4.1.26), and his aggressive response to Aguecheek and Toby are all the

more justified because his interactions with Olivia's household and his confusion at misidentification not only parallel Viola's final solo visit to Olivia
(duel for no cause, strangers claiming to know her) but also immediately
echo that experience. The simultaneity of the twins' experiences, "both
born in an hour" (2.1.19), is restored cinematically as simultaneous experiences registered in crosscutting. At the same time, the audience becomes
more aware of the confusion arising from mistaking the twins for each
other as Olivia pleads, "Be ruled by me" (4.1.63). His acceptance of her
and his willingness now to keep the madness or dream that has overcome
him find an echo transported from 3.4 as Nunn cuts away to Viola, sitting
by the sea: "Prove true, imagination, O prove true" (3.4.384). On the one
hand, from the audience's privileged position, "reading" Cesario's character at the end of the film apparently presents no problem; on the other hand,
the discontinuities perceived by the Illyrians, most by notably Orsino and
Olivia, disrupt that character completely, in part because "Cesario" is a
product of their imaginations supplying the "interior" logic of "his" character according to their own assumptions about servants and young gentlemen.

However, Nunn also significantly challenges the audience's superior
knowledge in his filming of the twins. He provokes *his* audience's confusion by substituting Imogene Stubbs for Steven Mackintosh when Olivia
spies Feste and "Cesario" outside her window just after this exchange. He
also uses the same sleight of film several other times, interchanging Mackintosh for Stubbs when "she" rides away from Olivia's house after her second visit and again when Malvolio, crossgartered and convinced of her
regard, peers through the window at Olivia and "Cesario" walking from
audience right to left outside the window. In turn, Stubbs stands in for
Mackintosh at the start of the first scene between Antonio and Sebastian on
the quayside and outside the church where Feste spies "him" with Olivia.
When asked about this cinematic indirection, Nunn acknowledges that "the
twin trick was played on the audience several times, though that wasn't
quite my intention—rather to imprint swift physical images on the audience's
collective retina so that the final moment of re-union would be credible and
moving."[38] In fact, Nunn himself is not sure how many times Cesario was
filmed for Sebastian or vice versa. Whenever such substitutions occur, the
film audience occupies the position of the Illyrians: they see the twin that
they expect to see, projecting the identity of the actor-as-character into the
situation that should present one or the other twin in terms of filmed and
filial coherence.

The dangers attached to believing the imagination, to projecting a complete character from a partial view, become the core of the next pair of
intercut scenes, foreshadowed by a brief cutaway to Malvolio ("they have
laid me here in darkness. The world shall know it").[39] The crosscutting

interleaving 4.2 and 4.3 hinges on the madness that Malvolio denies and Sebastian suspects. Malvolio's certainty that Olivia loves him finally rests on far less direct evidence than does Sebastian's; as a result, their responses prove different yet interrelated. The intercutting of these two scenes, while again drawing out the encounters with the Illyrians, explicitly uses references to madness as the cinematic pivot linking the gulling of Malvolio to the good luck of Sebastian. After all, Malvolio's insistence that the house is dark and that he is not mad leads immediately into Sebastian's opening speech in 4.3, in which he tries to determine who is mad:

> This is the air, that is the glorious sun,
> This pearl she gave me, I do feel't, and see't,
> And though 'tis wonder that enwraps me thus,
> Yet 'tis not madness.
>
> (4.3.1–4)

Unlike Malvolio, Sebastian wavers on the subject of his own sanity; he is "ready to distrust [his] eyes" (4.3.13) as he looks at his reflection in one of Olivia's mirrors. His reflection, echo to the doubling that makes the twins so confusing throughout the last two acts of the play, leads him to "wrangle with my reason that persuades me / To any other trust, but that I am mad" (4.3.14–15). Not so Malvolio whose immediate line following the cut back to 4.2 is "I am not mad" (4.2.41). Malvolio's encounter with Feste offers another possibility besides madness for the confusion that both Sebastian and Malvolio are experiencing. After Malvolio begs Feste to "convey what I will set down to my lady" (4.2.115–16), Nunn cuts back to Sebastian in 4.3: "Or else the lady's mad" (4.3.16). But the proof of Olivia's sanity surrounds him in her well-ordered gardens and household. As Sebastian notes, if she were mad, "She could not sway her house, command her followers, / Take and give back affairs, and their dispatch, / With such a smooth, discreet, and stable bearing" (4.3.17–19). Of course, the crosscutting underscores that at least one of her followers is not being swayed or commanded with "smooth, discreet and stable bearing."

As in the previous scene, where Sebastian accepts confusion and follows Olivia, here he again abandons his attempts to reason out his situation and promises, "I'll follow this good man, and go with you, / And having sworn truth, ever will be true" (4.3.32–33). Nunn then cuts away to Feste and Malvolio on truth and madness:

> *Clown.* [I will help you too't.] But tell me true, are you not mad indeed, or do you but counterfeit?
> *Malvolio.* Believe me I am not, I tell thee true.
>
> (4.2.116–18)

This telling interchange happens before Sebastian's promise of truth in the Folio; Nunn's filming and cuts make the parallels more direct and pointed. Sebastian's primacy apparently sets his logic as the more valid one, but "truth" itself is suspect since Sebastian, like Malvolio, is caught up in mistaken identity.

The extensive elongation of the very short 4.3 by crosscutting it with one of the play's longest scenes, 4.2 (even though substantially cut here), sets the evolution of Sebastian's mistaken involvement with Olivia against the consequences of Malvolio's erroneous belief that she loves him. Not only does Sebastian's hesitancy show well against Malvolio's unyielding self-delusion, but also the extended time frame and parallels develop both Sebastian's character and his relationship with Olivia beyond the two brief encounters they have before their marriage in the Folio text. In this way, the striking fragmentations and rearrangements of the play's text in Trevor Nunn's *Twelfth Night* not only answer the critical queries about Viola's sudden affection for Orsino, which extend from the eighteenth century, but also attempt comparable effects in making Olivia's mistake more acceptable. Nonetheless, this development is not and cannot be as thorough as the elaboration provided by the combination of 2.3 and 2.4 and by the dispersal of composite scenes between Viola and Orsino. Even though this mingling of 4.2 and 4.3 does extend Olivia's involvement with Sebastian and sets the level of confusion between the twins as high as possible, the layering of these fragments actually exposes how characters in Illyria interpret and try to make coherent their encounters with Cesario in assessing "his" character. Their mistaken reactions to the partial views offered them by Viola and Sebastian underscore how expectations set by gender and romantic ideology produce "Cesario" ultimately as an impossible character.

The twin relationship in Nunn's film calls into question the emerging fullness of "Cesario's" character by displaying Viola as complexly grounded in shifting ideologies of gender. Extending from the seventeenth-century text through the British nineteenth-century setting ("where the differences between men and women were at their greatest . . . the last years of the previous century took those attitudes to extremes exemplified in the dress silhouettes of the two genders")[40] to a twentieth-century audience, Nunn's film emphasizes Viola's abilities, once driven, to enact and dress the male part. The plausibility of mistaking one twin for the other derives not just from the excellent casting or even the camera tricks, but from the establishment of male and female characters whose talents, tricks, and even abilities prove closer to interchangeable than in any previous *Twelfth Night* film. In fact, the casting here is even more effective than those films that use a single actress for both roles and are consequently compelled to emphasize gender differences.[41] Nunn's film as a whole works through the equality and blend of genders predicted in their opening performance, largely because this *Twelfth Night* reflects a particularly twentieth-century Western set of assumptions about gender equity—given equal opportunity. Sebastian's incursions into Cesario's Illyria expose how the Illyrians' mistaken constructions of Cesario mirror our investment in "reading" Viola's character within her extended association with Orsino.

Trevor Nunn's *Twelfth Night* reveals our twentieth-century investment in character as a complex weave of gender identity and erotic alliance. The "depth" of Viola's character proves inextricably linked to the depth of her love, which can only be shown through her ongoing relationship with Orsino. The paradox, of course, is that both her character and their relationship are signaled by dispersed fragments of the text, echoed and emphasized by the comparable strategies applied to Sebastian's interactions with Olivia. As a result, the film exposes a peculiarly twentieth-century "filling up of subjectivities": scenic parallels both confuse and establish gender identity, and only short, disjointed interactions can produce the required continuity. In Nunn's *Twelfth Night*, our "natural perspective" on the twins, like that in Shakespeare's play, proves at once fragmented and continuous—and therefore ideological rather than "natural."

NOTES

1. Alan Sinfield, *Faultlines: Cultural Materialism and the Politics of Dissident Reading* (Berkeley: University of California Press, 1992), 62.
2. Sinfield, 63.
3. William Shakespeare, *Richard III*, ed. G. Blakemore Evans et al. (New York: Houghton Mifflin, 1974), 1.2.229. All subsequent references to Shakespeare's plays will refer to this edition and be noted parenthetically in the text.
4. Stanley Kauffmann, "Blanking Verse," *The New Republic*, 2 December 1996, 42.
5. John Podhoretz, "O for a Muse of Fire," *The Weekly Standard*, 18 November 1996, 46.
6. John Collick, *Shakespeare, Cinema, and Society* (New York: Manchester Press, 1989), 33-37.
7. Peter Donaldson, *Shakespearean Films/Shakespearean Directors* (Boston: Unwin Hyman, 1990).
8. See Barbara Hodgdon, *The Shakespeare Trade: Performances and Appropriations* (Philadelphia: University of Pennsylvania Press, 1998), and Douglas Lanier, "Drowning the Book: *Prospero's Books* and the Textual Shakespeare," in *Shakespeare, Theory, and Performance*, ed. James Bulman (London and New York: Routledge, 1996).
9. Lorne M. Buchman, *Still in Movement: Shakespeare on Screen* (Oxford: Oxford University Press, 1991), 107.
10. Franco Zeffirelli, "Filming Shakespeare," in *Staging Shakespeare: Seminars on Production Problems*, ed. Glenn Loney (New York: Garland Publishing, 1990), 261.
11. Kenneth Branagh, *Hamlet: Screenplay, Introduction, and Film Diary* (New York and London: W. W. Norton, 1996), 33.
12. Buchman, 108–9.

13. Joe Morgenstern, "Film: Vintage Wine in Hip Flasks." *The Wall Street Journal*, 25 October 1996, A12.

14. Trevor Nunn, *William Shakespeare's Twelfth Night: A Screenplay* (London: Methuen, 1996), xii. Unfortunately, Nunn's screenplay text does not include page numbers for his valuable introduction; I supply them as they would appear.

15. In "'The very names of the Persons': Editing and the Invention of Dramatick Character" in *Staging the Renaissance: Reinterpretations of Elizabethan and Jacobean Drama,* ed. David Scott Kastan and Peter Stallybrass (London and New York: Routledge, 1991), Randall McLeod examines the variations in stage directions in *All's Well* in order to argue that characters on stage seem to be reconfigured—and renamed—according to their relationships to other characters on stage. Such variable naming does not appear in the 1623 Folio *Twelfth Night*, except insofar as Orsino wavers between being called "Count" and "Duke." Some textual critics have taken this variation as a sign of textual revision in the play, but the naming has implications for characters as well since the counts in Shakespeare's plays have less authority and more involvement with love than do the dukes.

16. This distinction between "true love" and lust is a common feature in popular romance fiction, as analyzed by Janice Radway in *Reading the Romance: Women Patriarchy and Popular Literature* (Chapel Hill: University of North Carolina Press, 1984).

17. See Laurie Osborne, *The Trick of Singularity: Twelfth Night and the Performance Editions* (Iowa City: University of Iowa Press, 1996), 47–77.

18. Osborne, 92–96.

19. Francis Gentleman, *Twelfth Night* in *Bell's Edition of Shakspeare's Plays*, vol. 5 (London: Bell, 1774), 299.

20. Mrs. M. L. Elliott, *Shakespeare's Garden of Girls* (London: Remington & Company, 1885), 215.

21. Arthur Symons, introduction to *The Henry Irving Shakespeare*, ed. Henry Irving and Frank Marshall, vol. 4 (London: Blackie & Son, 1888), 355.

22. Nunn, xii.

23. Trevor Nunn, as quoted in *Twelfth Night: About the Film*, n.d., <http://www.flf.com/twelfth/index.html>16 July 2000.

24. For a discussion of how underanalyzed are the effects of romantic ideologies as they affect the reception of Shakespeare's plays, see Linda Charnes, "'What's Love Got to Do with It?' Reading the Liberal Humanist Romance in Shakespeare's *Antony and Cleopatra,*" *Textual Practice* 6, no. 1 (1992): 1–16.

25. Nunn, *Screenplay*, 16.

26. Stephen Holden, "There's Something Verboten in Illyria," *New York Times* 25 October 1996, B1.

27. Mark Rose, in *Shakespearean Stage Design* (Cambridge: Harvard University Press, 1981), draws attention to the roots of Shakespearean scenic structure in the visual arts, especially in the juxtaposition of scenes that "reflect upon" each other. Rose only addresses *Twelfth Night* specifically in his comments on the structural effects of the opening scenes; in *Shakespeare's Art of Orchestration* (Champaign-Urbana: University of Illinois Press, 1989), Jean Howard analyzes more fully the dynamic development from scene to scene between stasis and motioning the comedy.

28. Podhoretz, 47.

29. Nunn, 42.

30. Nunn, as quoted in Peter Marks, "So Young, So Fragile, So Vexed about Sex," *New York Times*, 20 October 1996, 13.

31. Rose, 9.

32. Nunn, *Screenplay*, 54.

33. Nunn allows Viola's glances to give this information almost as early as the first

scene. Certainly her interest in him is clear as early as the seaside scene when he first sends her to Olivia; however, it is an interest that we as the audience must supply out of our interpretation of the cinematic gaze she offers of him rather than the revelation of a spoken declaration.

34. Nunn, *Screenplay*, xii.
35. Symons, 257.
36. Rose, 9.
37. Sinfield, 63.
38. Trevor Nunn, Letter to Author, 8 May 1997. I wrote to inquire about the doubling I had noticed only to discover that the substitutions also appeared in places I had not recognized, despite several viewings.
39. Nunn, *Screenplay*, 101.
40. Nunn, *Screenplay*, 8–9.
41. Osborne, 124–36.

WORKS CITED

Branagh, Kenneth. *Hamlet: Screenplay, Introduction, and Film Diary*. New York and London:W. W. Norton, 1996.

Buchman, Lorne M. *Still in Movement: Shakespeare on Screen*. Oxford: Oxford University Press, 1991.

Charnes, Linda. "'What's Love Got to Do with It?' Reading the Liberal Humanist Romance in Shakespeare's *Antony and Cleopatra*." *Textual Practice* 6, no. 1 (1992): 1–16.

Collick, John. *Shakespeare, Cinema, and Society*. New York: Manchester Press, 1989.

Davies, Anthony. *Filming Shakespeare Plays*. Cambridge: Cambridge University Press, 1988.

Donaldson, Peter. *Shakespearean Films/Shakespearean Directors*. Boston: Unwin Hyman, 1990.

Elliott, Mrs. M. L. *Shakespeare's Garden of Girls*. London: Remington & Company, 1885.

Gentleman, Francis. *Twelfth Night*. In *Bell's Edition of Shakspeare's Plays*. Vol. 5. London: Bell, 1774.

Hodgdon, Barbara. *The Shakespeare Trade: Performances and Appropriations*. Philadelphia: University of Pennsylvania Press, 1998.

Holden, Stephen. "There's Something Verboten in Illyria." *New York Times*, 25 October 1996, B1, B16.

Howard, Jean. *Shakespeare's Art of Orchestration*. Champaign-Urbana: University of Illinois Press, 1989.

Kauffmann, Stanley. "Blanking Verse." *The New Republic,* 2 December 1996, 40–41.

Lanier, Douglas M. "Drowning the Book: *Prospero's Books* and the Textual Shakespeare." In *Shakespeare, Theory, and Performance*. Edited by James Bulman. London and New York: Routledge, 1996.

Marks, Peter. "So Young, So Fragile, So Vexed about Sex." *New York Times*, 20 October 1996, 13.

McLeod, Randall. "'The very names of the Persons': Editing and the Invention of Dramatick Character." In *Staging the Renaissance: Reinterpretations of Elizabethan and Jaco-*

bean Drama. Edited by David Scott Kastan and Peter Stallybrass. London and New York: Routledge, 1991.

Morgenstern, Joe. "Film: Vintage Wine in Hip Flasks." *The Wall Street Journal*, 25 October 1996, A12.

Nunn, Trevor. Letter to Author. 8 May 1997.

———. As quoted in *Twelfth Night: About the Film*, n.d., http://www.flf.com/twelfth/index.html 16 July 2000.

———. *William Shakespeare's Twelfth Night: A Screenplay*. London and New York: Methuen, 1996.

Osborne, Laurie. *The Trick of Singularity: Twelfth Night and the Performance Editions*. Iowa Studies in Theatre and Culture. Iowa City: University of Iowa Press, 1996.

Podhoretz, John. "O for a Muse of Fire." *The Weekly Standard*, 18 November 1996, 46–47.

Radway, Janice. *Reading the Romance: Women Patriarchy and Popular Literature*. Chapel Hill: University of North Carolina Press, 1984.

Rose, Mark. *Shakespearean Design*. Cambridge: Harvard University Press, 1981.

Shakespeare, William. *Richard III*. In *Riverside Shakespeare*. Edited by G. Blakemore Evans et al. New York: Houghton Mifflin, 1974.

———. *Twelfth Night, Or What You Will*. In *Riverside Shakespeare*. Edited by G. Blakemore Evans et al. New York: Houghton Mifflin, 1974.

Sinfield, Alan. *Faultlines: Cultural Materialism and the Politics of Dissident Reading*. Berkeley: University of California Press, 1992.

Symons, Arthur. "Introduction to *Twelfth Night*." In *The Henry Irving Shakespeare*. Vol. 4. Edited by Henry Irving and Frank Marshall. London: Blackie & Son, 1888.

Zeffirelli, Franco. "Filming Shakespeare." In *Staging Shakespeare: Seminars on Production Problems*. Edited by Glenn Loney. New York: Garland Publishing, 1990.

Films Cited

Hamlet. Directed by Kenneth Branagh. 3 hr. 58 min. Castle Rock Entertainment, 1996. Videocassette.

Looking for Richard. Directed by Al Pacino. 1 hr. 52 min. Fox Searchlight Pictures, 1996. Videocassette.

Twelfth Night. Directed by Trevor Nunn. 2 hr. 13 min. Fine Line Films, 1996. Videocassette.

William Shakespeare's Romeo + Juliet. Directed by Baz Luhrmann. 2 hr. Twentieth Century Fox/Bazmark Films, 1996. Videocassette.

The Marriage of
Shakespeare and Hollywood: Kenneth Branagh's
Much Ado about Nothing

SAMUEL CROWL

WHETHER BY ACCIDENT OR DESIGN, KENNETH BRANAGH THRIVES ON MIDDLES. His greatest achievement as an artist is as a synthesizer: between Belfast and London in his personal life and between Stratford and Hollywood in his professional career. Such a situation, of course, leaves him open to attack for being a Hollywood popularizer by the Shakespearean purists and for being a Thatcherite entrepreneur by the cultural materialists. What neither side seems prepared to admit is that Branagh is almost single-handedly responsible for the 1990s revival of the seemingly defunct genre of the Shakespeare film. This decade has already given us the greatest explosion of Shakespeare films since the 1960s, stimulated first by the artistic achievement of his *Henry V* (1989) and then by the surprise commercial success of his *Much Ado about Nothing* (1993). His *Henry V* was the first English-language Shakespeare film to be made since the box office failure of Roman Polanski's undervalued *Macbeth* in 1971 seemed to have doomed the genre.

In revitalizing the Shakespeare film, largely invented in the post–World War II era by Laurence Olivier and Orson Welles, Branagh absorbed the lessons of his masters but reached boldly beyond them by incorporating into his films echoes of Hollywood ranging from Errol Flynn and Tony Curtis to Wes Craven and George Lucas. As Robert Hapgood has pointed out, Branagh's Shakespeare films ultimately owe as much to the work of the Anglo-American outsider Franco Zeffirelli as to Olivier and Welles.[1] Branagh works and creates in the postmodern moment dominated, as Fredric Jameson and his followers argue, by a sense of belatedness, a sense that originality is exhausted and that only parody and pastiche and intertextual echo remain.[2] Rather than finding such a condition enervating, Branagh's work seizes its possibilities. The Shakespeare film that most thoroughly and successfully embraces the postmodern aesthetic, Baz Luhrmann's *William Shakespeare's Romeo + Juliet* (1996), would not have been possible, both conceptually and commercially, without the example of Branagh's *Much Ado*.

Hollywood elements and images infuse Branagh's Shakespeare films from initial images to last. Think first of Henry V's double entrance, first captured back-lit and in long shot framed in a huge door looming like some medieval version of Darth Vader, and then, moments later, caught in a tight close-up sitting dwarfed in a giant throne chair looking like Luke Skywalker. Then flash forward to the final moments of his 1996 *Hamlet* and his bravura Errol Flynnesque rope swing down from the high balcony to follow his foil's (and the huge candelabra's) fatal whistle through the great chamber and into Claudius's chest to discover evidence that Branagh reaches beyond even Zeffirelli in his willingness to marry Shakespeare and Hollywood. Courtney Lehmann has provided the most thorough and effective analysis of the ways in which Branagh's attempt to mix Shakespeare and film, Stratford and Hollywood, links up with the mingling of high and low culture in the cultural poetics of both the Renaissance and the postmodern eras. While her reading of Branagh's *Much Ado about Nothing* through the perspective of a Gramscian cultural critique ultimately finds the film failing to deliver on its theoretical potential, her persuasive essay indicates the seriousness with which some Shakespeareans are beginning to regard Branagh's films.[3]

I am more concerned (and impressed) with the positive impact Branagh's *Much Ado* has had on the revival of the genre including its obvious influence on the making of Oliver Parker's *Othello* (1995) and Trevor Nunn's *Twelfth Night* (1996). As Nunn argues: "It has become possible for many people to think in terms of filming Shakespeare almost entirely because of the achievement of Kenneth Branagh . . . the breakthrough success of his *Henry V*, followed by the even bigger box-office success of his *Much Ado about Nothing* has made the film world, and Hollywood in particular, become interested again when, for years, everything concerning the Bard was darkness."[4]

Branagh and Nunn (likè Olivier, Welles, and Zeffirelli before them), came to film Shakespeare via the stage. All three of Branagh's Shakespeare films grew from stage productions in which he starred but did not direct and from which he gleaned visual ideas that provided keys to the translation of his Shakespearean material into the language of film. Rain and grit and the garroting of Bardolph from Adrian Noble's production of *Henry V* for the Royal Shakespeare Company; the hot Italian sun and festive energy from Judi Dench's *Much Ado about Nothing* for Branagh's own Renaissance Company; and the nineteenth-century period and the use of a full text collation of Q2 and F1 from Noble's *Hamlet* again for the RSC. But in each instance, Branagh's synthesizing sensibility reached out to link stage ideas with film images, traditions, and techniques. I have already suggested a few examples of this phenomenon in the opening shots of his *Henry V* and the closing ones of his *Hamlet*. His *Much Ado about Nothing* brazenly lifts images and ideas from films as diverse as *The Magnificent Seven* (dir. John Sturges, 1960), *Singing in the Rain* (dir. Stanley Donent and Gene Kelly, 1952), and *Some Like It Hot* (dir. Billy Wilder, 1959), but Branagh's greatest achievement is to link ideas in Shakespeare's play with the witty Hollywood comedies of the 1930s that have come to be labeled as "screwball."[5]

As I indicated earlier, Branagh's film of *Much Ado about Nothing* has its source in Judi Dench's stage production and, Branagh tells us, the specific images of the film's opening sequence: "heat haze and dust, and horseflesh, and a nod to *The Magnificent Seven*" all flashed through his mind one evening as his stage Benedick listened to Balthazar's song, "Sigh no more, ladies."[6] Russell Jackson, text consultant for Branagh's Shakespeare films, places the film in the screwball tradition, and it is clear from the film's casting and its production values that Branagh wanted his film to merge Shakespeare and Hollywood.[7]

The most profound treatment of those wonderful films including *It Happened One Night* (dir. Frank Capra, 1934), *The Awful Truth* (dir. Leo McCarey, 1937), *The Lady Eve* (dir. Preston Sturges, 1941), *The Philadelphia Story* (dir. George Cukor, 1940), and *Bringing Up Baby* (dir. Howard Hawkes, 1938) is by Stanley Cavell in his *Pursuits of Happiness: The Hollywood Comedy of Remarriage*. Cavell traces the structure of these films back to Shakespeare's comic romances and their Old Comedy antecedents. Cavell argues that these Depression-era films embraced the "creation of a new woman" who was the symbolic daughter of the leaders of the first phase of the American feminist movement, which culminated in winning the right to vote in 1920. These Hollywood comedies "may be understood as parables of a phase of the development of consciousness at which the struggle is for the reciprocity or equality of consciousness between a woman and a man" with the recognition that this is "a struggle for mutual freedom, especially of the views each holds of the other."[8] Such films are romances and they "harbor a vision which cannot be fully domesticated, inhabited, in the world we know" for "they express the inner agenda of a nation that conceives Utopian longings and commitments for itself."[9]

Cavell sees that the intelligent wit play that distinguishes the romantic commerce between the heroes and heroines of these films represents a movement towards a recognition of freedom and equality between the sexes in which each freely rechooses the other after the relationship has been ruptured, strained, or literally—in the case of Tracy Lord and Dexter Havens in *The Philadelphia Story*—divorced. Thus Cavell's decision to classify these films as comedies of remarriage. The witty bickering in these comedies leads "to acknowledgement; to the reconciliation of a genuine forgiveness; a reconciliation so profound as to require the metamorphosis of death and revival; the achievement of a new perspective on existence; a perspective that presents itself as a place, one removed from the city of confusion and divorce."[10] Shakespeareans, of course, can hear echoes of Northrop Frye and C. L. Barber in Cavell's language here as he rediscovers the structure and romantic energy of Shakespearean comedy buried in the heart of these remarkable films.[11]

While Cavell never mentions *Much Ado about Nothing* when he spins out from his close readings of individual films to seek and work a Shakespearean resonance, it strikes me that *Much Ado* is the Shakespearean comedy that most resembles Cavell's remarriage pattern. Though Beatrice and Benedick have not been previously married, the play does suggest a past romantic attachment between them which Benedick, as Beatrice reports, has broken off: "Indeed, my lord, he [Benedick] lent it [his heart] me awhile, and I gave him use for it, a double heart for his single one. Marry once before he won it of me with false dice; therefore your Grace may well say I have lost it."[12] Beatrice and Benedick are surely the prototypes for the bantering pairs (most commonly played by Katharine Hepburn and Cary Grant) who distinguish Cavell's Hollywood comedies. The entire movement of the contrasting romantic plots in *Much Ado* is to bring each pair of lovers, in very different fashions, through the metamorphosis of separation and even feigned death into the revival of forgiveness and reconciliation. Beatrice and Benedick's progress through this pattern is self-created and unique while Hero and Claudio's is socially generated and conventional.

Shakespeare's two plots are intimately linked in Cavellian terms because it takes Claudio's immature and cruel disruption of the socially sanctioned ritual of marriage to spur the creation of Beatrice and Benedick's privately conceived and imagined ceremony of reconciliation and reengagement. Claudio's slander of Hero spurs Benedick to exercise his independent intelligence in moving from the male camp to the female in response to Beatrice's wildly apt but unconventional rejoinder—"Kill Claudio"—to his hyperbolic, male wooing sentiment: "Come, bid me do *anything* for thee" (4.1.287–88 [emphasis added]). These two experienced and wounded lovers then create their own private pact as Benedick promises to enact Beatrice's consciousness of gender inequality (thus acknowledging her equality) when seeking revenge for slander ("Oh God, that I were a man! I would eat his heart in the market place!" [4.1.305–6]) by allowing her anger to be expressed through his action: "Enough. I am engaged" (4.1.330).[13] This moment is the triumph of their unconventional courtship and represents their engagement as equals. Claudio and Don Pedro, along with the conventional patriarchal social order they represent and embody, can only be threatened and exposed by the united action of a woman and a man (Beatrice and Benedick) acting as a single consciousness and sensibility.

Theirs is a singular social revolution, which is too often, in production and criticism, swallowed by an overemphasis on their "merry war of words."

I evoke Cavell here not because I believe Branagh was directly aware of his work, but because I do think Branagh had the screen comedies Cavell champions in mind as one of several Hollywood ingredients he wished to bring to his treatment of Shakespeare's play as film. Rather than seeing his film—as many stage productions do—as solely a vehicle for Beatrice and Benedick, Branagh is on record as desiring to give equal visual attention to Claudio and Hero by imagining them as younger versions of the older lovers: "Emma Thompson and I both wanted to suggest former lovers who had been genuinely hurt by their first encounter, which perhaps occurred at the tender age of Hero and Claudio in the play. ("For our own purposes we deliberately made the younger lovers around twenty . . . and Beatrice and Benedick a significant ten years older or so.")[14]

Much Ado occupies a swing position in the development of Shakespeare's comedies. Its emphasis on the confusions of courtship and wooing places it with the earlier festive comedies, but its city setting, its concern with social mores and fashion, and its flirtation with rape and death all echo elements in the problem comedies that follow.[15] Branagh's film clearly seeks to highlight the play's festive elements made most apparent in his transfer of the play's locale from Sicily's Messina to Tuscany's Villa Vignemaggio: from city street to country estate. Anne Barton remarks that *Much Ado* is one of the most "resolutely urban of Shakespeare's comedies," and that in Branagh's film "Messina has disappeared" to be replaced by the "boldly rural and open air" which entails a "virtual obliteration of Shakespeare's carefully structured social hierarchy."[16] That hierarchy is probably well lost on film as its subtle distinctions are difficult to capture for a contemporary international movie audience and, as I will argue later, Branagh wants his film to create a utopian green world vision based on the powers of imagination and intelligence rather than on social status.[17]

Shakespeare's comedies have been notoriously difficult to translate successfully into film. Zeffirelli's *The Taming of the Shrew* (1966) is primarily a star vehicle for Richard Burton and Elizabeth Taylor, though the film's gaudy opening sequence visually celebrating the carnival atmosphere surrounding the beginning of term at the University of Padua, all taken in with wide-eyed amazement by Lucentio and Tranio, provided a cinematic model for the visual impact of Branagh's lush, fleshy, dynamic opening to his *Much Ado*.[18] Peter Hall's *A Midsummer Night's Dream* (1968) certainly is the most textually faithful and probably comes closest of all the filmed comedies to making a synthesis between H. R. Coursen's desire for film productions of Shakespeare that merge "'conservative' criteria like clarity in the speaking of the lines" with a "radical [approach] to freshness and originality."[19] But much of what seemed filmically fresh and original in

1968, from the women's miniskirts to the use of a handheld camera to an editing style distinguished by the jumpcut, has come to seem in a mere thirty years seriously dated in its impact. Christine Edzard's *As You Like It* (1992) found its inspiration in a series of Dickensian parallels between the homeless in Mrs. Thatcher's London and the exiles in Shakespeare's Arden. Edzard's idea is provocative, but her film never fully releases the potential energy of its invention. The film lacks an animating visual energy to transport us willingly into its ideological conceit.

Derek Jarman's *Tempest* (1980) and Peter Greenaway's *Prospero's Books* (1991) are both the work of film auteurs who use Shakespeare, often stunningly, as one element in their own idiosyncratic aesthetic biographies. Jarman's film is, I think, the most interesting low budget radical appropriation of Shakespeare on film, but it never sought (and certainly did not find) a popular film audience. The commercial success of Branagh's *Much Ado* created a climate that made possible the financing of Trevor Nunn's recent film of *Twelfth Night*, produced by Branagh's own Renaissance Films Production Company. Nunn's version of Shakespeare's comedy makes an instructive contrast with Branagh's. If Branagh went for sun and flesh and festive energy, Nunn created a darker, more complex treatment of Shakespeare's farewell to festivity by emphasizing *Twelfth Night's* affinities with Chekhov and our own culture's fascination with issues relating to gender, cross-dressing, and androgyny.

Hall, Edzard, Jarman, and Greenaway—each in his or her own way— used their Shakespearean comic material to make personal films intended for a very small slice of the potential international film audience. Branagh's plan for his *Much Ado*, encouraged by the surprising success of his *Henry V*, was more Zeffirelli-esque. Building on the popular approach to Shakespeare established by his Renaissance Company's stage productions, Branagh wished "to tell the story with the utmost clarity and simplicity" for audiences "relatively unfamiliar with Shakespeare . . . [W]e wanted audiences to react to the story as if it were here and now and important to them. We did not want them to feel they were in some cultural church."[20] Branagh's insistence on a realistic, plain style of performing Shakespeare turned him once again to America and to Hollywood: "The film presented a rare opportunity to utilize the skills of marvelous film actors who would embrace this naturalistic challenge. . . . In crude terms, the challenge was to find experienced Shakespearean actors who were unpracticed on screen and team them with experienced film actors who were much less familiar with Shakespeare. Different accents, different looks . . . [producing] a Shakespeare film which would belong to the world. I naturally wished to include some U.S. actors [as] the best American acting [is distinguished by an] emotional fearlessness."[21]

There's an echo of Peter Quince (and Andy Hardy) here as Branagh assembles his cast and sets out to compete with Hollywood's one venture into big budget, big studio Shakespearean comedy on film: Warner Brothers' 1935 *A Midsummer Night's Dream* (dir. William Dieterle and Max Reinhardt). That film, too, featured a crazy quilt cast of some of Hollywood's top stars including Branagh's own icon, Jimmy Cagney and, of course, Andy Hardy himself—Mickey Rooney.[22] Now, some sixty years later, Branagh surrounds his Benedick and Emma Thompson's Beatrice with young male Hollywood stars: Denzel Washington (Don Pedro), Keanu Reeves (Don John), and Robert Sean Leonard (Claudio), which gives his film something of the flavor of Beatrice and the Brat Pack.

Branagh's visually romantic film, buoyed by the sophistication of his maturing cinematic imagination (several sequences, including the final swirling dance, are beautifully effective in their fluid use of a steadicam), and Patrick Doyle's lush score, locates this version of *Much Ado* firmly within the festive tradition. Branagh shapes his translation of Shakespeare's text into the visual language of film through four sweeping cinematic moments where the soundtrack abandons dialogue for swelling score or song. The film's opening sequence captures the men pounding home from war with a comic fist-pumping brio lifted from *The Magnificent Seven*, while the women make a mad dash to prepare to welcome them. Then Branagh gives us two wordless contrasting inner sequences where Benedick and Beatrice celebrate the release of their romantic emotions in fountain and swing and, later, Claudio and Don Pedro lead a winding torch-lit vigil up to Hero's tomb. Finally, the film concludes with an evocation of Benedick's insistence on dancing before wedding in which the cast—intentionally absent Don Pedro—swirl out from the chapel, through the villa's courtyard, and into the garden while "Sigh, no more, ladies" chorically swells on the soundtrack and confetti pirouettes in the air.

Shakespeare is imagined here by Branagh as the first of a long line of English authors who send their characters to Italy to discover the joys of the flesh. Branagh can infuse his film with so much ripe romantic energy without destroying the more subtle and unconventional elements in Shakespeare's tale because of Emma Thompson's remarkable performance as Beatrice. She is the film's radiant, sentient center. Intelligence and wit illuminate every moment of her performance. Thompson's Beatrice can register emotion, underline irony, change mood, raise alarm, deflect attention, suppress sorrow, and enhance wit by the mere tilt of her head, the cock of an eyebrow, the flick of an eyelid, or the purse of her lips. She can also capture just the right inflection for Shakespeare's muscular prose and deliver it in a rhythm properly suited to the camera. The economy with which she allows us to understand her previous romantic entanglement with Benedick and her embarrassment at unintentionally encouraging Don Pedro's marriage proposal is film acting worthy of association with

Katharine Hepburn, Barbara Stanwyk, and Irene Dunne: the heroines of the great screwball comedies.

The film cleverly leads us into its romantic landscape by allowing word and voice to precede image. The words of the first verse of Balthazar's bittersweet song, "Sigh no more, ladies," unfold on a blank screen, half-line by half-line, spoken by Miss Thompson to the accompaniment of a guitar and cello. No bouncing ball appears above the words as in the sing-a-longs that preceded silent films, but Thompson's carefully nuanced reading invites us to murmur the words with her and to register wry amusement at the way in which the song's description of male inconstancy and deception speaks not only to Shakespeare's comic concerns with the worlds of war and wooing but also to Branagh's delicate balancing of one foot on the verbal shore of the play and one in the visual sea of the film. As we move into the song's second verse, the screen is suddenly filled with a painting (in progress) of a Tuscan landscape. As Doyle's score swells, the camera slides—in a single pan shot lasting over a minute—from the canvas to reveal the painter (Leonato) and the landscape itself peopled with lolling picnickers and then moves on from their tanned and laughing faces across the splendid vista to discover Emma Thompson's Beatrice perched in a tree reading Shakespeare's song to her fellow revelers as a bee buzzes about her face and birds chirp on the soundtrack. "A good song," as Don Pedro later observes and one intelligently used here by Branagh to establish the mood of the women trying to distract themselves while the men are away at war as well as to prepare us for the fickle behavior of those men once war gives way to wooing. This opening also allows him to move rapidly and cleverly from text, to scenic representation (Leonato's painting) as we might find it in a stage production, to his "on location" Tuscan film landscape.[23]

In a flash the messenger arrives and down in the valley the men are seen thundering home as the women make a mad dash down the hill to greet them. The screen is filled with the rush of flesh and frenzy as men and women strip and plunge into baths and showers. For an instant Branagh's camera catches Beatrice and Hero framed in a high window—a shot he will repeat several times in the film—placing them with amused detachment above the splashing and shouting of the boys below and slightly separated from the shrieks and giggles of the girls wriggling out of their clothes and into the confusion of romantic excitement in the next room. Branagh concludes this sequence with an overhead shot of the women emerging from the house to welcome the newly spruced up men marching through the archway into the villa's courtyard. The two groups form a large X underlining the film's prime interest.

Branagh's visual insistence in these opening moments on landscape and the formation of the distinct groups of men and women serves his under-

standing of Shakespeare well.[24] *Much Ado's* Messina setting and its concerns with social fashion has led some critics to place it, among the comedies, somewhere between Falstaff's Windsor and Vincentio's Vienna, where
Shakespeare explores and tests comic themes in a recognizable social /
urban context, rather than with the green world, festive comedies where
Branagh's setting chooses to align it. The festive comedies explore, like
Much Ado, the gender confusions of love and loyalty prompted by wooing
and tested by wedding. Here it is the men, specifically Claudio and Benedick,
who are so prompted and so tested by the tension between male bonding,
the confusions of wooing, and the commitments of wedding. By setting his
film against the sunburnt Tuscan landscape (only Don John, the anticomic
villain, is repeatedly shot indoors, usually in the villa's cellarage) Branagh
establishes the green world's liberating, socially leveling spirit, which carries over into costume design; all the women wear similar sheer cotton
camisoles under mock corsets, and the men are either in identical uniforms
or in white linen vests worn over white shirts with open collars. Andrew
Lane's response to these costumes was to remark that "*Much Ado* could
become Ralph Lauren's favorite movie."[25] But Lane fails to see that
Branagh's approach attempts to stress the democratic tendencies in
Shakespeare's comic art with its youthful egalitarian yearnings of emotion
and romance. It's part of the stripping away of fashion to bare flesh which
begins the film and provides one explanation for Claudio's eventual confusion of Hero and Margaret as both maiden and maid are dressed in almost
identical white cotton dresses.

Branagh's film has its climax and its finest moment where wooing and
wedding meet and clash: Claudio's shameful despoiling of his marriage to
Hero and the genuine union of Beatrice and Benedick that rises from its
ashes. It is also in these two antithetical moments that the film most closely
approaches Cavell's comic paradigm. Robert Sean Leonard's Claudio is an
insecure boy for whom confusion and embarrassment flush upon his face
as quickly as does the blush of romance. By setting the wedding outside of
the villa's small chapel, Branagh's camera gives ample space to Claudio's
petulant tantrum. He savagely shoves his bride to the ground and makes a
triumphant circuit of the scene overturning benches and ripping away deco-
rations before nestling in next to Denzel Washington's elegant Don Pedro
to reestablish what he smugly believes to be the primacy of the male order.
By contrast, Branagh's Benedick goes to his knees to join Beatrice at Hero's
side and looks on in amazement as Leonato, with an ugly violence, makes
the opposite move to join the male hierarchy by condemning his own child.

Now Beatrice and Benedick move into the chapel where, first through
her tears and anger and then through his commitment to her passion, they
create a ceremony and construct a vow that issues not from social practice
and tradition but from their own emotional and imaginative response to

Hero's crisis. Branagh shoots a kneeling Beatrice in profile over Benedick's left shoulder so that we see and react to her through his perspective. They aren't squared to the camera because they aren't yet square with each other. Beatrice's anger, and her frustration with her gender's limitations when it comes to taking appropriate action on that anger in the male world of "honor," leads her to kick over, in an exasperated parody of Claudio's earlier behavior, the communion bench she has been kneeling on as she cries out: "O that I were a man for his sake, or that I had any friend would be a man for my sake!"

Branagh's Benedick is transformed by her passion. Earlier we had seen his nervous cocky jester melt into the explosive comic romantic in the gulling scene. Now both of these excessive portraits are clipped, darkened, and matured as we watch his mind absorb and understand the issue that spurs Beatrice's fury. For the first time in the film Branagh allows Benedick to look directly into the camera's eye as he determinedly confronts his emotional commitment to Beatrice.[26] Here he steadies and fixes his gaze because to engage the camera is to engage Beatrice. Branagh plucks out the word "soul" to underscore in his quiet query, "Think you in your soul that Count Claudio hath wronged Hero?" because it is a word Claudio himself has flung about recklessly. Thompson chooses to underline "thought" in her reply, "Yea, as sure as I have a thought or a soul" completing the marriage of mind and heart, thought and soul, between them, which is then sealed by the vow the entire scene has moved toward: "Enough. I am engaged; I will challenge him." Benedick's commitment to action completes Beatrice's outrage and creates a surprise: a constant man. The words that lead man to woo and to wed will now be as consequential as those that lead him to war.

This scene is a perfectly realized Shakespearean antecedent to the "equality of consciousness between a man and a woman" that Cavell uncovers at the center of his Hollywood comedies. This intelligent moment, like Thompson's performance throughout, is what allows us to release our critical, skeptical selves to freely enjoy the film's exuberant excesses captured by Branagh's Gene Kelly-like splashing in the fountain superimposed on Thompson's high flying in a swing crowning the neatly segued scenes of the unmaskings of their true affections. Branagh's foregrounding of the absolutely serious gender issues at work in the play, which come into precise focus in his treatment of the chapel scene, makes possible the film's seemingly paradoxical indulgence of its high-flying romanticism. Even as Shakespeare's comedies critique the follies and cruelties of love's social conventions, they provide evidence—however fleeting—for love's powers to cross class and gender divisions as witness the relationships of Titania and Bottom, Ganymede and Orlando, Caesario and Orsino, Toby and Maria.

Branagh's film makes us laugh—a rarity in even the best films of Shakespeare's comedies. *Much Ado* wrests smiles from us from Thompson's wry reading of "Sigh no more," to the men pounding home lifting in and out of their saddles in slow motion, to Branagh's struggle to position himself properly at the fountain to receive Beatrice's call to dinner (inspired, his screenplay tells us, by Tony Curtis's imitation of Cary Grant in *Some Like It Hot*) to Thompson's fiercely reluctant march down one of the garden's hedge-lined corridors to deliver that message, to the way each reads, admires, and seeks to improve the sonnets each has written to the other demonstrating "our hands against our hearts."[27] The Dogberry comedy, however, is another matter, and my first reaction was that it did not fit with the rest of the film's style. I found it cartoonish and fashioned after Michael Keaton's performance in *Beetlejuice* (dir. Tim Burton, 1988) and the villains in the recent *Superman* and *Batman* films. But Dogberry is another reminder of the ways in which Shakespeare uses humor, along with imagination, as a device for crossing class lines in his comedies. Dogberry, working determinedly (and comically wrong-headedly) up from the bottom, does, like Beatrice and Benedick, finally get it right. It is another example of Shakespeare's utopian playfulness that, in comedy at least, the comics (high and low) should be the ones to expose and foil the villains.

Keaton and Branagh create a Dogberry who seems equal parts mixture of The Three Stooges, Monty Python, and some of the eccentrics who play off against the lovers in Cavell's comedies of remarriage. (I am thinking here primarily of the major, the psychiatrist, and the town cop in Howard Hawkes's *Bringing up Baby*.) Keaton, who chews the text into tatters, misses much of the ways in which Dogberry creates unintended humor by proudly misappropriating the language of his social superiors. But, in compensation, he does create a similar visual comedy by a malapropism of gesture. Keaton's Dogberry and Ben Elton's Verges, for instance, imitate the thundering riders of the film's opening sequence as they mock gallop in and out of the frame carried only by their own legs.[28]

The one corner of the play—and an important one—that is not well served by Branagh's lush emphasis on sunburnt romance and comic mirth is his visual treatment of Claudio and Hero. His film fails to drive home the ways in which the play repeatedly favors the independent, unruly, intelligent wooing behavior of Beatrice and Benedick with the empty, socially conventional path followed by Claudio in his courtship of Hero. Claudio doesn't have to be played as a cad, as Anne Barton suggests, but the text is at pains to underline his shallowness.[29] He seeks to confirm his love's beauty by soliciting the opinion of another male ("I pray thee [Benedick] tell me truly how thou lik'st her"); he is quick to ascertain her fortune ("Hath Leonato any son, my lord [Don Pedro]?"); and even quicker to seize upon the opportunity to allow a more powerful sponsor to conduct his wooing for him ("How sweetly you [Don Pedro] do minister to love, / That know love's grief by his complexion!"). Though Branagh cuts these last lines, they provide an accurate description of Robert Sean Leonard's Claudio, whose complexion seems equally flushed by love or grief. Balthazar's song "Sigh no more, ladies" is even more apt for this lad who is constantly registering love's delight or pain with an open mouth and watery eye. Branagh's camera lingers on Leonard's face and finds no distinction there between the shy smiles he flashes at Hero in the opening sequences and the tormented grief he displays first when he mistakenly believes Don Pedro has wooed Hero for himself and then later when he sees Borachio supposedly making love to Hero at her bedroom window. Branagh's decision to visualize for us this off-stage moment and to make graphic Borachio's lusty coupling (rather than the text's more modest "talking") by capturing its effects on Claudio's face shot in tight close-up, severely skews the audience's reaction. This moment rarely fails to elicit an almost audible flow of sympathy—particularly from the teenagers who became the prime market for the film—streaming towards Leonard's grief. After all, this was the same actor who, as many of them know, had already suffered and died for Shakespeare in his previous film, *Dead Poets Society* (dir. Peter Weir, 1989).

Branagh and Leonard are, it seems to me, illustrating here a particularly American sentimentality about the precariousness of youthful innocence. American culture champions innocence over irony and the literature of its high school curriculum is dominated by the tales of the misunderstood and threatened young from Romeo and Juliet to Oliver and Pip to Tom and Huck and on to our century's contributions from Salinger's Holden to Harper Lee's Jem and Scout and Dill. Neal Perry (Leonard's role in *Dead Poets Society*) is a film equivalent of these characters, and Leonard's playing of Claudio in a similar manner imposes this American sentimental tradition on Shakespeare's more tough-minded tale. Though, as I have already indicated, Branagh and Leonard do make Claudio's wedding tantrum properly ugly and savage, the power of the moment's impact has been decidedly lessened. Rather than revealing Claudio's insecure and immature male malice (in contrast to Benedick's immediate move to support Hero's innocence) based on his superficial acceptance of the assumptions of the patriarchal order, Branagh's film asks us to understand the wounded lover's anger and to sympathize with Claudio rather than to judge him. This has the effect of making Claudio and Hero's reconciliation as romantically inviting and welcome as that of Beatrice and Benedick, allowing them a less problematical place in the concluding moments of Branagh's film than the one they occupy in Shakespeare's text.

Only in his handling of Claudio does Branagh's desire to be lushly cinematic conflict with his otherwise sure and intelligent translation of Shakespeare's comic energies into film rhythms and images. Branagh is not bashful about wanting his films to entertain; it's all wrapped up with his infatuation with the heyday of Hollywood from the 1930s to the 1950s. His cinematic imagination here incorporates a range of American impulses from the egalitarian issues Cavell sees at work in *It Happened One Night* and *Adam's Rib* (dir. George Cukor, 1949) to the sentimentalizing of the young. Branagh's *Much Ado* is a marriage, resembling that of Beatrice and Benedick, between Shakespeare and Hollywood. With an intelligent, if necessarily inconstant, foot in both worlds, Branagh provides us with the most successful version we have of a Shakespearean comedy on film.[30]

NOTES

1. See Robert Hapgood, "Popularizing Shakespeare: The Artistry of Franco Zeffirelli," in *Shakespeare, the Movie*, ed. Lynda E. Boose and Richard Burt (London and New York: Routledge, 1997), 92–93.

2. See Fredric Jameson, *Postmodernism, or, The Cultural Logic of Late Capitalism* (Durham, N.C.: Duke University Press, 1991), 55–67, and Ihab Hassan, "Pluralism in Postmodern Perspective," *Critical Inquiry* 12 (1981): 503–20.

3. See Courtney Lehmann, *"Much Ado about Nothing*? Shakespeare, Branagh, and the 'National-popular' in the Age of Multinational Capital," *Textual Practice* 12, no. 1 (1998): 1–22.

4. Trevor Nunn, *William Shakespeare's Twelfth Night: A Screenplay* (London and New York: Methuen,1996), ii.

5. I find "screwball" an unfortunate term for these great comedies. For an understanding of its genesis see Kristine Karnick, "Commitment and Reaffirmation in Hollywood Romantic Comedy," in *Classical Hollywood Comedy*, ed. Kristine Karnick and Henry Jenkins (London and New York: Routledge, 1995), 123–46.

6. Kenneth Branagh, *Much Ado about Nothing: Screenplay, Introduction, and Notes on the Making of the Movie* (New York and London: W. W. Norton, 1993), viii.

7. In his interview with me about his performance of Hamlet for the Royal Shakespeare Company in 1992–93 as he was editing his film of *Much Ado*, Branagh remarked: "If I can't make Shakespeare live for a broad audience with all the Hollywood that got packed into the film, then I doubt I will be able to raise the financing for a *Hamlet* film." *Shakespeare Bulletin* 12 (1994): 8. For Jackson's remarks see his "Shakespeare Comedies on Film," *Shakespeare and the Moving Image*, ed. Anthony Davies and Stanley Wells (Cambridge: Cambridge University Press, 1994), 116–19.

8. Stanley Cavell, *Pursuits of Happiness: The Hollywood Comedy of Remarriage* (Cambridge: Harvard University Press, 1981), 17–18.

9. Cavell, 18.

10. Cavell, 19.

11. Several essays in *Classical Hollywood Comedy*, particularly those by Kristine Karnick and Charles Musser, try to rework Cavell's formulations without significantly improving on them.

12. William Shakespeare, *Much Ado about Nothing*, in *The Complete Works of William Shakespeare*, ed. David Bevington, updated 4th ed. (New York: Longman, 1997), 2.1.265–68.

13. Beatrice is the most liberated of Shakespeare's comic heroines and shares the greatest affinity with Cavell's "new woman" because, unlike Rosalind and Viola, she speaks out of

her own voice as a female without having to assume a masculine identity to express an independent, witty perspective on love and romance.

14. Branagh, xi.

15. For instance, C. L. Barber does not include *Much Ado* in his *Shakespeare's Festive Comedy* (Princeton: Princeton University Press, 1959).

16. Anne Barton, "Shakespeare and the Sun," *New York Review of Books*, 27 May 1993, 11.

17. Perhaps spurred by Branagh's film, a recent highly acclaimed stage production of *Much Ado* by the Cheek by Jowl Company relentlessly underlines the play's class and gender divisions. See Jane Collins's review in *Shakespeare Bulletin* 16 (1998): 10–11.

18. See Jack Jorgens, *Shakespeare on Film* (Bloomington: Indiana University Press, 1977), 73–74 for an excellent analysis of the festive comedy atmosphere that pervades Zeffirelli's film.

19. Samuel Crowl, *Shakespeare in Production: Whose History?* (Athens: Ohio University Press, 1996), 116.

20. Branagh, ix. Branagh's film reportedly cost about 16 million dollars to make and has grossed over 45 million in worldwide sales not counting television or video rental revenues.

21. Branagh, ix–x.

22. Branagh's first full-length play, *Public Enemy*, dramatizes the life of a young man coming of age in Belfast in the 1960s through the lens of several Jimmy Cagney films from the 1930s.

23. There is also a potential echo here of Olivier's more elaborate move from stage to painted sets to Ireland's Powerscourt (and back again) in his film of *Henry V.*

24. While Vincent Canby shares my amusement with this opening sequence in his review of the film in the *New York Times*, 7 May 1993, C16, many have failed to be charmed. Here's the response of a senior colleague in my department generally sympathetic to the tastes and habits of the young: "I was disappointed with the film. I can literally hear the director shouting 'Come on. Get some life! You over there by the window, show some teeth! Remember Errol Flynn! A little more swash and less buckle!' That opening sequence gave me the Stanford football team on their way to a tryst with a Southern Cal sorority's summer camp."

25. Anthony Lane, Review of *Much Ado about Nothing*, *The New Yorker*, 10 May 1993, 97.

26. Barton notes that Branagh's problem in delivering Benedick's soliloquies comes from "his insistence upon looking everywhere except into the camera." I agree with Barton that had Branagh's Benedick confronted the camera directly he would have given us a less edgy and contorted performance, a version of the more self-assured Benedick we both have come to expect—perhaps a Benedick played with the cool control demonstrated in the film by Denzel Washington. But Branagh clearly wants to stress the insecurity of his Benedick's antiromantic stance. This Benedick can't be comfortable with himself or the camera until he has confronted and confessed his affection for Beatrice.

27. Branagh comments on the fountain scene: "Benedick has thrown what he thinks to be a gallant and sexy leg up on the edge of the fountain He strikes a pose and a tone of voice that reminds one of Tony Curtis as Cary Grant in *Some Like It Hot*. It is a face frozen in a grin that is trying to convey sex, romance, intelligence, wit, and warmth all at once. In short, he looks ridiculous" (Branagh 47).

28. Branagh admits that Shakespeare's clowns escape him; "In the Dogberry scenes we cut the unfunniest lines. (I realize this is an entirely subjective issue, but having played one of the great unfunny Shakespearean clowns—Touchstone in *As You Like It*—I speak from bitter experience)." Branagh also acknowledges that, from the beginning, he and Keaton

had determined that Dogberry "should be not only a verbal but a physical malaprop" (Branagh xiii, xv).

29. Barton, 11.

30. This essay develops and enlarges upon ideas first presented in my review of the film in *Shakespeare Bulletin* 2 (1993): 39–40.

WORKS CITED

Barber, C. L. *Shakespeare's Festive Comedy*. Princeton: Princeton University Press, 1959.

Barton, Anne. "Shakespeare and the Sun." *New York Review of Books*, 27 May 1993, 11.

Branagh, Kenneth. *Much Ado about Nothing: Screenplay, Introduction, and Notes on the Making of the Movie*. New York and London: W. W. Norton, 1993.

Cavell, Stanley. *Pursuits of Happiness: The Hollywood Comedy of Remarriage*. Cambridge: Harvard University Press, 1981.

Coursen, H. R. *Shakespeare in Production: Whose History?* Athens: Ohio University Press, 1996.

Crowl, Samuel. "An Interview with Kenneth Branagh." *Shakespeare Bulletin* 12 (1994): 5–8.

_____. "Review of Branagh's Film of *Much Ado about Nothing*." *Shakespeare Bulletin* 11 (1993): 39–40.

Frye, Northrop. *A Natural Perspective*. New York: Columbia University Press, 1965.

Hapgood, Robert. "Popularizing Shakespeare: The Artistry of Franco Zeffirelli." In *Shakespeare, the Movie: Popularizing the Plays on Film, TV, and Video*. Edited by Lynda E. Boose and Richard Burt. London and New York: Routledge, 1997.

Jackson, Russell. "Shakespeare's Comedies on Film." In *Shakespeare and the Moving Image: The Plays on Film and Television*. Edited by Anthony Davies and Stanley Wells. Cambridge: Cambridge University Press, 1994.

Jameson, Fredric. *Postmodernism, or, The Cultural Logic of Late Capitalism*. Durham, N.C.: Duke University Press, 1991.

Jorgens, Jack. *Shakespeare on Film*. Bloomington: Indiana University Press, 1977.

Karnick, Kristine, and Henry Jenkins, eds. *Classical Hollywood Comedy*. London and New York: Routledge, 1995.

Lane, Anthony. Review of *Much Ado about Nothing*. *The New Yorker*, 10 May 1993, 97.

Lehmann, Courtney. *"Much Ado about Nothing?* Shakespeare, Branagh, and the 'National-popular' in the Age of Multinational Capital." *Textual Practice* 12, no. 1 (1998): 1–22.

Nunn, Trevor. *Twelfth Night: A Screenplay*. London and New York: Methuen, 1996.

Shakespeare, William. *Much Ado about Nothing*. In *The Complete Works of William Shakespeare*. Edited by David Bevington. Updated 4th edition. New York: Longman, 1997.

FILMS CITED

Much Ado about Nothing. Directed by Kenneth Branagh. 1 hr. 51 min. Samuel Goldwyn, 1993. Videocassette.

Shakespeare in Love:
Romancing the Author, Mastering the Body

COURTNEY LEHMANN

LONG BEFORE THE QUEST TO "PRODUCE THE BODY" BECAME AN OBSESSION OF detective fiction, it was a staple of Shakespearean scholarship. Shakespeare's status as a missing person from the scene of authorship, coupled with his sparse paper trail, have sent forensic specialists, private investigators, and curious bibliophiles like Washington Irving in search of the Bard's textual and bodily remains, hoping to unearth some startling new discovery about the "real" author of the plays in Shakespeare's hallowed Stratford-upon-Avon tomb. Something of a nineteenth-century Geraldo Rivera in search of Al Capone, Irving returned from his pilgrimage empty-handed, having recovered "no coffin, no bones, nothing but dust."[1] Irving's humorous entry into the authorship debate uncannily foretells the future of Shakespeare's "corpus" in contemporary theory, where "Shakespeare"—now housed in obligatory quotation marks—has been disembodied to a fault.

Since the advent of poststructuralism in 1968, critical theory has traded in its long romance with the solitary figure of the Author to embrace the multiple pleasures of the text. Compared with the rapid influx of critiques of the Author in other literary periods, however, the deconstruction of Shakespeare has occurred rather belatedly. But what Shakespeare studies may have lost in time, it has made up for in violence. In the last fifteen years, Shakespeare has not merely been pronounced dead but also dismembered: unnamed by Margreta De Grazia, unstitched by Michael Warren, unemended by Randall McLeod, and unedited by Leah Marcus.[2] While this exorcism of the Author in academic culture presents us with a striking image of the body-in-pain, popular culture—and Hollywood film in particular—has resurrected Shakespeare in the form of an authorial body-in-pleasure, as recent films like *Shakespeare in Love* (dir. John Madden, 1998) and *Love's Labour's Lost* (dir. Kenneth Branagh, 2000) demonstrate. Cinema has always argued the ontological priority of bodies over texts, claiming,

125

from its earliest moments, that the movies "give us back our bodies, and
particularly our faces, which have been rendered illegible, soulless, unex-
pressive by the centuries-old ascendancy of print."[3] Films like *Shakespeare
in Love* and *Love's Labour's Lost*, which approach the Shakespearean text
by fetishizing the human body, seem to realize this cinematic dream with a
vengeance. But what exactly explains the return of Shakespeare's much
maligned corpus in the full-bodied fleshiness of sexual desire and dance,
respectively? What might this sexualized body tell us about Shakespeare's
textual remains? Focusing on Shakespeare's latest incarnation as a cinematic romance hero in *Shakespeare in Love*, I shall explore the way in
which this corpus, in all its incarnations—bodily, textual, commercial, and
critical—returns from the dead to implore us not to love, but rather, to
"enjoy."

☆ ☆ ☆

In *Shakespeare in Love* "enjoyment" revolves deliriously around the act of
consumption. Thus, rather than aligning Shakespearean authorship with
the production-driven energies associated with early capitalism and the
Elizabethan theatrical marketplace, this film ultimately positions Shakespeare-
the-Author as an invention and, in fact, endorsement of *late* capitalism. As
Slavoj Žižek explains, the experience of enjoyment-as-consumption is a
prerogative of late capitalistic society, deriving from a crucial mutation in
the status of cultural authority, specifically, the authority of the "Master."
Precapitalistic society is structured by a belief in the regulatory function of
a singular authority or Master, a figure who reflects a stable paternal signifier and exists as a model of the "ethics of self-mastery and 'just measure.'" Whether constituted as an ideological illusion or a material reality,
the figure of the Master is central to "the entire precapitalistic ethics," which,
according to Žižek, "is aimed to prevent the excess proper to the human
libidinal economy from exploding." Within capitalism, however, this regulatory function of the Master "becomes suspended, and the vicious circle
of the superego spins freely."[4] In other words, the nature of the Master's
function as a collective superego changes; rather than serving as an agent
of prohibition, the Master's imperative is reconstituted as an *invitation* to
consume and, therefore, to enjoy "freely"—without restraint. In this context, then, "to obey" *is* "to enjoy."[5] Poised on the brink of transition from
feudalism to capitalism, the Elizabethan England of *Shakespeare in Love*
is a society in the throes of economic and social chaos, seeking a Master
who can articulate a new conception of "value"—monetary *and* human—
appropriate to the fiscal and ethical changes demanded by the rise of capitalism. As we shall see, "Master Will" fits this bill, but only in the guise of

the *late* capitalistic Master of enjoyment, for rather than emerging as a producing text, he materializes as a consuming and, indeed, consummating body.

In its portrait of a theatrical marketplace beset by the "plague" of early capitalism, *Shakespeare in Love* localizes the culturewide growing pains of Elizabethan England in its opening images of the body-in-pain. The first such body we encounter belongs not to Shakespeare but to Philip Henslowe (Geoffrey Rush) who, the film informs us, is "a businessman with a cash flow problem," a phrase which smacks anachronistically of late-capitalistic slang. But the subsequent title card sends us swiftly back to the Elizabethan marketplace with an advertisement for a play called THE LAMENTABLE TRAGEDIE OF THE MONEYLENDER REVENG'D. Engaged in a real-life drama, Henslowe is strapped to a chair on stage, where he is being tortured with hot coals for his failure to pay his debts to the vengeful moneylender, Hugh Fennyman (Tom Wilkinson). Tabulating Henslowe's debt, Fennyman's thug claims that they have been "bitten" for "Twelve pounds, one shilling and four pence . . . including interest."[6] Curiously inflected with an image of orality, this line suggests the ravenous mouth of a marketplace fully committed to usury, burning its bottom-line mentality into the bottom of Henslowe's boots.[7] Prone, enfeebled, feminized, and filthy, Henslowe's body is more than just a body-in-pain, for in this scene it acquires the more specific contours of what Susan Jeffords calls a "*soft*body." In her book entitled *Hardbodies: Hollywood Masculinity in the Reagan Era*, Jeffords explains that the "softbody" typically emerges during a time of national crisis, when patriarchal authority—embodied in the symbolic figure of the Master or, to use Robert Bly's terms, the "Father-King"—is in a state of atrophy, weakened by some emasculating economic, social, or political threat.[8] As suggested by the opening scene of *Shakespeare in Love*, Elizabethan England is a culture in need of a Master to regulate its strumpet-like embrace of exchange values within the emergent theatrical marketplace, as well as to restore enabling models of distinctly male power during the emasculating reign of Elizabeth I. Henslowe's last-ditch offer to Fennyman of a partnership in a new comedy by "*Will* Shakespeare," a name conspicuously foreshortened to connote desire itself, seems to initiate precisely this quest.

But the next body we encounter in *Shakespeare in Love* does little to placate the sense of dis-ease that permeates this opening image of Elizabethan culture, for this body is, as Henslowe memorably puts it, "Nobody": it's "[t]he author" (50). And so we are introduced to Will Shakespeare (Joseph Fiennes), a playwright whose humble surroundings, composed of crumpled paper balls and broken quills, playfully suggest the dismembered status of the Shakespearean corpus. Will's "corpus," meanwhile, is in even worse shape. Ignoring Henslowe's desperate entreaties for the completion of his new play, Will heads to his analyst, bitterly complaining about his writer's block: "It's as if my quill is broken," he exclaims. "As if the organ of the imagination has dried up. As if the proud tower of my genius has collapsed." If Henslowe's body is threatened with indigence, Will's body is threatened by impotence; clearly, Will is not only unable to produce poetry, he is also unable to consume women. "Broken," "dried up," and "collapsed," Will's body, by his own admission, is also a "softbody."

Will's softbody, however, is more complicated than Henslowe's because at this point it expresses alienation from rather than complicity with the succubus-like forces of the burgeoning Elizabethan marketplace. "Once," Will laments, "I had the gift . . . I could make love out of words as a potter makes cups out of clay . . . for sixpence a line I could cause a riot in a nunnery" (9–10). Will's complaint revolves around the fact that his poetic inspiration came freely to him so long as it was, in fact, a "gift." The problem is that now, the work of his hands can no longer be separated from its market value. Indeed, Will's equation of poetry first with "pottery" and then with "pence" alludes to the much larger cultural shift from use value to exchange value beginning to take place in early modern culture. For like pottery, Will's poetry once had a "riotous" and distinctly human quality; now, however, both poetry and pottery fall victim to the leveling, quantity-intensive logic of the commodity form which, as Herbert Marcuse argues, reduces not only all forms of art, but also all realms of culture, to commercials, so that "[t]he music of the soul is also the music of salesmanship."[9] Echoing this tune, Will laments his futile search for a "soulmate" in a world in which love is for sale from Black Sue, Fat Phoebe, Rosaline, and Aphrodite, and where, consequently, there is no place for true love poetry—only the relentless demand for "Comedy . . . and a bit with a dog."

At this point in the film, then, Will's professional and personal failures may be read as a form of resistance to the alienating forces of the marketplace that seek to coopt and corrupt his art and life for "sixpence a line." Will's loss of poetic and sexual prowess, in other words, may signal at least an unconscious refusal to buy into the crass consumer logic that prostitutes his genius and his person. As Jeffords might conclude, Will's inability to generate poetic lines defies not only the all-important *bottom* line, but also the idea of social definition more generally—"the hard edges, determinate lines of action, and clear boundaries" that distinguish the socially legible hardbody from the anomalous, "messy" and "confusing" softbody.[10] In this state, Will resembles the disruptive figure of the "rebel-poet" who, Marcuse explains, flouts the established order by refusing to "earn a living, at least not in an orderly and normal way." It is at the beginning, therefore, rather than the end of the film that Will represents the "poet of true love" because only here does he maintain a properly "romantic" existence—one that exudes "aesthetic incompatibility with the developing society."[11] And, while the historical setting of *Shakespeare in Love* suggests a society in the throes of a developing capitalistic economy, we know very well that the dilemma between art and commerce is a cliché of late, not early, capitalism. Accordingly, it soon becomes apparent that Will's aesthetic incompatibility with the world around him stems from his failure to engage in proper *consumption* and, consequently, from his failure to adopt the late capitalist solution: *"enjoy!"*

☆☆☆

[A]musement always reveals the influence of business, the sales talk, the quack's spiel. But the original affinity of business and amusement is shown in the latter's specific significance: to defend society. To be pleased means to say yes.
— Max Horkheimer and Theodor W. Adorno,
Dialectic of Enlightenment

In *Shakespeare in Love*, what begins as a critique of the dehumanizing drive to *produce* within early capitalism quickly becomes an endorsement of the desire to *consume* associated with late capitalism. Will's quack, Doctor Moth (Antony Sher), encourages him to say "yes" to this latter choice, persuading Will to engage in desublimation by giving free rein to his repressed passions which, rather than being channeled into art, can be enjoyed in life. In short, Dr. Moth supplies Will with a prescription for pleasure, a distinctly capitalistic form of therapy that foregrounds consumption as a cure-all for the incommensurate ailments of the soul. Offering Will an asp-shaped bangle for a modest fee, Dr. Moth instructs him to write his name on a piece of paper, feed it through the mouth of the snake and, finally, place the snake charm on his lady's wrist. Presumably, his lady will proceed to dream of him and his poetic "gift" will be restored. The fact that this gift is no longer free, however, indicates that Will has begun to buy into the logic of the marketplace; he has been charmed by the snake and is now falling from pseudoalienation into willing complicity with the forces of capitalism.

In its role as a mystical go-between for Will and his lady, as well as for Will and his poetry, the magic snake bracelet alludes to the ways in which the fetishization of commodities within capitalism reduces social relations between people to "the fantastic form of a relation between things."[12] Not surprisingly, this axiom also describes the brief course of Will and Rosaline's relationship. With the help of the snake charm, Will doesn't even really need Rosaline for inspiration or, for that matter, sexual gratification. He is able to produce the first scene of *Romeo and Rosaline* with little more than a passing kiss from his lady-muse; and his far more passionate act of kissing his new-wrought pages—followed by the climactic exclamation "God,

I'm good!"—renders his satisfaction with "things" virtually complete. But Will is being groomed for a *late* capitalistic variation on this theme, which stipulates that gratification can be obtained immediately through "relations" with people that produce "things"—and in this case, the play's the thing— we need only recognize the exchange value "Juliet" commands over "Rosaline" in *Romeo and Juliet.* Quite provocatively, then, the image of the snake with the mouth that *consumes before it can produce* presents us with a virtual tableau of the libidinal economy destined to restore Will's gift—but only at the expense, as we shall see, of the lady of *his* dreams.

If, as Marcuse explains, proper desublimation involves "replacing me-diated with immediate gratification," then in *Shakespeare in Love*, it is not until Will's conversional encounter with the Master of the Revels that he learns how to enjoy without limits.[13] From a historical perspective, the Master of the Revels is a figure easily aligned with the "Master" of precapitalist society, for both are authority figures who exist to censor and restrict the excess traditionally associated with the human libido. More specifically, the Master's function "is to dominate the excess by locating its cause in a clearly delimited social agency."[14] In Elizabethan England, one such potentially dangerous social agency was the institution of the public theater, and the Master of the Revels was the figure who, represent-ing the Crown's interests, maintained regulatory power over it. But in *Shakespeare in Love*, the Master of the Revels (Simon Callow) is more accurately described as a "master of revel*ing*," for he reopens the theaters *not* because they have been purged of the social threat of plague and moral corruption, but because of his own naked self-interest in enjoying Burbage's (and Will's) mistress, Rosaline:

> *Will.* You have opened the playhouses?
> *Tilney.* I have Master Will.
> *Will.* But the plague . . .
> *Tilney. (Sighs.)* Yes, I know. But he [Burbage] was always hanging around the house. (26)

Clearly, when the censor himself has reopened the playhouses solely for the purposes of getting the men *out of their houses*, the new ethos of self-indulgence has overtaken the old ethics of self-mastery and restraint.[15] As this scene makes abundantly clear, within capitalism, there is no "clearly delimited social agency" to guard against, for everyone—even the Master charged with protecting society—is a potential threat. But rather than in-creasing the prohibitions already in place in this every-man-for-himself environment, capitalism "solves" the problem of social antagonisms inher-ent to it by taking the path of least resistance, that is, by encouraging every-one to busy themselves with consumption and, in so doing, increase the cycle of production.

Following the Master of the Revels' cue, then, Will becomes a kind of "no holds Bard," allowing his repressed desires to roam free. In this incarnation, Will most resembles the subject of late capitalism who, according to Žižek, is not so much a person as a "place" traversed by free-ranging and often conflicting desires associated with the confusing affective cues of consumer culture. Consequently, Žižek explains, the subject of late capitalism is a subject in search of "images which regulate his or her passions"— a figure on a billboard or a face on TV capable of mastering and making sense of the myriad desires which the subject seems to experience all at once. [16] Similarly, before emerging as a figure capable of "mastering" his own and others' desires as a Hollywood Hard*Bardy*, Will becomes a site of multiple, even subversive passions, for the first image that momentarily regulates *his* desire is that of a "handsome young man," Thomas Kent (33). Of course, the off-screen audience is privy to the fact that this handsome young man with whom Will becomes infatuated is really a lovely young lady, Viola de Lesseps (Gwyneth Paltrow), and so the subversive potential of Will's desire is quickly "straightened out." But even Will's patently heterosexual desire for Viola is potentially subversive in its rejection of existing hierarchies of class and gender. For example, when Will learns that Viola is betrothed against her will to the aristocrat Wessex, "Thomas" asks him if "a lady born to wealth and noble marriage can love happily with a Bankside poet and player?" Without thinking, Will responds: "Yes, by God! Love knows nothing of rank or riverbank!" (66). At this point, Will and "Thomas" kiss, as if to seal their pledge of socially disruptive desire. But the revolutionary romantic energy of *Shakespeare in Love* stops here— where the buck begins—as the bottling up of Will's impromptu speech in convenient couplets like "rank" and "bank" implies. Indeed, Will *will* take his desire straight to the bank, once he realizes that in consuming Viola, he can (re)produce her—as a play—and so work becomes play and play becomes the masterwork of *Romeo and Juliet*.

This mystifying merger of work and play is precisely the logic that *Shakespeare in Love* applies to its representation of authorship which, I shall argue, also represents the interests of what Theodor Adorno and Max Horkheimer call "the culture industry." The culture industry is a catchall phrase for sites of mass entertainment within late capitalism: television, record companies, Harlequin romance novels, and above all, Hollywood. The culture industry refers to the commercialization of culture and the process whereby "art," masquerading as culture, becomes an industrial product, created not by some solitary genius, but by market trends, mass production, tailorization, reproduction and, of course, consumption. The way that the culture industry disguises this industrial process and seduces consumers into believing that mass entertainment is "high" art or culture is by disguising work in play, business in pleasure, labor in leisure. For the culture industry and its products are, according to Adorno and Horkheimer, "sought after as an escape from the mechanized work process" in order to "recruit strength in order to be able to cope with it again." [17] But enjoyment, in this context, *also* becomes mechanized—courtesy of two-hour movies, three-day miniseries, sixty-minute records—to the point where it "is entirely extinguished in fixed entertainments." The idea is that the more efficiently we spend our leisure time, the better workers we become, and so the culture industry and its products convince us to work more so we can play more. In its most insidious form, then, entertainment within late capitalism, according to Adorno and Horkheimer, ultimately becomes an "after-imag[e] of the work process itself." [18]

Shakespeare in Love adopts a similar approach to authorship, by representing the work of playwrighting as something that is enhanced by play itself. Materializing Shakespeare's dismembered and, at worst, nonexistent "corpus" as a smooth, sexually viable hardbody is part and parcel of this late capitalistic fantasy. But before this body can become a playmaking and lovemaking machine, it must be established that it exists in the first place—a feat which the film accomplishes in the following exchange between Will and Viola:

> *Viola*. Answer me only this: are you the author of the plays of William Shakespeare?
> *Will*. I am. (68)

In an instant, the four-hundred year-old memory of Shakespeare's missing body and Will's "messy" softbody is erased, for the success of this multiple-Oscar winning film hinges on our willingness to believe not only that this *is* Shakespeare, but that this is Shakespeare "in love." What follows is a vision of the *Author*-as-Master, a figure whose ability to produce "riotous" passions in others is ideally suited both to meet and to manufacture the needs of late capitalist culture. For this is a Master who *enjoys*—and who can teach us how to enjoy—by leading us through the confusing byways and detours of desire within contemporary consumer culture. Indeed, *Shakespeare in Love* banks on the fact that, as subjects of late capitalism, we, too, are in need of images to "regulate our passions"; and what better image to lend meaning to our own potentially wayward desires than the specter of Shakespeare raised from the dead through the special effects and sublime affect of love?

Born of the unmistakable style of the culture industry, Will and Viola's love generates an extraordinarily efficient merger of work and play. This merger is inscribed, appropriately, in the film's magnificent montage effects, as dress rehearsals from "The Rose Theatre" are intercut with *un*dressed rehearsals in "Viola's bedroom." In both locations, lines of the play we recognize as *Romeo and Juliet* are uttered and lived, blurring the boundaries between business and pleasure, work and play, even further. The result is something akin to method acting meets "the rhythm method":

> *WILL and VIOLA are both out of bed, halfway through dressing. Still rehearsing.*
> *Will.* Good night, Good night. As sweet repose and rest
>   Come to thy heart as that within my breast.
>   O wilt thou leave me so unsatisfied?
> *Viola.* That's my line!
> *Will.* Oh, but it is mine too!
>
> INT. THE ROSE THEATRE. STAGE. NIGHT.
>
> *Viola as Romeo.* O wilt thou leave me so unsatisfied?
> *Sam as Juliet.* What satisfaction can'st thou have tonight?
> *Viola as Romeo.* The exchange of thy love's faithful vow for mine.
>
> INT. DE LESSEPSES' HOUSE. VIOLA'S BEDROOM. NIGHT.
>
> *WILL and VIOLA are back on the bed, kissing and making love.*
> *Will.* My bounty is as boundless as the sea,
>   My love as deep. . . .
> *Viola and Will (Continuing the speech with him).*
>   . . . the more I give to thee
>   The more I have, for both are infinite . . . .
> *Will.* Stay but a little, I will come again. (82–83)

As dramatic collaboration is reduced to copulation, rhymed couplets emerge from the rhythms of orgasm, and the seminal work of *Romeo and Juliet* is born. "I would not have thought it," Viola exclaims after making love with Will. "There is something better than a play" (70). What Viola doesn't realize at this point is that lovemaking is the same thing as playmaking; she is Master Will's masterpiece-in-the-making, and the more they play, the more *of* the play, *Romeo and Juliet*, they produce. And there is no chicken-and-egg confusion as to who or what "comes" first here, for the film makes it very clear that Will's authorship of *Romeo and Juliet* is based on his sexual enjoyment of Viola as foreplay to his creation of *the* play.

Brilliantly reversing the Marxist dictum that within capitalism, relations between people take the form of relations between things, *Shakespeare in Love* convinces us that people can "have relations" to produce things—and as we all know, the play's the thing. Will and Viola's effortless creation of *Romeo and Juliet* thus represents a fantasy of what we might call "good capitalism," which naturally appears to privilege human values over exchange values. The central value of "good capitalism" is, therefore, love. But not just any love will do, for this must be a love, as Viola dreamily puts it, "that overthrows life. Unbiddable, ungovernable, like a riot in the heart, and nothing to be done, come ruin or rapture. Love like there has never been in a play" (21). Because Will and Viola's love has at least the *potential* to transgress the institutional boundaries of class, gender, sexuality, and the theater itself, it anticipates the "riot" of the bourgeoisie revolution, following which, sexual and economic success were widely considered to be the fruits of individual initiative and industry, rather than property and pedigree.[19] Viewed through the lens of good lovin', then, this is "good capitalism."

But what is really at stake in the film's vision of "good capitalism" is its privileging of an all-consuming desire that leads to the consummate production of a most profitable play. And plays cannot ultimately be isolated from things—from the vicious cycle of commodity production—just as bodies engaged in the voluptuous spectacle of lovemaking cannot ultimately be insulated from the specter of (alienated) labor. Accordingly, the more art imitates life and work mirrors play in *Shakespeare in Love*, the more we are reminded of Adorno and Horkheimer's sarcastic observation that "[w]hat repeats itself is healthy, like the natural or industrial cycle."[20] The film's attempt to naturalize, if not idealize, the industrial cycle of commodity production is etched in the healthy, buffed surfaces of Will's laboring body, and particularly, in the film's focus on Will's tricep muscle, which becomes an icon of "the hard edges, determinate lines of action, and clear boundaries" that distinguish his new and improved hardbody from its impotent precursor. Supporting him as he hovers intimately over Viola, Will's tricep leads down in a hard, straight line to the hand that writes *Romeo and Juliet*, suggesting the teleology of Shakespearean authorship as a labor that begins and ends in the mystery of love.

What gets truly mystified in this film, however, is not love, but labor. For Will's apotheosis as the Hollywood HardBardy assumes the form of a chiseled physique that churns away in the business of pleasure without sweating or showing any other symptoms of exertion.[21] This ease is possible because the only labor at stake in the film's vision of authorial production is, in fact, consumption; and, as suggested in Will and Viola's erotic dialogue, the more Viola gives to Will, the more he has, for both her supply and his demand are "infinite." Thus, consumption begets production which, in turn, leads to more consumption—an ideology decidedly connected to the deterritorializing logic of late capitalism, which seeks to convince us that by enjoying without limits, we actually become *more* creative, productive, and satisfied individuals. But by the same token, *Shakespeare in Love*'s vision of *sexual* desublimation as the key to authorial creativity exposes the film's complicity with the industrial cycle—that is, the reality of alienated labor it takes pains to naturalize through the *chic* of sex. For sex is not associated with production so much as it is associated with *re-production*—and reproduction, as Adorno and Horkheimer conclude, serves to confirm only "the immutability of circumstances."[22] Far from producing "infinite" pleasure, then, *Shakespeare in Love*'s vision of desublimation is, in fact, repressive.[23]

The paradox of repressive desublimation hinges on the way enjoyment masquerades as freedom within the cultural logic of late capitalism. Žižek explains that capital exercises "the ultimate power of 'deterritorialization,'" liberating us from the constraints of "every fixed social identity." This free-dom from socially prescribed roles is extended even further within late capitalism, wherein "the traditional fixity of ideological positions (patriar-chal authority, sexual roles, etc.) *becomes an obstacle to the unbridled commodification of everyday life*."[24] If we read between the lines, we find that this freedom from ideological fixity is actually a ruse of late capital-ism, for the only true freedom it grants is the unbridled freedom *to con-sume* and, by extension, to enjoy. Knowing that all people do not have equal access to enjoyment, it is also clear that late capitalism deterritorializes desire only to reterritorialize society according to its own economic inter-ests. Indeed, what *Shakespeare in Love* cannot ultimately conceal beneath the spectacle of sex, the drug of romance, and the rocking and rolling of heavenly bodies is the fact that there *are* consequences to consumption, and one person's enjoyment is another person's exploitation.

In *Shakespeare in Love*, the specter of repressive desublimation emerges most emphatically in the *other* transactions that take place behind closed doors in the de Lesseps household: the property dealings over and for Viola's body. The film cleverly convinces us to buy into Will and Viola's compara-tively liberated working relationship by situating it in relation to the prac-tice of "bad capitalism" exercised by figures like Viola's father, Lord Wessex and, to a lesser extent, Fennyman. While Will and Viola are engaging in the pleasures of the flesh, Lord Wessex (Colin Firth) and Sir Robert de Lesseps (Nicholas Le Prevost) are trafficking in it—"bargaining for a bride," as Viola's mother (Jill Baker) coldly describes the dowry negotiations (37). Inquiring about the quality of the goods, Wessex asks: "Is she fertile?" The vulgarity of this question is topped only by Robert de Lesseps's reply: "She will breed. If she do not, send her back." The horrors of this bad capitalism culminate in the following phallocratic exchange between father and fu-ture son-in-law:

Wessex. Is she obedient?
Sir Robert. As any mule in Christendom. But if you are the man to ride her, there are rubies in the saddlebag.
Wessex. I like her. (42)

With the deal thus made, Wessex is quick to lay claim to his purchase, informing Viola that he has purchased her from her father and that he is her new "six-day lord and master." This, of course, is Master *Will's* cue to rescue Viola from the exploitative clutches of bad capitalism and to introduce her to the ways of good capitalism, writ large in the "mystery" of playmaking through lovemaking, or, production through consumption.

Quite deftly, then, by generating a decoy for its own heartless business maneuvers in the figures of Wessex and Robert de Lesseps, the film encourages us to enjoy Will and Viola's happy, hardy, liberating breed of capitalism without seeing its soft, slimy underbelly. Representing a caricature of "bad capitalism," Wessex and de Lesseps, we are led to believe, reflect "a criminal aberration from the norm [of capitalism], rather than the norm itself," as Fredric Jameson might argue. But the film's displacement of properly economic issues onto the sphere of ethics is a diversionary tactic designed to generate a false "solution" to irresolvable "social contradictions" which, Jameson concludes, "is a very different proposition from that diagnosis . . . whose prescription would be social revolution."[25] Accordingly, the principal deception *Shakespeare in Love* performs lies in the fact that the "revolutionary" freedoms it grants in the name of desublimated desire are not free at all; rather, the frenzied emotions of liberated love and unmitigated enjoyment merely mimic the capriciousness of the commodity form itself. And not even Will and Viola's love is immune to the shattering effects of the glass ceiling, for as we shall see, it is not long before Viola is called upon to perform the role of the commodity she always already was. In the meantime, however, by deflecting its own exploitative economic practices onto the exaggerated evil of characters like Wessex and de Lesseps, the film slyly substitutes the fiction of bad capitalism for the reality that *all* capitalism is bad from the standpoint of those denied the "freedom" to consume and enjoy.

☆☆☆

Exchange value, not truth value counts. On it centers the rationality of
the status quo, and all alien rationality is bent to it.
                    —Herbert Marcuse, *One Dimensional Man*

Shakespeare in Love goes even further in its attempt to "bend" all alien rationality" to its "feel good" vision of capitalism by reterritorializing the desire of the vicious financier, Fennyman. As the only internal spectator witnessing the piecemeal evolution of *Romeo and Juliet*, Fennyman's increasingly enrapt gaze is implicitly aligned with our gaze. His conversion from bad capitalism to good capitalism, therefore, is designed to mitigate potential skepticism on the part of the off-screen audience. Through the combined magic of love and theater, Fennyman grows convinced that his latest investment is shaping up as something more than a profit-or-perish phenomenon; he eventually assumes a part in the play himself and even becomes a "born again theatre groupie" (87). [26] As Fennyman crosses over the river that divides the base, repressive business practices of the Wessex-de Lesseps merger from the elevated, desublimated bliss of Will and Viola's transactions, he thus becomes more than a patron of the arts: he becomes the leading patron of the culture industry. But "[t]he deception" central to the culture industry, as Adorno and Horkheimer explain, lies not in the fact it "supplies amusement but that it ruins the fun by allowing business considerations to involve it in the ideological clichés of a culture in the process of self-liquidation."[27] The closer we get to the end of *Shakespeare in Love*—at which point all the liberal claims about men and women being free to follow their desires uninhibited by gender, class, or custom come tumbling tragically down—the more the film relies on its clichéd quest to show us "the truth of love." With Fennyman now among those converted by the shared truths of love, theater, and "good capitalism," the only remaining obstacle to the film's complete reterritorialization of the collective libido is Queen Elizabeth herself—the figure who, historically, "just said no" to enjoyment. When the subject of love is raised at a royal function, the queen (Dame Judi Dench) complains that "playwrights teach nothing about love, they make it pretty, they make it comical, or they make it lust. They cannot make it true." Viola, lost in her rapturous love for Will, naturally forgets her place and objects: "Oh, but they can!" The result is a wager that Will (disguised as Viola's country cousin) sets at the amount of fifty pounds, to which the queen responds: "Fifty pounds! A very worthy sum on a very worthy question. Can a play show us the very truth and nature of love? I bear witness to the wager, and will be the judge of it as occasion arises" (94–95). Working together like a well-oiled machine, Will and Viola hereby establish the terms of their own "self-liquidation," for this is the bet that will liberate Will from the life of a hired player at the price of selling Viola into domestic slavery.

Perhaps the single most disturbing deception enacted by *Shakespeare in Love* is its representation of a love which, in the beginning, creates riot in the heart, but in the end, prefers ruin to rapture. In the final third of the film, troubling questions are raised about Will and Viola's relationship—questions, for instance, about Will's present wife and Viola's future husband, which threaten to destroy the pleasing homeostasis achieved by their lovemaking. When pressed about her betrothal to Wessex, Viola says to *Will.* "What will you have me do? Marry you instead?" Will replies:

> To be the wife of a poor player?—can I wish that for Lady
> Viola, except in my dreams? And yet I would, if I were free
> to follow my desire in the harsh light of day.
> *Viola.* (*Tartly.*) You follow your desire freely enough in the night. . . . (89)

These mutual snipes, which point to irreconcilable tensions between Will
and Viola, are abandoned in favor of a sexual resolution. Similarly, when
Viola temporarily leaves Will, having learned of his Stratford wife, Will
claims in his defense:

> My love is no lie. I have a wife, yes, and I cannot marry
> the daughter of Sir Robert de Lesseps. It needed no wife come from Stratford
> to tell you that. And yet you let me come to your bed. (112)

And he will "come again," as Will once promised Viola, for here, too, conflict is displaced onto and replaced with sexual pleasure. "Pleasure," as
Adorno and Horkheimer explain, "always means not to think about anything, to forget suffering even where it is sham. Basically it is helplessness.
It is flight; not, as is asserted, flight from a wretched reality, but from the
last remaining thought of resistance." Indeed, toward the end of the film,
we must wonder what has happened to Will and Viola's revolutionary desire to wreak havoc with social conventions and their come-what-may commitment to love each other without limits. Will's uninspired response to
the brutal force of circumstances that divides him from Viola is to convert
his play to tragedy, while Viola ultimately consents to marry Wessex, albeit
with a wry twist: "I see you are open for business," she says to him as she
witnesses the dowry changing hands, "so let's to church" (128). Will and
Viola's increasing complicity with the oppressive social order that surrounds
them suggests the insidious influence of capital which, having deterritorialized
their desire and freed them from "all fixed social identities" in order to facili-
tate their enjoyment of each other, now *re*territorializes their desire in its own
image: Viola generates a socially conservative merger of money and land,
while Will wins the £50 wager and with it, entry into the lucrative, up-
wardly mobile "company" of the Lord Chamberlain's Men.

☆☆☆

> In love enjoyment was coupled with a deification of man,
> who vouchsafed it; it was the human emotion proper.
> Finally it was revoked as a sexually conditioned value
> judgment. In the pietistic adoration of the lover, as in

the boundless admiration he commanded from his
sweetheart, the actual slavery of woman was glorified anew.
—Max Horkheimer and Theodor W. Adorno,
Dialectic of Enlightenment

What, then, is the truth of love in *Shakespeare in Love*? The truth of love in *Shakespeare in Love* is more accurately described as the irony of romance. "It is perhaps the most extravagant irony in the history of women," observes Jan Cohn, "that romantic love, with its source in the celebration of woman in chivalric romance, should have become a means for exacerbating the powerlessness of women."[28] At the conclusion of *Shakespeare in Love*, Will becomes the poet of true, or rather, "romantic" love, and Viola, now powerless in petticoats, is sold into a life of domestic slavery on a Virginia tobacco plantation. The film's choice of the feminized landscape of "Virginia" furnishes subtle clues into the stark reality of Viola's pending violation as Wessex's wife, for we know that both flesh and land are fertile sites destined to be pillaged for profit. Even before Viola is shipped off to Virginia, the film suggests that the empowerment she once shared with Will was, in fact, illusory; for in her emergency appearance in the debut of *Romeo and Juliet*, Viola no longer plays the young wayfarer, Romeo, but rather, the Capulet commodity Juliet—a reminder that she "wears the pants" only in fiction—not in the real performance where money is on the line and the "truth of love" is at stake. And, as Adorno and Horkheimer observe, "Language based entirely on truth simply arouses impatience to get on with the business deal it is probably advancing."[29] There is no doubt about the business transaction taking place at the end of *Shakespeare in Love*, wherein the trafficking in female flesh proceeds by royal decree. Were "the very truth and nature of love" really at stake here, the queen would keep the business deal for Viola from advancing. Instead she demands that Wessex pay Will for losing the wager, though it is obvious that it is Viola who is being purchased at this price, confirming the fact that in this culture of consumption, "exchange value, not truth value counts."

It seems only appropriate that the Master of the Revels should return for an encore performance at this time, emerging somewhat curiously as the Old Master of prohibition, inveighing against public lewdness. But it is too late for the old order of "self-restraint" and "just measure" to be established. As if to signify how completely this culture has been retrained to enjoy, the queen herself overrules the Master of the Revels in favor of the new Master, Master Will, whose play of *Romeo and Juliet*—if the truth be told—comments on the defeat of true love and "the triumph of invested capital, whose title as *absolute master* is the meaningful content of every film, whatever plot the production team may have selected." [30] The final apotheosis of the figure of the Master in *Shakespeare in Love* represents a compromise between the Old Master of precapitalism and the New Master of enjoyment, combining archaic prohibitions with reckless hedonism. For Master Will encourages us to *cultivate the will*: to work not for hire, but for a higher purpose, that is, to "play." The merger that occurs at the end of the film to sanctify this new understanding of work and play is the implied merger of Will and Fennyman, playwright and financier.

Becoming joint patrons of the culture industry, Will and Fennyman will work together to convert what Adorno and Horkheimer call the liberating "festival" of enjoyment into the repressive "farce" of socially controlled satisfaction: "The[se] masters introduc[e] the notion of enjoyment as something rational, a tribute paid to a not yet wholly contaminated nature; at the same time they try to decontaminate it for their own use, to retain it in their higher form of culture . . . until, ultimately, it is entirely extinguished in fixed entertainments."[31] These "fixed entertainments" serve a crucial purpose in *Shakespeare in Love*, by reminding us to *master our wills* when the more painful affects and effects of love threaten to spoil the fun at the film's conclusion. Indeed, to mitigate the pain we might feel for Viola, *Shakespeare in Love* convinces its off-screen audience that her tragic fate also has a higher purpose: she will be *recycled*. Thus, as she undertakes her future "with tears and a journey" (150), we are encouraged to enjoy the journey—assured, like the wildly applauding on-screen audience—that Will will "write her well" for *Twelfth Night*. And, as the film closes with Will's handwriting superimposed on an image of Viola trekking across a sandy coastline, *Shakespeare in Love* brilliantly relocates Shakespeare-the-Author from early modern England to our own postmodern consumer society, recycling the Bard not as the Marlboro Man of Southern Virginia, but as the daydream believer of Southern California: Hollywood.

☆ ☆ ☆

For all the academics who have "just said no" to the popular pleasure promised by the cinematic celebration of the Author in *Shakespeare in Love*, the film makes good on its attempt to offer something for everyone by staging the death of the Author. In the closing moments of *Romeo and Juliet*'s debut, Will, the Author, counterfeits Romeo's death so convincingly that Viola's Nurse (Imelda Staunton) believes Will himself is dead, a realization that prompts her to cry out in agony from the audience. The Nurse's exclamation—"Dead!"—which momentarily ruptures the diegesis of the play, also reminds the film audience that this author will, in fact, not "come again." But the film's more obvious privileging of the name "Will" as a synonym for interminable desire, as well as for the last "will" and testament that survives the death of the physical body, frustrates the potential for a proper poststructuralist burial of the Author at the conclusion of *Shakespeare in Love*. Indeed, this is one "corpus" that will, happily, *never* rest in peace; for it is clear that, while academic and popular culture strongly disagree about Shakespeare's status as an author, both share an undeniable fascination, whether expressed through violence or veneration, with the authorial body. In short, no matter how we slice—or splice—it, the Shakespearean corpus and the historical haggling over it bespeaks the presence of an enduring *surplus* value and, as such, suggests the ultimate commodity fetish. Significantly, Marx thought it apt to liken commodity fetishism to the experience of "mystery," "magic," and "necromancy," the very terms used to describe authorship in *Shakespeare in Love*. For many years, these terms also described the equally romantic fetishization of the Author in academic culture. But even though we can now clear ourselves, at least in *theory*, of the charge of romancing the dead, we might consider the possibility that the status of the Author's body in academic discourse has always been less about theoretical revelations than it is about the revolutions of our own desires. By way of concluding, I would argue that one reason why we take so much pleasure in dismembering the Author—and Shakespeare in particular—is because the Author is guilty of what Žižek calls the "theft of enjoyment."

According to Žižek, enjoyment is precisely what is ascribed to the Other because we cannot come to terms with it in ourselves. The "theft" of enjoyment, therefore, is what is "imputed to the Other, and . . . conversely, the hatred of the Other's enjoyment is always the hatred of one's own enjoyment."[32] Is it possible to substitute "Author" for "Other" here? After all, isn't the figure of the Author guilty of robbing all the other agents involved in literary production—silent collaborators, invisible prompters, compositors, printers, audiences and, chiefly, *critics*—of their fair share of the pleasure pie? But notice how, in the same breath, textual scholars like Margreta De Grazia and Peter Stallybrass cathect their own critical desire into the space vacated by the figure of the Author:

> This [authorial] genius is, after all, an impoverished, ghostly thing, compared to the complex social practices that shaped, and still shape, the absorbent surface of the Shakespearean text. Perhaps it is these practices that should be the objects not only of our labors but also of our desires.[33]

What is so instructive about recent films that romance the Bard is that they expose what always already exists in the Shakespearean corpus: the inextinguishability of enjoyment and the bodies that perpetuate it—whether they belong to authors, actors or, for that matter, academics. Unwittingly, then, the ultimate act of mystification undertaken by a film like *Shakespeare*

in Love lies in its preservation of the "mystery" housed in the *critical* enter-
prise, for by boldly imputing enjoyment to a figure for whom we cannot
even locate a body—let alone a single, authoritative textual corpus—it provides the perfect alibi for the desire we refuse to locate in ourselves: the
enjoyment of our own authority.

NOTES

1. Washington Irving, "Stratford-on-Avon," in *The Sketch-Book*, ed. Susan Manning
(Oxford and New York: Oxford University Press, 1996), 229. I wish to thank Cynthia Dobbs
and Skip Willman for their helpful suggestions for revision.

2. See, for instance, Margreta De Grazia's "Shakespeare in Quotation Marks" and
Michael Warren's work on "unstitching" and "unbinding" facsimile versions of *Lear* in *The
Complete King Lear, 1608-1623* (Berkeley: University of California Press, 1989). See also
Randall McLeod's various articles on "un-emending" Shakespeare and his edited collec-
tion *Crisis in Editing: Texts of the English Renaissance* (New York: AMS Press, 1994) as
well as Leah Marcus's recent book on *Unediting the Renaissance: Shakespeare, Marlowe,
Milton* (London and New York: Routledge, 1992).

3. Susan Sontag is paraphrasing the words of early filmmaker Bela Belazs. See her
essay on "Film and Theatre," in *Film Theory and Criticism*, 4th ed., ed. Gerald Mast, Marshall
Cohen, and Leo Braudy (Oxford and New York: Oxford University Press, 1992), 373.

4. See Žižek's *Tarrying with the Negative: Kant, Hegel, and the Critique of Ideology*
(Durham, N.C.: Duke University Press, 1993), 210.

5. In *Tarrying with the Negative*, Žižek explains the imperative to enjoy within late
capitalism through the following example drawn from the commercialization of everyday
life: "consider the labels on food cans full of pseudoscientific data—this soup contains so
much cholesterol, so many calories, so much fat . . . (Lacan, of course, would discern behind this replacement of direct injunction by the allegedly neutral information the superego
imperative '*Enjoy!*')" (218). Two provisos must be articulated at this point in order to
contextualize my reading of *Shakespeare in Love*. First, it is important to note that Lacan
distinguishes between "enjoyment" (as *jouissance*, or, pleasure-in-pain) and "pleasure." I
use these terms interchangeably in my argument, which relies more heavily on social materialism than psychoanalysis for its theoretical foundations. Second, it must also be acknowledged that, for the sake of clarity, I am oversimplifying the ethics of "precapitalism," setting
it up as a kind of "straw man," rather than exploring the various nuances in and abuses of its
system of "self-mastery and just measure."

6. Marc Norman and Tom Stoppard, *Shakespeare in Love: A Screenplay* (New York:
Hyperion, 1998), 1–2. All subsequent references to this work will be noted parenthetically.

7. Thomas Moisan observes that usury, while exploited not only by "capital-hungry
merchants" but also by "Parliament and the Queen herself," was still considered to be a
morally suspect practice in Elizabethan England (192). See Moisan's essay, "'Which is the
merchant here? and which the Jew?': Subversion and Recuperation in *The Merchant of
Venice*," in *Shakespeare Reproduced: The Text in History and Ideology*, ed. Jean E. Howard
and Marion F. O'Connor (London and New York: Methuen, 1987; reprint, London and New
York: Routledge, 1990), 192. Significantly, the name alone of the principal "capital-hungry" entrepreneur in *Shakespeare in Love*, Fennyman, reflects his entrenchment in the emergent Elizabethan marketplace, for "Fennyman" is an Anglicization of the word "Pfennigmann"
or "pennyman."

8. Susan Jeffords, *Hardbodies: Hollywood Masculinity in the Reagan Era* (New
Brunswick, N.J.: Rutgers University Press, 1994), 12.

9. Herbert Marcuse, *One-Dimensional Man: Studies in the Ideology of Advanced Industrial Society* (Boston: Beacon, 1964), 57.

10. Jeffords, 27.

11. Marcuse, 59–60.

12. This phrase is Karl Marx's famous assessment of commodity logic in *Capital, Volume One. The Marx-Engels Reader*, 2nd ed., ed. Robert C. Taylor (New York and London: W. W. Norton, 1978), 321.

13. Marcuse, 72.

14. Žižek, *Tarrying with the Negative*, 210.

15. This image of the Master of the Revels as a Master of Enjoyment is strikingly similar to the Freudian figure of the pre-oedipal or totemic father who monopolizes enjoyment by hoarding all the women and, therefore, must be killed. From the standpoint of cinematic intertextuality, the fact that Simon Callow plays this figure after having played the celibate priest, Mr. Beebe, in *A Room with a View* (dir. James Ivory, 1987) and the openly gay Scotsman in *Four Weddings and a Funeral* (dir. Mike Newell, 1994), is particularly interesting.

16. Žižek, *Tarrying with the Negative*, 218.

17. Adorno and Horkheimer's reflections on "the culture industry" may be found throughout their *Dialectic of Enlightenment*, trans. John Cuming (1944; reprint, New York: Continuum, 1999). See especially "The Culture Industry: Enlightenment as Mass Deception," 120–67 (page citations are to reprint edition).

18. Adorno and Horkheimer, 105–6, 137.

19. The two models of marriage represented in *Shakespeare in Love*, namely, the Wessex-Viola union and the Will-Viola union, correspond to what Lawrence Stone describes in as the "clear dichotomy between marriage for interest, meaning money, status or power, and marriage for affect, meaning love, friendship or sexual attraction." Viola and Will are clearly ahead of their time, for the latter model of marriage does not come into vogue until after the bourgeois revolution. See Stone's *The Family, Sex, and Marriage in England: 1500–1800* (New York: Harper and Row, 1977), 86.

20. Adorno and Horkheimer, 148.

21. As Marcuse observes: "It has often been noted that advanced industrial civilization operates with a greater degree of sexual freedom—'operates' in the sense that the latter becomes a market value and a factor of social mores. Without ceasing to be an instrument of labor, the body is allowed to exhibit its sexual features in the everyday work world and in work relations. This is one of the unique achievements of industrial society—rendered possible by the reduction of dirty and heavy physical labor; by the availability of cheap, attractive clothing, beauty culture, and physical hygiene" (74).

22. Adorno and Horkheimer, 149.

23. When "sex is integrated into work and public relations," Marcuse explains, it "is thus made more susceptible to (controlled) satisfaction." Thus, sex is particularly susceptible to what Marcuse calls "repressive desublimation," whereby the "range of socially permissible and desirable satisfaction is greatly enlarged," but "through this satisfaction, the Pleasure Principle is reduced."

24. Žižek, *Tarrying with the Negative*, 216 (emphasis added).

25. See Fredric Jameson, *Signatures of the Visible* (London and New York: Routledge, 1992), 32.

26. We witness a similar smoke-and-mirror trick of "good capitalism" when, shortly after the Master of the Revels closes The Rose, Burbage offers The Curtain to his chief competitors, Henslowe's players—another gesture designed to conceal the realities of vicious market competition in the "gentlemen's agreements" associated with the film's fantasy of good capitalism.

27. Adorno and Horkheimer, 143.

28. See Jan Cohn's *Romance and the Erotics of Property: Mass-Market Fiction for Women* (Durham, N.C.: Duke University Press, 1988), 129.

29. Adorno and Horkheimer, 147.

30. Adorno and Horkheimer, 147 (emphasis added).

31. Adorno and Horkheimer, 105-6.

32. Žižek, *Tarrying with the Negative*, 206.

33. See Margreta De Grazia and Peter Stallybrass's important essay entitled "The Materiality of the Shakespearean Text," *Shakespeare Quarterly* 44 (1993): 283.

Works Cited

Adorno, Theodor W., and Max Horkheimer. *Dialectic of Enlightenment*. Translated by John Cuming. 1944. Reprint, New York: Continuum, 1999.

Burt, Richard. *Unspeakable Shaxxxspeares: Queer Theory and American Kiddie Culture*. New York: St. Martin's Press, 1998.

Cohn, Jan. *Romance and the Erotics of Property: Mass-Market Fiction for Women*. Durham, N.C.: Duke University Press, 1988.

De Grazia, Margreta. "Shakespeare in Quotation Marks." In *The Appropriation of Shakespeare: Post-Renaissance Reconstructions of the Works and the Myth*. Edited by Jean Marsden. New York: St. Martin's Press, 1991.

De Grazia, Margreta, and Peter Stallybrass. "The Materiality of the Shakespearean Text." *Shakespeare Quarterly* 44 (1993): 255–83.

Irving, Washington. "Stratford-on-Avon." In *The Sketch-Book*. Edited by Susan Manning. Oxford and New York: Oxford University Press, 1996.

Jameson, Fredric. *Signatures of the Visible*. London and New York: Routledge, 1992.

Jeffords, Susan. *Hardbodies: Hollywood Masculinity in the Reagan Era*. New Brunswick: Rutgers University Press, 1994.

Marcus, Leah. *Unediting the Renaissance: Shakespeare, Marlowe, Milton*. London and New York: Routledge, 1996.

Marcuse, Herbert. *One-Dimensional Man: Studies in the Ideology of Advanced Industrial Society*. Boston: Beacon, 1964.

Marx, Karl. *Capital, Volume One. The Marx-Engels Reader*. 2nd ed. Edited by Robert C. Taylor. New York and London: W. W. Norton, 1978.

McLeod, Randall, ed. *Crisis in Editing: Texts of the English Renaissance*. New York: AMS Press, 1994.

Moison, Thomas. "'Which is the merchant here? and which the Jew?': Subversion and Recuperation in *The Merchant of Venice*." In *Shakespeare Reproduced: The Text in History and Ideology*. Edited by Jean E. Howard and Marion F. O'Connor. London and New York: Methuen, 1987. Reprint, London and New York: Routledge, 1990.

Norman, Marc, and Tom Stoppard. *Shakespeare in Love: A Screenplay*. New York: Hyperion, 1998.

Sontag, Susan. "Film and Theatre." In *Film Theory and Criticism*. 4th ed. Edited by Gerald Mast, Marshall Cohen, and Leo Braudy. Oxford and New York: Oxford University Press.

Stone, Lawrence. *The Family, Sex, and Marriage in England, 1500–1800.* New York: Harper and Row, 1977.

Warren, Michael. *The Complete King Lear, 1608–1623.* Berkeley: University of California Press, 1989.

Žižek, Slavoj. *The Sublime Object of Ideology.* New York: Verso, 1989.

———. *Tarrying with the Negative: Kant, Hegel, and the Critique of Ideology.* Durham, N.C.: Duke University Press, 1993.

FILMS CITED

Shakespeare in Love. Directed by John Madden. 2 hr. 2 min. Miramax Films/Universal Pictures, 1998. Videocassette.

Part III
The Politics of the Popular:
From Class to Classroom

"Art thou base, common and popular?":
The Cultural Politics of Kenneth Branagh's
Hamlet

Douglas Lanier

No single figure has been more central to the recent flowering of Shakespeare on film than Kenneth Branagh. The founder of the Renaissance Theatre Company and director of four major Shakespeare films, Branagh has shown a particular genius for finding Shakespeare a broad audience, and his entrepreneurial savvy has quieted the perennial fear among producers that Shakespeare is box-office poison. Perhaps even more important, Branagh has reinvigorated the ideal of a "popular Shakespeare," a Shakespeare set free from the taint of elitism and "restored" to his proper status as a commercially viable, accessible playwright for the masses. In fact, Branagh has been quite explicit, proudly so, about the "life-enhancing populism"[1] of his theatrical and cinematic Shakespeare productions: "I wanted to reach a large group of potential Shakespeare-lovers, beyond the obvious range of RSC die-hards. . . .We wanted to present popular art. Not poor art or thin art or even 'arty' art, but popular art that would expand the mind and the senses and really entertain" (*Beginning* 174, 193).

In his films Branagh has sought, often with great inventiveness, to accommodate Shakespeare to the apparatus of mass-market cinema, its visual and dramatic vocabulary, genres, star system, modes of production and marketing techniques. Indeed, I will argue that Branagh's Shakespeare films thematize the conditions of their own reception; they constitute an extended meditation on the ideal of Shakespeare (re)integrated into the cultural life of the common man, a meditation conducted from within the institutional imperatives of the contemporary stage and screen. Given those concerns, his 1996 *Hamlet* emerges as a pivotal work, for *Hamlet* and its cinematic paratexts *Swan Song* (1992) and *A Midwinter's Tale* (1995) turn from Branagh's early populist utopianism to a more conflicted account of the competing priorities involved in popularizing Shakespeare.[2]

Many elements of Branagh's "populist" approach to Shakespearean film can be traced to the performance style of his Renaissance Theatre Company. Its emphases lay in the clarity, accessibility, and immediacy of the interpretive line, a goal to which all else was subordinated. In the case of his *Henry V* (1989), for example, Branagh claims that his textual cuts were made on "the altar of instant understanding."[3] His working assumption is that his audiences have never seen a particular Shakespeare play before, and thus will not be engaged in assessing a production's place in performance history. Rather, their concern is with simply following the action and forging an immediate identification with the characters' emotions expressed in an unfamiliar idiom. Branagh's first theatrical experience of *Hamlet* (the Prospect Theatre Company's 1978 production, with Derek Jacobi) exemplifies the ideal: "The story was gripping, and I wanted at every moment to know 'what happened next.' Much of the language I did not understand, and yet the actors' commitment to each line convinced me that I knew what they were feeling."[4]

This kind of immediacy can be achieved, Branagh claims, through a naturalistic, colloquial delivery, in which the lines seem to spring naturally from a clear emotional process occurring before the viewer's eyes. He self-consciously distinguishes his mode of delivery from the "incomprehensible booming and fruity voiced declamation"[5] that, he observes, popular audiences find so unnatural and intimidating. Instead, Branagh's emphasis falls on the clarity and intensity of emotions rather than the beauties of poetic language, moments of deep feeling or energy rather than the dramatic *grande ligne*.

Branagh's working methods also contribute to the impression of emotional "freshness" and spontaneity. In interviews, Branagh has tended to focus not on the "high concept" of his films but on the fluid nature of the acting process—the ways in which one actor intuitively, even unexpectedly, responds to another in mid-performance. Such moments, he explains, encourage the "natural," "truthful," style for which he aims: "Julie Christie used to say to me, 'You do it different every time, don't you?' I said, 'If you say it different to me, I'll say it different to you.' It's just however it comes out."[6] His Shakespearean films, he claims, depend upon and foreground the collaborative process between the actors, rather than simply realizing an a priori directorial "vision" or recording some cherished performance from the theater. Russell Jackson's film diary of *Hamlet*, for example, documents the ways in which performances evolved during rehearsal and changed from take to take. That is one reason that Branagh typically favors the long steadicam shot rather than editing, since the former preserves the integrity of the give-and-take between the actors within a scene.[7] It also explains why in his introductions to his published screenplays Branagh so underscores the importance of the ensemble to the production. The fundamental unit of Branagh's Shakespearean productions is not the director-auteur but the acting company, whose "full emotional commitment to the [individual] characters"[8] rather than reverence for the Shakespearean text or performance tradition assures the accessibility of the performance.

This ideal of the theatrical company is crucial to Branagh's concept of a popular Shakespeare and the cultural politics that inform it. For Branagh the egalitarian camaraderie and "family feeling" of the theatrical company becomes both substitute and symbol for the organic community he left behind on York Street in Belfast, a "strong community life" held together by storytelling, "the collective yarn session" (*Beginning* 13). The flyleaf pictures for his autobiography underline the analogy: the front photograph is of Branagh's immediate family in Ireland; the back photograph is of the cast of the *Henry V* film, gathered for the first read-through. Little wonder, then, that Branagh's production methods work so explicitly toward creating the ideal of egalitarian community in the acting company itself and that this communal ideal is so central a thematic touchstone in his readings of Shakespeare. In fact, in Branagh's films the community within the fiction and the company performing the fiction typically collapse into one another. The first meeting of the *Henry V* cast he describes in terms of Henry's brotherhood of "dear friends": "This was the one time they would all be together, and I wanted this to be a 'Company' picture. Here was the one opportunity to establish the tone and taste of the movie so we all understood. . . . A disaster it might be, but a singular one. Everyone was glad to be there. We few, we happy few" (*Beginning* 222). And that company ideal is also at the heart of Branagh's treatment of Henry, who as a politically weak monarch must cobble together a united army from a diverse, potentially fractious collection of underclass men. Mud becomes the mark of the English king's identification with his "debased" troops and symbol of the terrible costs of war that, despite Henry's victory, both French and English share on the Agincourt battlefield.[9]

Similarly, in his *Much Ado about Nothing* (1993), the travel-brochure Tuscan setting situates the play's action within an idealized vision of village life, an idyllic family-community temporarily broken apart by Don Pedro and Claudio, who are overly concerned with class-coded notions of masculine honor.[10] But, if the film's publicity is to be trusted, the location was also designed to provide something of a sun-drenched Italian group holiday for the cast and crew. Actors were encouraged to share villas, Keanu Reeves recalls, in an effort to build a family feeling among the company.[11] Branagh's signature shot in *Henry V*, *Much Ado*, and *Love's Labour's Lost* (2000), a long, complex single take in which nearly all of the cast appears, brings together the community that is each film's essential subject—the English army, the village community of Messina, the Navarrian and French lovers and their entourages, as well as the company of actors who in effect take their bows.

Even Branagh's penchant for casting Hollywood stars, begun with *Much Ado*, contributes to the sense of immediate familiarity between players and audience, for the star system encourages viewers to feel a certain intimacy with film celebrities. For Branagh, the production's success depends on the extent to which the organic society within the Shakespearean fiction and the organic "family" of the theatrical company meld into one.[12] This homology of communities becomes the catalyst for a third organic community, that forged between the popular audience and the Shakespearean players, united in their enjoyment of and identification with the "collective yarn session" that is—or should be—a popular Shakespearean performance. One can find no better emblem of this communal ideal than the opening sequence of *Much Ado*, where we as viewers join Leonato's extended family to watch Beatrice recite Shakespearean verse with a romanticized village in the background.

Branagh characterizes his brand of Shakespearean populism as "actor militancy" (*Beginning* 46). It sprang, he claims, from the peculiar institutional circumstances of contemporary Shakespearean theater in Britain and was sharpened by his frustrating experience with the RSC in the mid 1980s. The central conundrum for postwar British theater has been that with the advent of mass media, particularly film, it has occupied an increasingly marginal place in the hierarchy of performance media, and yet it has retained the aura of preeminent cultural authority, not least because stagework still serves to establish the actor's artistic credentials through unique handmade—rather than technologically mediated—performances. The contradiction of a theater both institutionally marginal and symbolically central is particularly acute in the case of Shakespeare, for despite the occasional successes of Shakespeare on film, in the popular imagination Shakespeare has remained primarily a figure of (and for) the *stage*. And as the very essence of the classical theater, Shakespeare has become at once the epitome of high cultural authority and the relic of a once popular, now residual cultural institution displaced by film and TV, living on by celebrating its cultural mystique with a much smaller and more select audience.

The British "solution" to this problem has been state subsidies and the formation of "national" theatrical companies (like the National Theatre and the RSC) specifically charged with responsibility for maintaining the heritage of British theatrical culture. From Branagh's perspective, the results of this approach have been mixed. The artistic directorship of Sir Peter Hall in the sixties, he observes, initiated an official RSC philosophy that the company was "one big family," a premise "based on the experience of a small, close-knit group of actors and other artists" based at a single Stratford venue and offering a small number of productions (*Beginning* 159). But as the company grew and its venues became more dispersed and productions more expensive, the organization was forced toward "directors' Shakespeare," so that actors were increasingly expected to serve production concepts established well before the rehearsal process began. The scale of the RSC meant that "it simply wasn't practical or economic to make lots of last-minute decisions about production details" (*Beginning* 157). As a result, Branagh asserts, the individual actor's creative contribution and the company's organic esprit de corps became necessary sacrifices to the director's great account. Other pressures also contributed to the predominance of directors' Shakespeare. In the face of diminished institutional stature and an expanding academic bardbiz, Shakespearean theater has tended to address itself not to first-time viewers but to an audience already familiar with the plays, its productions becoming "interpretive essays" self-consciously contributing to the plays' critical and performing traditions.[13] And subsidized theater's relative freedom from commercial pressures has also meant that it has been somewhat protected from popular horizons of reception, shaped as they are by film and TV, institutions against which the theater defined its cultural mission.

As Peter Womack has shown, the emphasis on "quality" in the Arts Council model has been shaped by class-coded standards of "good taste": where the marketplace might be seen as promoting mediocrity and vulgarity, government subsidy can "protect the quality of drama from the ill effects of social and economic egalitarianism."[14] Thus, we are faced with the odd paradox of a putatively "national" Shakespeare company that showcases the (often brilliant) "high" concepts of director-intellectuals in centralized venues largely insulated from their local constituencies and pitched, so Alan Sinfield argues, primarily to the university-educated bourgeois class.[15] However, Branagh's name for his theatrical company—*Renaissance*—implies that he sees his project as a matter of *returning* Shakespearean theater to its once organic relationship to a popular audience. And film has been integral to that goal. Presenting *Henry V* on film, Branagh has claimed, was at first merely a practical choice: it allowed his audience the widest possible access to intimate acting without subjecting his company to the trials of constant touring (*Beginning* 205). But in retrospect it can also be seen as a gesture of rejection, a decision that allowed Branagh to pursue his cultural-political ideal outside of the dominant institutional form of British Shakespearean theater.

Even so, using the film medium to promote Shakespeare, still so potent a symbol of the theater *as an institution*, is not without its ironies and contradictions, many of which have surfaced in Branagh's later Shakespearean projects. The politics of medium surface as early as 1992, when Branagh directed a film short, *Swan Song*, for Renaissance Films, a project financed by prize money he won for *Henry V. Swan Song*, Hugh Cruttwell's free adaptation of Chekhov's one-act by the same name, decries the vanishing audience for Shakespeare. Its central image is of a darkened, empty playhouse, that is, of theater's absent constituency. There the aging actor Svetlovidov laments to itinerant prompter Nikita that his artistry as an actor has never been appreciated by the public, and as if to prove it, he gives Nikita a private taste of his Shakespearean talents, ending, significantly enough, with "Othello's occupation's gone."

Given that lament for the unappreciated Shakespearean, Branagh's choice of medium for *Swan Song*, film, takes on an added meaning. That choice seems to acknowledge that theater, particularly Shakespearean theater, can continue to fulfill its social mission only on screen, reconstituting its lost cultural authority by lamenting its own passing in the very medium that has replaced it. What *Swan Song* records is Branagh's first attempt to articulate the incongruent relationship between Shakespearean theater and the film medium, and the cultural issues that attend upon that incongruence. Only with the film camera can one fully take up the perspective of the thespian looking out at his (absent) audience, and only with film can one preserve, and make available for scrutiny and appreciation, what is evanescent in live theater: the particularities of a Shakespearean star's performance—in this case, John Gielgud. But lost in the process is the frisson of presence, the power of a communal event shared by audience and performer.

Branagh undertook a more throughgoing consideration of the cultural politics of Shakespearean theater in his 1994 film *In the Bleak Midwinter* (released in America with the title *A Midwinter's Tale*), the cinematic prolegomenon to his *Hamlet*. It is a study in black and white, a morality play in which the protagonist, Joe, the downtrodden director of a Shakespearean troupe, must choose between his ragtag, seemingly doomed production of *Hamlet* in the dilapidated village church of Hope and a financially secure career in Hollywood, playing the sidekick in a B-picture knockoff of *Star Wars*. The film builds toward a moment of truth that sets in stark relief the film's thematic oppositions—cynical pragmatism versus Romantic idealism, commercialism versus genuine artistry, film versus theater, vapid American popular culture versus the glories of Shakespeare. Of course, Joe ultimately chooses Shakespeare and the theater, even though he acknowledges that bouts of despair about money and the value of art are sure to return. *In the Bleak Midwinter* juxtaposes the fantasy of a Shakespearean "poor theater" revitalizing merrie old English village life with the reality that the communal experience so essential to live performance has become a relic of the past. His film details how fully the sense of community has eroded, both for the actors (who have damaged family relations or none at all) and for the town of Hope (which, Molly observes, has "nowhere for people to go, apart from the pub . . . there's no village hall, there's no arts centre").[16] At first the troupe is just another example of noncommunity, a gathering of misfits whose vanities, self-serving acting tics, and mutual antagonisms threaten to undermine the show. In the course of rehearsing *Hamlet*, how-

ever, the actors subsume their own egos in the collective project and transform themselves into a genuine ensemble of players.

Within the fiction of the film, the catalyst for this transformation is
Shakespeare. Under the pressure of creating a show, the actors discover in
Hamlet refractions of their own insecurities and come to confront them. As
he directs Ophelia's mad scene, Joe claims that Shakespeare can serve as a
point of emotional identification between otherwise isolated individuals, a
reservoir of deeply shared feelings that extends outward from the players
to the audience:

> You're all shying away from the power of this play. Now this scene is about
> loss. The loss of sense, Ophelia's madness, the loss of a sister, the loss of a
> relationship between Claudius and Gertrude, and crucially the loss, the death
> of someone they have all in their own ways experienced a profound love for,
> that's a human emotion we can all share—that's where we connect with the
> audience in Hope or wherever. (Branagh, *Midwinter's,* 69–70)

The lack of intimate community is precisely the underlying cultural issue that in different ways bedevils the actors, the village in which they
play, and the modern theater, but Shakespeare's articulation of this loss,
Branagh seems to argue, provides a remedy, in the form of a community
composed of audience and actors united in their nostalgia for primal familial bonds and mutual recognition of their loss. Accordingly, in the course
of the film the actors' initial antagonisms fall away as the group gradually
recognizes in *Hamlet* its shared professional failings and personal losses.
By film's end, Nina speaks of the troupe as her "family." The bonds within
the company even take on an erotic charge, as Fadge's hardened nipples
before each performance and the occasional slide into sexual innuendo
indicate. In the case of the men, their homosocial bonding is half-expressed,
half-denied through the "theatrical camp" Terry introduces into the group;
by playfully addressing each other by women's names and, in Joe's case,
waggishly complimenting Vernon's arse, the men can express their mutual
affection without becoming maudlin.[17] Bonds within the stage ensemble,
in short, do the work of family, lovers, and village.[18] When the troupe ultimately pulls together in a dazzling performance of *Hamlet*, the village
audience's enthusiastic response and the backstage reconciliation afterward
of Terry and Carnforth with their families demonstrates how a "poor"
Shakespeare might catalyze a renaissance of small-scale community founded
on the model of the theatrical company. Given its Christmas setting, the
performance in an abandoned church, and the pointed allusion to Christina
Rossetti's carol, it is not too much to see Shakespearean theater emerging
from this film as a secular substitute for the salvific holy family and the lost
communion of religious congregation.

Against this fantasy of an organic connection between the players and

their local public, Branagh sets the fallen state of the modern theater as an
institution. Once, Henry Wakefield reminisces, theatrical companies were
an integral part of rural British culture, but no more:

> Used to read about the old Shakespeare companies. You know, eight plays in
> six days. Traveling from town to town on a Sunday. Hundreds of people
> waving the actors off from the platform. So romantic. Unfortunately I was
> born out of my time. When I joined the business all that was gone. It was
> divided in two, there was the "proper" theatre, you know Stratford and all
> that, and then there was the commercial stuff. Well, a little suburban oik like
> me, had no chance of the tights and the fluffy white shirts. I was straight into
> understudying old men and "anyone for tennis?" (63)

The operative word here is "business": what makes contemporary Shakespearean theater "proper" is its state subsidy and thus its freedom from financial dependence upon constant touring and such vulgar fare as the Christmas
pantomime and "Puss 'n' Boots." But that class-coded freedom from the
taint of trade comes at a price, the price of Shakespeare's isolation from the
public, the very suburban and village "oiks" he once nourished. The unacknowledged backdrop to this emergence of "proper" stage Shakespeare is
the rise of the cinema and the resulting dependence of the theater upon
dwindling arts subsidies. When Joe's village *Hamlet* quixotically seeks to
restore Shakespearean theater to its original cultural function, from the start
his chief, insurmountable problem is money. In true romance fashion, only
by symbolically embracing the "higher" spiritual value of the Shakespearean
stage over the financial security of the cinema does Joe manage to get both,
in the form of an artistically *and* commercially successful show.

Of course, to formulate the movie's ideological stance in this way is to
focus almost exclusively upon Joe. As several reviewers observed, he clearly
stands in for Branagh the idealist, the populist Shakespearean director whose
despair mirrors Branagh's personal crisis on the heels of the public breakup
of his self-mythologized marriage and romance with Emma Thompson and
the critical failure of his 1994 *Mary Shelley's Frankenstein*. Yet Branagh
complicates the scenario with a second alter-ego, the humble, enterprising
Vernon. It is Vernon who voices the bond of love between actors in its
purest form, without the safe distance of camp: "I love you," he tells
Carnforth, "as an audience member, I love you. As a company member, I
love you. As a human being, I love you" (90). And early on it is Vernon
who worries about "tickets, box-office, the cash-advance, advertising" (51),
and it is his commercial savvy and ingenuity that rescues the show. He, not
Joe, dons a sandwich board and sells tickets to the people of Hope; he taps
into the tourist market at nearby Chelford Castle, drumming up business
with his "occasional cabaret act, of crooning and conjuring" (66); he orga-
nizes the company's pooling of funds to cover's Joe's shortfall; and he

makes sure that the audience is provided such money-making amenities as programs and ice cream. Vernon's talent for promotion, far more than Joe's "pure" devotion to his art, secures the play's success. When Tom pronounces his willingness to hawk tickets "vulgar," Vernon's reply is pointed: "Don't you want anyone to see it?" (73). It is difficult not to regard Vernon as Branagh's case for vulgar entrepreneurialism in the service of the political ideal represented by Shakespearean performance.

So powerful is this metatheatrical fantasy that one might easily forget that it takes the form of a *film*, and Branagh's case extends to the film medium itself. In one respect, *In the Bleak Midwinter* sets the cinema squarely against Shakespearean theater. Whereas Shakespeare is quintessentially British, emotionally sustaining, "artistic" rather than commercial, the cinema is American, uncreative, tastelessly concerned with money, epitomized by Nancy Crawford, the producer of *Galaxy Terminus*. Though Joe's *Hamlet* makes little impression on her, Crawford is taken with two-dimensional superficialities, with Fadge's cardboard cutouts of the audience and with Tom's broad shoulders and silly accents. For her, historic Chelford Castle is just one more cheap location, "the ruins of an ancient city on the planet Zarbok" (85) and her actors mere bodies on which to plaster latex prostheses. While Joe finds in Shakespeare a vitality capable of speaking, as he puts it, directly to his "chief reproductive organ" (43), Crawford offers the world Smegma, the aptly named alien of her sci-fi epic. But stark as these distinctions seem at first, the film acknowledges a rather different institutional reality. For one thing, Joe's "pure" Shakespeare production is indirectly underwritten by film, through his agent Margaretta's seed money (which has its ultimate source in her film deals) and later, when Tom gets the film role, through Margaretta's offer of "compensation to the management." For another, Vernon—in another of Branagh's self-references—films the rehearsal process for posterity, an action he connects in his fight with Tom with creating an audience for theater:

> Tom. Can't we work in private for once? Why does everyone have to see behind the scenes, these days? Whatever happened to all the bloody mystery?
> Ver. (Enraged, snaps.) I'm recording our history love. It was discussed, right Joe. I think it's the least I deserve. I'm the only one who's got off his ass to sell this show. (73)

Most important, Branagh draws attention to the hybrid nature of his own film, its attempt to dovetail, rather than oppose, stage and screen, popular culture and "proper" Shakespeare. Indeed, he underscores *Midwinter*'s debts to a particular film genre, the backstage melodrama, which both idealizes the theater and puts its institutional mechanics before the viewer. When Nancy Crawford congratulates Joe and Molly after their performance, she glosses the cinematic source: "Mickey and Judy. You two were fine. Keep it up kids" (115).

At the level of form, then, Branagh makes the case for a hybridized sort of Shakespearean performance that blends rather than rigorously distinguishes theater and the popular cinema. *Midwinter*'s climax, which poses a painful choice between the financial rewards of film and the spiritual rewards of theater, posits a myth of theatrical "integrity" from which Branagh's own stage-screen hybrid—and his *Hamlet* to come—can claim artistic legitimacy. This myth, framed by acknowledgment of commercial realities, allows Branagh to stand apart from questions about how the institutional demands of mass-market film complicate and potentially compromise Branagh's political ideals for Shakespearean theater. It allows, for example, Branagh to sidestep the problem of film stardom. Starting with *Much Ado* and continuing with *Hamlet* and *Love's Labour's Lost*, Branagh has cast Hollywood film stars alongside British theatrical stalwarts in an effort not merely to provide Shakespeare some box office punch but also, so he asserts, to create a community of actors that crosses the boundaries of screen and stage, Britain and America. Even so, the very nature of stardom—the cult of the individual talent—runs counter to the ideal of organic camaraderie exemplified by the ensemble. It is symptomatic then that, unlike the Shakespearean films before and after it, *Midwinter* eschews "big star" casting, as if tacitly acknowledging that stardom were at some level at odds with the company ideal. *In the Bleak Midwinter* begs to be read against the momentary dip in Branagh's film career, marking a recuperative return to his theatrical roots and making a case for commercial failure as a mark of artistic integrity. But *Midwinter* also looks forward to Branagh's film *Hamlet*, locating, as if in preemptive reply to his critics, *Hamlet*'s ultimate origin and claim to "popularity" in an intimate community of humble stageplayers and their audience, an origin otherwise difficult to imagine in the presence of the film's grand production values.

Indeed, the problem of grand scale is at the heart of *Hamlet*'s contradictory politics. The film takes up the relationship between the family-community and a larger political order, between, in Branagh's words, "a personal, domestic story about a family and its problems" and "the epic dimension that reflects the effects of those problems on the nation." With this change in focus Branagh's *Hamlet* makes a break with the optimism of *Henry V* and *Much Ado*. Like the film that precedes it, this *Hamlet* is a midwinter's tale. The vast winter palace and the vaguely czarist iconography obliquely recalls David Lean's 1965 epic *Dr. Zhivago*,[20] evoking the Romanovs in the last season of an aristocratic age, on the eve of a new, mass political regime. Though the epic scale is intended to lend the play's events and characters greater impact, it also dwarfes the characters in icy landscapes and vast halls, often stressing their isolation in Elsinore's public spaces. Instead of the dark metaphysical shadows of conventional productions, Branagh offers an Elsinore glittering with surface splendor that masks an emotional chill. The opulent state room in which we first meet the court manifests the character of its public life—a flamboyant, gilded hall of mirrors that opens onto a warren of private chambers and hidden passages where the court's real life of secret machination is conducted. When the court first gathers in the state hall to celebrate Claudius and Gertrude's marriage, the bonds between its members seem heartfelt and familiar— Claudius becomes effusive when he thanks the gathered nobles for having "freely gone / With this affair along."[21] But the snowy confetti that falls as Claudius and Gertrude make their triumphal exit suggests that an affective winter has descended upon this community.

Later scenes reveal that the seeming familiarity between king and courtiers masks class-coded hypocrisy and political calculation. The motif of fencing, for example, suggests how conflict at court has become formalized and genteel, given a wintery-white costume and rendered a bloodless and faceless ritual.[22] Elsinore is an aristocratic clique insulated from the commons (and, only temporarily, from the military threat to its status posed by Fortinbras), an elite class bound by polite codes of decorum. And Branagh's Hamlet offers a series of escalating affronts to that decorum. In his opening scene, he stands aloof from the ordered ranks of wintry-white courtiers, his bowed head and ramrod-straight posture a private protest that nevertheless suggests the prince's initially aristocratic bearing. The emphasis in Hamlet's "O that this too too solid flesh" soliloquy falls on how court propriety prevents him from voicing his private grief over his father's death and mother's insult to his memory. But as the film progresses, Branagh's Hamlet becomes less and less willing to abide by that propriety. He angrily mocks Polonius because Claudius's sycophant seems the epitome of court hypocrisy, and his public refusal to behave himself at the Mousetrap elicits as much court discomfort as any revelation of Claudius's crime. Hamlet's "madness" is designed to push Claudius's public restraint to the breaking point, a point Claudius finally reaches when after the closet scene he explodes, "Where is Polonius?" and strikes the prince.

This code of aristocratic propriety, the principal means by which Claudius maintains political sway in the first half of the film, is contrasted to the bonds of family, particularly the deep, reverent love between fathers and children. Branagh pointedly parts company with the oedipal readings of Olivier's and Zeffirelli's films,[23] making Hamlet's idealization of his father the centerpiece of his performance. The film begins and ends with the larger-than-life statue of the elder Hamlet, and the prince is repeatedly overwhelmed with grief at the thought of his lost father, a feeling most intense in the closet scene when Hamlet watches with tearful, anguished desperation as the melancholy ghost of his father fades away. Branagh locates this intensity of feeling not in some defect in Hamlet's character but in the utopian ideal of the family. When the Ghost narrates the circumstances of his murder, in flashback we see royal father, mother, and son engrossed in a game of curling in the corridor, with Claudius the odd man out insinuating himself into the group. The flashback establishes the extraordinarily loving bond between father and son, a bond so strong that as the two commune with each other, Gertrude is left open to Claudius's blandishments.

This brief idyll suggests the informality of their relationship, their sheer pleasure in family fun, the sense that the bonds between these family members stand outside the codes of propriety that govern the public life of the court and are thus more authentic, free of the taint of class. This idealization of filial bonds extends to Polonius and Laertes as well. Polonius's parting advice to Laertes, so often played for comedy, becomes a touching, intimate, entirely unironic expression of a father's love for his son, their relationship gently sacralized by virtue of setting the scene in the palace chapel. Even so, Branagh distinguishes the two fathers: Polonius's love is tainted by the proprieties of class, a motive that underlies his stinging rebuke of Ophelia for her relationship with Hamlet and his contract with Reynaldo to spy on his own son.

Given Branagh's identification of "company feeling" with the ties of family, it is not surprising that Branagh chooses to portray the players as a theatrical family. Though it is clear from its tatty dress that the troupe has fallen from a former grandeur,[24] Hamlet immediately adopts an affectionate intimacy with them, acting as if he were welcoming long-lost relatives rather than a group of actors, treating them as a substitute for the family unit he has lost. (That affection also characterizes Hamlet's instruction to the players, handled not as directorial criticism so much as informal advice from a long-standing friend of the family, addressed principally to the young.) In Branagh's handling, the First Player's speech describes not the fall of a political order but the demise of a family, and the theatrical company—and the profoundly moving tale it tells—becomes a compensatory substitute for what has been so irretrievably lost.

With elegiac music providing emotional punctuation, the First Player's delivery is full of pathos attached to fathers. The inserts picture not Pyrrhus or his hesitation at the moment of revenge, the ostensible focus of the speech, but Priam amidst the burning ruins of Troy in terrified close-up as his death-blow falls. That Priam is played by John Gielgud—declaiming but without voice—adds an additional layer of piquancy to the link between family and theatrical company, since we are watching not merely Priam's death but also the leave-taking of the last living patriarch of British theater's golden age. The insert of an anguished Hecuba helps clarify that Priam's fall is a family tragedy, for in the foreground to the left, as Hecuba wanders the burning ruins, is huddled a group of children orphaned by the disaster. By filming the First Player over the shoulders of the actors seated on the stage, Branagh specifies that the principal audience for the Player's speech is, at least at first, his own troupe. A quick reaction shot of mother, son, and father suggests that because the players are a family, they are naturally moved by the extraordinary pathos of the player-patriarch's performance and the poignant narrative of familial tragedy. When the First Player turns to deliver the speech directly to the camera, it is as if we (along with Hamlet) have been invited into this small community of players and spectators joined by shared anguish at the death of fathers. Polonius, by contrast, remains unmoved throughout. He breaks the mood—the background score even falls momentarily silent—by caviling at what he sees as violations of theatrical decorum. When he objects to the prince's request to use the players "according to their desert," Hamlet erupts in fury at Polonius's snobbery and insists, with obvious metatheatrical significance, that he "use them after [his] own honour and dignity."

This short scene plays out Branagh's by now familiar ideal of a popular Shakespeare, a quasi-familial community of players and spectators absorbed in the experience of intense feeling. However, the very epic scale of the film raises difficult questions of cultural politics. *In the Bleak Midwinter* could focus on utopian possibilities for a truly popular cultural-political order because Branagh was working on the intimate scale of the village. But when in *Hamlet* he turns to imagining how the company-family might translate to some broader political order, he runs into difficulties. We might notice, for example, that the community temporarily forged by the First Player's acting is pointedly small, a happy few composed of disenfranchised players (and in Hamlet's case, a theatrical enthusiast). As in *Swan Song*, those best able to appreciate the Player's performance are actors themselves, into whose inner circle we are briefly invited. And like *Swan Song* and *In the Bleak Midwinter*, much of the intensity of feeling springs from our awareness that past glories—particularly the joys of family—have been or will be irremediably lost. In the case of *Hamlet*, that lost ideal finds a specific correlative in dead fathers, but it extends as well to the diminished place of the theater (and of Shakespeare) that the shabbily genteel players represent, and, finally, to the fact that the gorgeous trappings of high culture–the royal palace, the cabinets of antiques, the statue of father Hamlet—fall into the hands of Fortinbras in the final reel.

Indeed, Branagh's shaping of the Fortinbras plot highlights the film's conflicted cultural politics. In the film's second half, the question of the commons intrudes with increasing urgency: the mob following Laertes or Fortinbras's army all threaten to invade the pristine state room. Branagh's prince reflects that shift in emphasis. To speak in the most general terms, his Hamlet moves from a tightly wound prince incensed by the polite aristocratic fictions of Elsinore to a man self-identified—albeit ambivalently—with the commons. He is amused rather than irritated by the Gravedigger's irreverence to the dead, seems more at peace with the death of his father and the grand order he represents and, before the duel, is poignantly aware of his own impending fall. One index of this change is Hamlet's costume. When he returns to Elsinore, he has exchanged his tailored black uniform for the rougher garb of the commons and players. The pivotal moment occurs, we are encouraged to think, when Hamlet encounters Fortinbras's army, perhaps the film's most hotly debated sequence and cinematically one of its most elaborate. From a promontory overlooking a vast icy plain crawling with Fortinbras's soldiers in antlike ranks, Branagh delivers "How all occasions do inform against me" as a rousing declaration of heroic resolve. The performance, reprising his "Crispin Crispian" speech in *Henry V* in theme and delivery, pivots on this passage:

> Rightly to be great
> Is not to stir without great argument,
> But greatly to find quarrel in a straw
> When honour's at the stake.
>   (Branagh, *Hamlet* 122)

As Hamlet speaks, the camera pulls back until he is a tiny figure in the snowy expanse, shouting his determination to the world with outstretched arms: "O, from this time forth / My thoughts be BLOODY . . . or be NOTHING worth!" (122).

Clearly this bravura shot is intended to show the epic scope of Hamlet's newfound resolution, pitched as it is against insurmountable forces. But the heroic gesture's place within the film's larger political scheme seems unclear at best. Several commentators have argued that the odd grand futility of it all is its point: in Samuel Crowl's words, "he's been isolated, cut off, frozen, and reduced in filmic terms to making grand gestures of impotent frustration while Fortinbras gets on with the business of doing."[25] Judged within the traditional question of Hamlet's inaction, such a reading seems attractive, yet the film itself doesn't dwell upon or condemn that inaction (as Olivier's version does), nor can one easily claim that the shot is intended to ironize Hamlet's declaration, particularly given the heroic tenor of the accompanying music. In my view, this sequence articulated a much different issue, for the operative visual contrast in this shot is in fact not between Hamlet and Fortinbras, but between Hamlet and *Fortinbras's army*. That army, a swarm of grey shock troops, forms the next frame out, the modern mass-political movements that will ultimately sweep the *ancien regime* from power. And judging from their brutality in taking Elsinore, what most characterizes those troops is their utter disregard for honor or fellow feeling, an indiscriminate destruction of aristocratic lives and cultural finery in the pursuit of raw political power.

This film's Fortinbras is hardly motivated by retribution, for unlike Hamlet and Laertes, whose tender relationships with their fathers provide them motives for revenge, Fortinbras shows no sentiment toward his surrogate father, his uncle Norway, even though the text (1.1.83–107) provides Branagh with ample basis for showing the elder Fortinbras in flashback. Instead, this Fortinbras is an emotionless Bolingbroke-like figure who, like his army, exudes a ruthless will to power and a contempt for diplomatic and ceremonial niceties. When his army storms the palace gates and crashes through the windows into the state room, indiscriminately destroying everyone in its path—and Fortinbras barely registers the magnitude of the tragedy when he discovers the slain Danish court—we are witnessing the entrance of a new political order, founded not on the warm bonds of the family but on an icy will to power. The dominant note of Fortinbras and his army is not revenge or resoluteness of purpose, but their incapacity for sentiment.

The "How all occasions" sequence, then, articulates Hamlet's attitude toward the mass political order represented by Fortinbras's army and, with it, something of the film's ambivalence when it considers the cultural status of the masses. Branagh's delivery of the speech emphasizes Hamlet's identification with Fortinbras's "divine ambition" and his newfound stress upon gentlemanly "honour at the stake," misrecognized in Fortinbras's crusade. Yet the visual setup articulates a far more conflicted message. With his back to the distant army on the wasteland below, Hamlet at first stands apart from the undifferentiated masses, but as the camera pulls back and he is absorbed into the wintry landscape and its army, the question arises: does Hamlet participate in or resist the historical process in which he finds himself? The problem is, the shot seems to suggest, how to move from the relative intimacy of Elsinore, grounded in the ideal of the royal family (and, in the case of the players, its surrogates), to the brutal world of mass politics, where, the film suggests, the bonds of the nation-community are devoid of affective attachment?

This dilemma structures Branagh's portrayal of a changed Hamlet in the film's second half. For while the prince's changed costume suggests a level of identification with the commons, his attitude toward the court, and particularly his allegiance to principle of honor, becomes far less antagonistic and mocking. He treats the pompous Osric, for example, with amusement rather than, as with Polonius, open contempt, and he offers Laertes a deeply sincere apology, with full recognition of the demands of public honor. What emerges under the pressure of the political alternative represented by Fortinbras and his army is, in other words, a recuperative shift in sympathy in the direction of the Danish court and its aristocratic codes of conduct. It is the court, with its intimate scale and familial foundations, that offers the possibility for affective bonding so central to Branagh's vision of community, no matter how corrupt Claudius's court may have become.

If, as so many commentators have approvingly remarked, Branagh's inclusion of the Fortinbras plot allows him to address the wider political contexts of Hamlet's tragedy, the film's final images offer a deeply pessimistic disquisition on the possibility of cultural continuity within the politics of mass culture. The final image, of the statue of old Hamlet being toppled and broken up, alludes to a contemporary image of the end of a political era, the toppled statues of Lenin in the former Soviet Union. At first glance, this razed monument might seem to signify, as it has for at least one reviewer, "the perils of aristocratic and royal authority" and to celebrate "the plebeian forces that contest the ownership of power and privilege."[26] But considered within *Hamlet*'s crypto-Romanov design, that image takes on a far more ambivalent cast: the "plebeian forces" bring high culture low (literally) by obliterating that last remaining symbol of a lost familial social order and with it, the very name of Hamlet and, not incidentally, of Shakespeare's play. Those forces institute, as the Bolsheviks do in *Dr. Zhivago*, a gray tyranny far worse than the duplicitous aristocracy that precedes it, one that brings not a triumph of popular community but the fall of paternal icons and the utopian potential they signify. As the Brahmsian dirge during the credits makes clear, Branagh's emphasis ultimately falls on the tragic break in the cultural-political-patrilineal line and, insofar as we identify the monumental elder Hamlet with Shakespeare the cultural icon, on the irrecoverable loss of a romanticized cultural past to the brutality of mass modernity. But to lament that loss requires one to become nostalgic for the class-coded order that, however flawed, comes to offer the film's only attractive political alternative. That this nostalgia seems entirely at odds with Branagh's populism points, I think, to the difficulty of reconciling his utopian vision of the cultural politics of Shakespearean theater with the mass-market medium that purveys it.

As if unsatisfied with the (ir)resolution offered by his *Hamlet*, Branagh returns to the problem of community in the final moments of *Love's Labour's Lost*, structured in terms of not one but three signature shots of the ensemble. An uneasy marriage of thirties musical and wit-driven Shakespearean farce, analogously residual forms, the film seems deeply contradictory on the question of class, for it offers a fantasy of upper-class sophistication, all lightly ironized, while making the case that Shakespeare's play is really about rejecting Oxbridge stuffiness in favor of love. As in *Hamlet*, Branagh includes a set-piece that celebrates the camaraderie and faded glories of the stage–for the pageant of the Nine Worthies, he substitutes "There's No Business Like Show Business," at first performed by Nathan Lane as something of a wistful elegy for the film musical, and then rousingly by the full cast (leaving, strangely, no one except the filmgoer as an audience for the show). Once again, the question of large-scale political community is precipitated by a father's death, here the death of the French king, which bars the union of the royal lovers and, more important, ushers in global war, dispelling the apolitical romantic innocence—recreated from the musical—that so dominates the film's first half.

The pain of separation forms the backdrop for Branagh's second company shot, a group reprise of the end of *Casablanca* set to a melancholy rendition of "They Can't Take That away from Me." In both text and tone that musical selection neatly captures the final reel's mood of loss and nostalgia, the sense that the young lovers recognize the depth of their affections only under the threat of separation, and the gathering clouds of war broaden the film's concerns to include the potential loss of the nation and with it the cultural legacy to which the king and his men have putatively committed themselves. Though in keeping with Shakespeare's text the courts do part, "you this way, us that way," Branagh adds a coda in the form of a poignant wartime newsreel that recreates images of wartime solidarity and patriotic sacrifice. In it, Branagh recasts the purifying penance of the royals: it is to join the masses in the trenches, tending to the wounded (an allusion to Rosaline's exhortation to Berowne that he "visit the speechless sick and still converse / With groaning wretches"), handing out Red Cross packets, piloting a bomber, aiding the Resistance. (Again, the end of an earlier, more innocent political era is punctuated by a father's death, here Boyet, surrogate parent to the French entourage.)

As in *Henry V*, war briefly obscures all class distinctions and, so Branagh suggests with stock footage of cheering V day crowds, it also once created a fleeting sense of organic British community that could transcend cultural classes and extend to the entire nation. The film's final company shot, ostensibly a photo of the reunited lovers and their attendants taken by Constable Dull, implicitly connects that "remembered" sense of community to the film's cast and thus, at least in theory, to the present, by way of the Shakespeare/Hollywood hybrid the actors have just performed. Indeed, the image underlines the point by shifting from black-and-white "documentary" to technicolor "present" and by never quite settling into the lifelessness of a still from an irrecoverable past. This interpolated ending, one that takes the entire film (and play) in an unexpected direction, suggests how even in this, the most self-consciously frivolous and nostalgic of his film adaptations of Shakespeare, Branagh's commitment to his ideals for Shakespearean performance remain, albeit in what risks becoming a revisionary afterthought.

Branagh's historical importance to the current Shakespeare boom seems beyond debate, yet he remains a controversial figure, particularly among academic critics. For even as scholars have recognized his role in revitalizing film Shakespeare, they have by and large expressed reservations about his status as a genuine Shakespeare auteur. If the job of a Shakespeare auteur is to offer an original interpretive take on the plays, so the argument goes, Branagh's films lack a strong overarching directorial concept or have not carved out a distinctive place within a performance tradition. There is certainly some truth to the observations that elements of his productions have the quality of glossy pastiche, ideas and images cobbled together from other sources; that his films at times pursue sentimentality and poignance, that is, contrived emotional intensity, at the expense of thematic clarity or ideological coherence; that his putative position as member of an acting ensemble rests uneasily with his status as a director or entrepreneur; that his productions shy away from radical experiments in form and content; and that his Shakespearean pursuits might be read in terms of the psycho-dynamics of the colonized subject, as a more-British-than-thou self-efface-ment of his Irish identity. Yet the thread I have been tracing, Branagh's abiding concern with the political potential of a popularized Shakespeare, suggests that his work cannot easily be dismissed as *simply* reproducing a dominant cultural order, particularly since his films seek so insistently to part company with an institutionalized and arguably dominant mode of production for Shakespeare in performance.

Like so many documents of popular culture, Branagh's Shakespeare of-fers a cultural politics that is, particularly in his later films, maddeningly inconsistent and conflicted, an unstable mix of populist utopianism and reactionary nostalgia, institutional iconoclasm and mass-market commer-cialism. Yet the progressive elements of his vision offer a cultural-political potential and a critique of certain canons of Shakespearean "authenticity" that should not be underestimated. At the very least, the ideological cross-currents of his *Hamlet* illuminate the odd institutional space that recent Shakespeare film has sought to occupy and, more generally, the contradic-tions built into the current cultural fantasy of a popular Shakespeare, a fantasy at once dependent upon and distrustful of mass culture. Perhaps despite itself, his *Hamlet* poses not one but two questions foundational to contemporary efforts to popularize Shakespeare. It asks not just, as the opening Noel Coward song in *In the Bleak Midwinter* asks, "Why must the show go on?" but "How?"

NOTES

1. Kenneth Branagh, *Beginning* (New York: Norton, 1989), 197. All subsequent refer-ences to this work will be noted parenthetically in the text.

2. My use of the term "utopianism" draws upon Richard Dyer's discussion of the relationship between entertainment and inchoate political aspirations. Dyer observes that in response to specific social inadequacies entertainment—he is speaking specifically of the musical—does not present coherent political programs but rather operates "at the level of sensibility," expressing "alternatives, hopes,wishes . . . what utopia would feel like rather than how it would be organized" ("Entertainment and Utopia," in *Only Entertainment* [Lon-don and New York: Routledge, 1992], 18).

3. Kenneth Branagh, *Henry V. by William Shakespeare: A Screen Adaptation by Kenneth Branagh* (London: Chatto & Windus, 1989), 11.

4. Kenneth Branagh, *Hamlet, by William Shakespeare: Screenplay, Introduction, and Film Diary* (New York and London: W. W. Norton, 1996), xii.

5. Kenneth Branagh, *Much Ado about Nother: Screenplay, Introduction, and Notes on the Making of the Movie* (New York and London: W. W. Norton, 1993), viii.

6. Cary Mazer, "Great Dane," *City Paper*, January 1997, available at <http://www.citypaper.net/rad/articles/article009.html#story1>. In the same interview, Branagh notes that several scenes in his *Hamlet* were shot in one take. That choice, he observed, "puts some real flame under the actors. . . . It actually helped to create conditions, as I thought, that were conducive to bringing out that sort of extra under-the-skin kind of tingle that the audience can feel, I'm sure, *when it's happening right in front of you, and you don't know what's going to happen next*" (emphasis added).

7. Russell Jackson, "The Film Diary," in Branagh, *Hamlet*, 175–208.

8. Branagh, *Hamlet*, xv.

9. For a critique of the politics of this motif, see Don Hedrick, "War Is Mud: Branagh's Dirty Harry V and the Types of Political Ambiguity," in *Shakespeare, the Movie: Popularizing the Plays on Film, TV, and Video*, ed. Lynda E. Boose and Richard Burt (London and New York: Routledge, 1997). In this regard, Branagh's declaration as Henry that "I am Welsh" at the movie's climax gains resonance, for Henry's identification with the ethnically marked Fluellen becomes in Branagh's performance an affirmation of his transcultural aesthetic, the ability of Branagh to declare his ethnic difference *and* lay claim to Henry's (and Shakespeare's) quintessentially English cultural authority. As Courtney Lehmann suggests in her discussion of *Much Ado*, Branagh's insistence that actors perform Shakespeare in their own accents, leaving their national differences intact, is intended "as a personal act of reclamation for him," demonstrating his claim that Shakespeare is a potential source of multinational and popular, and not exclusively British upper-class, cultural capital ("*Much Ado about Nothing*? Shakespeare, Branagh, and the 'National-popular' in the Age of Multinational Capital," *Textual Practice* 12, no. 1 [1998]: 5).

10. Lehmann sets Branagh's desire to suspend ethnic, national, and class differences in his casting, to make Shakespeare available to all actors, against the ways in which Denzel Washington's casting as Don Pedro brings uncomfortable and unresolved issues of race into the production of *Much Ado* (see Lehmann, "*Much Ado*?," esp. 11–15). Lehmann critiques Branagh's utopian vision of "collective and social unity" throughout the film with great subtlety, setting it within the conceptual paradigms of multinational postmodern capitalism.

11. Alison Light, "The Importance of Being Ordinary," *Sight and Sound* 3, no. 9 (1993): 45. See also Branagh, *Much Ado*, xiii.

12. This thematic territory is also at the center of *Peter's Friends*, which Branagh directed in 1992 from a script by Martin Bergman and Rita Rudner. A British counterpart of *The Big Chill* (dir. Lawrence Kasdan, 1983), the film details the New Year's reunion of members of a Cambridge student revue troupe who, despite their seeming successes many years later, harbor a need for community and family, a need that takes the form of dysfunctional pairings and neurotic attachments to children, pets and, in Peter's case, his housekeeper. At film's end, the group rediscovers its emotional bonds when Peter, the host of this now disastrous reunion, announces that he is HIV-positive. Having recently lost his father and now without a family, Peter sees his fellow troupers as a surrogate and model for an organic social unit that can replace the familial attachments he now lacks, and that his fellow troupers equally turn out to need. In fact, Andrew (played by Branagh) drunkenly identifies Peter as a "savior" who will "send us out into the world on New Year's Day resurrected" (a quasi-sacramental allusion to which Branagh returned in *In the Bleak Midwinter*).

The production has a special metatheatrical meaning for those viewers who recognize that the film's cast reunites members of the Footlight *Cellar Tapes* company. As if to underline the point, the "Underground Song," which frames the film narrative self-consciously reprises a revue song first heard in Footlight's 1977 revue, and the film begins and ends with Branagh's signature shot, a long take in which all the members of the cast join in communal activity.

13.   Robert Smallwood, "Directors' Shakespeare," in *Shakespeare: An Illustrated Stage History*, ed. Jonathan Bate and Russell Jackson (Oxford: Oxford University Press, 1996), 177; see also Stanley Wells, "Directors' Shakespeare," *Shakespeare Jahrbuch* 113 (1976): 64–78. For a strong defense of the "conceptualizing director" that specifically targets Branagh's methods and philosophy, see Charles Marowitz, "Free Shakespeare! Jail Scholars!" in *Recycling Shakespeare* (New York: Applause Books, 1991), 53–68.

14.   Peter Womack, "Post-War Theatre and the State," in *English Drama: A Cultural History*, eds. Simon Shepherd and Peter Womack (New York: Blackwell, 1996), 310. Womack's observation helps clarify the larger ideological context for Branagh's assertion that "greater quality can mean greater accessibility" (*Beginning* 46). For a specific account of the RSC from this perspective, see Alan Sinfield, "Royal Shakespeare: Theatre and the Making of Ideology," in *Political Shakespeare: New Essays in Cultural Materialism*, ed. Jonathan Dollimore and Alan Sinfield (Ithaca: Cornell University Press, 1985), 158–81.

15.   Sinfield, "Royal Shakespeare," 164–72. The RSC has recently acknowledged the danger of its becoming mere "heritage" theater. With its move away from the Barbican for the summer tourist season to venues in Plymouth and Newcastle, the RSC has sought to forge bonds with a much wider public; company publicity characterizes the change as a means to put 75 percent of the British population within forty-five minutes of an RSC production in the course of a year.

16.   Kenneth Branagh, *A Midwinter's Tale: The Shooting Script* (New York: Newmarket Press, 1995), 30. All subsequent citations from this filmscript will be cited parenthetically. For an extensive analysis of the thematic oppositions in *A Midwinter's Tale*, as well as the *Star Wars* subtext and its relationship to Branagh's own conflict of theater versus film, see Courtney Lehmann, "Shakespeare: The Savior or Phantom Menace? Kenneth Branagh's *Midwinter's Tale* and the Critique of Cynical Reason," *Colby Quarterly* (forthcoming).

17.   Branagh goes out of his way to develop analogues between camp subculture and his conception of a theatrical community. The link is first signaled with Joe's ad for his "profit-share, spirit-share" production, misprinted in the *Theatre Weekly*: instead of reading "six fellow journeymen to enter the world of the gloomy dane," it reads "six fellow journeymen to enter the gloomy dane," at which Margaretta sardonically observes, "Great darling. Expect a lot of new-age gays looking for a workout" (5). When Henry first discovers Terry's homosexuality, he complains with disgust that "the entire British Theatre's dominated by the class system and a bunch of Oxford homos" (24). Soon, however, he comes to appreciate (and even adopt) Terry's campy sensibility.

18.   Characteristically, Branagh stresses how the circumstances of the shoestring film production mirrored those of the theatrical production within the film:

> It was the cumulative experience of this group that informed and changed the script...The film was made in the spirit of the story. Everyone—actors and crew—received the same initial payment, and everyone who worked throughout the shoot received a profit participation. The very fact of this affected the tone of the final movie. The spirit of generous collaboration...made for a shoot...which, as Hamlet would say, held "the mirror up to nature."(Branagh, *Midwinter's*, vi)

19.   Quoted in Robert Hapgood, ed., *Hamlet, Prince of Denmark*, Shakespeare in Production Series (Cambridge: Cambridge University Press, 1999), 93.

20.   Samuel Crowl, "Hamlet," *Shakespeare Bulletin* 15 (1997): 34. Gail Paster notes

that among the many visual reminders of *Zhivago* is the casting of Julie Christie—she played Lara in *Zhivago*, Gertrude in *Hamlet*; see John F. Andrews, "Kenneth Branagh's *Hamlet* Launched at National Air and Space Museum," *Shakespeare Newsletter* 46, no. 3 (1996): 1. By making *Hamlet*'s production values so very grand and panoramic (nearly every reviewer singled out the film's incredible splendor for praise), Branagh self-consciously sets himself within the legacy of epic British filmmaking last practiced by David Lean, also the last British filmmaker before Branagh to use 70mm cinematography. That tradition carries with it a nostalgia for the age of empire that becomes, I think, rather more ambivalent in Branagh's hands.

21. Branagh, *Hamlet, by William Shakespeare: Screenplay*, 12. Quotations from *Hamlet* are taken from Branagh's screenplay, which uses an emandated version of the Oxford Edition of the *Complete Works*, ed. Stanley Wells and Gary Taylor, 1988. All subsequent references to this work will be noted parenthetically.

22. See Richard Alleva, "A Sixteen-Wheeler: Branagh's 'Hamlet,'" *Commonweal*, 28 March 1997, 18–19.

23. Lisa S. Starks traces how these three *Hamlet* films engage the oedipal subtext (and differentiate themselves) in "The Displaced Body of Desire: Sexuality in Kenneth Branagh's *Hamlet*," in *Shakespeare and Appropriation*, ed. Christy Desmet and Robert Sawyer (London and New York: Routledge, 1999), 160–78. Starks emphasizes that in Branagh's film it is the usurping figurative "son," Fortinbras, who "inherits" the paternal legacy. The consequences of Branagh's counter-oedipalism is searchingly critiqued in Courtney Lehmann and Lisa S. Starks's "Making Mother Matter: Repression, Revision, and the Stakes of 'Reading Psychoanalysis into' Kenneth Branagh's *Hamlet*," *Early Modern Literary Studies* 6, no. 1 (May 2000): 2.1–24 <URL: http://purl.oclc.org/emls/06-1/lehmham1.htm>. Lehmann and Starks stress the relationship between paternal filiation in his *Hamlet* and Branagh's oedipal relationship to theatrical predecessors in the role, particularly to Derek Jacobi; they read Jacobi's passing Forbes Robertson's copy of Hamlet, for example, as a codification of Branagh's status as a British theatrical "peer." For me, the theme of paternal filiation resonates just as powerfully with Branagh's concern about how the cultural authority of Shakespeare—as theatrical monument, as primal father—can be carried into a mass-cultural age. That cultural authority finds its visual equivalents in the film's images of the elder Hamlet, as a towering Colossus come to life and ultimately destroyed, in the "remember me" scene as a giant mouth in closeup (that is, voice itself), in the closet scene as a pitiable fading ghost. In the final film's final images, Branagh stresses not continuity but the potential break in the cultural-political-patrilineal line and thereby the fragility of the Name-of-the-Father that the film–and Branagh's performance as lamenting son–seeks to honor. The paradox is that the potential for loss becomes precisely what gives Branagh's company ideal such urgency and Shakespeare such cultural power.

24. See Russell Jackson's discussion of the conception of the players in "The Film Diary" in Branagh, *Hamlet,* 181. Of particular interest is the impulse to concoct metatheatrical parallels: "We imagine that the actor who plays the poisoner fancies himself as an innovator and may have an eye on the Hamilton troupe for himself" (181). It is equally noteworthy that filming began with the long tracking shot of Hamlet instructing the players (182).

25. Crowl, "Hamlet," 34. See also Robert F. Willson, Jr., "Kenneth Branagh's *Hamlet*, or the Revenge of Fortinbras," *Shakespeare Newsletter* 47, no. 1 (1997): 7, and H. R. Coursen, "Words, words, words: Searching for *Hamlet*" (paper presented at the annual meeting of the Shakespeare Association of America, Washington, D.C., April 1997), 2.

26. Mark Thornton Burnett, "The 'Very Cunning of the Scene': Kenneth Branagh's *Hamlet*," *Film-Literature Quarterly* 25, no. 2 (1997): 82.

Works Cited

Alleva, Richard. "A Sixteen-Wheeler: Branagh's 'Hamlet.'" *Commonweal*, 28 March 1997, 18–9.

Andrews, John F. "Kenneth Branagh's *Hamlet* Launched at National Air and Space Museum." *Shakespeare Newsletter* 46, no. 3 (1996): 1, 62, 66.

Branagh, Kenneth. *Beginning*. New York and London: W. W. Norton, 1989.

———. *Hamlet, by William Shakespeare: Screenplay, Introduction, and Film Diary*. New York and London: W. W. Norton, 1996.

———. *Henry V by William Shakespeare: A Screen Adaptation by Kenneth Branagh*. London: Chatto & Windus, 1989.

———. *A Midwinter's Tale: The Shooting Script*. New York: Newmarket Press, 1995.

———. *Much Ado about Nothing: Screenplay, Introduction, and Notes on the Making of the Movie*. New York and London: W. W. Norton, 1993.

Burnett, Mark Thornton. "The 'Very Cunning of the Scene': Kenneth Branagh's *Hamlet*." *Film-Literature Quarterly* 25, no. 2 (1997): 78–82.

Coursen, H. R. "Words, words, words: Searching for *Hamlet*." Paper presented at the annual meeting of the Shakespeare Association of America, Washington, D.C., April 1997.

Crowl, Samuel. "Hamlet." *Shakespeare Bulletin* 15, no. 1 (1997): 34–35.

Dyer, Richard. "Entertainment and Utopia." In *Only Entertainment*. London and New York: Routledge, 1992.

Hapgood, Robert, ed. *Hamlet Prince of Denmark*. Shakespeare in Production Series. Cambridge: Cambridge University Press, 1999.

Hedrick, Don. "War Is Mud: Branagh's Dirty Harry V and the Types of Political Ambiguity." In *Shakespeare, the Movie: Popularizing the Plays on Film, TV, and Video*. Edited by Lynda E. Boose and Richard Burt. London and New York: Routledge, 1997.

Lehmann, Courtney. "*Much Ado about Nothing*? Shakespeare, Branagh, and the 'National-popular' in the Age of Multinational Capital." *Textual Practice* 12, no. 1 (1998): 1–22.

———. "Shakespeare: The Savior or Phantom Menace? Kenneth Branagh's *Midwinter's Tale* and the Critique of Cynical Reason." *Colby Quarterly*. Forthcoming.

Lehmann, Courtney, and Lisa S. Starks. "Making Mother Matter: Repression, Revision, and the Stakes of 'Reading Psychoanalysis into' Kenneth Branagh's *Hamlet*." *Early Modern Literary Studies* 6, no. 1 (May 2000): 2.1–24 <URL: http://purl.oclc.org/emls/06-1/lehmham1.htm>.

Light, Alison. "The Importance of Being Ordinary." *Sight and Sound* 3, no. 9 (1993): 45.

Marowitz, Charles. "Free Shakespeare! Jail Scholars!" In *Recycling Shakespeare*. New York: Applause Books, 1991.

Mazer, Cary. "Great Dane." *Philadelphia City Paper*. January 1997. <URL: http://www.citypaper.net/articles/012397/article011.shtml>.

Sinfield, Alan. "Royal Shakespeare: Theatre and the Making of Ideology." In *Political Shakespeare: New Essays in Cultural Materialism*. Edited by Jonathan Dollimore and Alan Sinfield. Ithaca: Cornell University Press, 1985.

Smallwood, Robert. "Directors' Shakespeare." In *Shakespeare: An Illustrated Stage History*. Edited by Jonathan Bate and Russell Jackson. Oxford: Oxford University Press, 1996.

Starks, Lisa S. "The Displaced Body of Desire: Sexuality in Kenneth Branagh's *Hamlet*." In *Shakespeare and Appropriation*. Edited by Christy Desmet and Robert Sawyer. London and New York: Routledge, 1999.

Wells, Stanley. "Directors' Shakespeare." *Shakespeare Jahrbuch* 113 (1976): 64–78.

Willson, Robert F., Jr. "Kenneth Branagh's *Hamlet*, or the Revenge of Fortinbras." *Shakespeare Newsletter* 47, no. 1 (1997): 7, 9.

Womack, Peter. "Post-War Theatre and the State." In *English Drama: A Cultural History*. Edited by Simon Shepherd and Peter Womack. New York: Blackwell, 1996.

FILMS CITED

Hamlet. Directed by Kenneth Branagh. 3 hr. 58 min. Castle Rock Entertainment, 1997. Laserdisc.

Henry V. Directed by Kenneth Branagh. 2 hr. 28 min. Renaissance Films and BBC, 1989. Laserdisc.

Love's Labour's Lost. Directed by Kenneth Branagh. 1 hr. 33 min. Shakespeare Film Company and Miramax Entertainment, 2000. 35 mm.

A Midwinter's Tale. Directed by Kenneth Branagh. 1 hr. 39 min. Castle Rock Entertainment and Midwinter Films, 1995. Laserdisc.

Much Ado about Nothing. Directed by Kenneth Branagh. 1 hr. 51 min. Renaissance Films and Samuel Goldwyn, 1993. DVD.

Peter's Friends. Directed by Kenneth Branagh. 1 hr. 41 min. Renaissance Films and Samuel Goldwyn, 1992. Videocassette.

Swan Song. Directed by Kenneth Branagh. 23 min. Samuel Goldwyn, 1992. Videocassette.

From the Cinema to the Classroom:
Hollywood Teaches *Hamlet*

Elizabeth A. Deitchman

THE TWENTIETH CENTURY HAS COME TO AN END, YET SHAKESPEARE'S PLACE IN contemporary culture continues to seem divided. On the one hand, nearly four hundred years after audiences first heard Othello assert "I have done the state some service, and they know't,"[1] Shakespeare himself has long been drafted into service for the state on behalf of worldwide boards of education. Indeed, Shakespeare has come a long way from the early modern Globe and Blackfriars Theatres into postmodern high school and university classrooms. For as Gary Taylor claims:

> In our society Shakespeare has become the subject, in most schools and universities, of "required courses"; for almost a century now, students have been compelled to study him, as they were once compelled to study Greek and Latin. The badge of cultural elitism and the instrument of pedagogical oppression, Shakespeare now finds himself needing to be constantly justified against the determined boredom, the soaking resentment, of conscripts. Captivated audiences have become captive classrooms.[2]

On the other hand, Shakespeare's place in popular culture continues to expand. In an early episode of NBC's television situation-comedy *Third Rock from the Sun*, for example, Hamlet's most famous soliloquy was attributed not to Shakespeare's most famous play but to "some Mel Gibson movie," an allusion to Franco Zeffirelli's 1990 film starring Mel Gibson as the melancholy Dane. If we understand the premise of this television program—a superior (in other words, more technologically advanced) yet constantly confused group of alien explorers comes to Earth to study its life-forms—this joke serves as a cultural commentary about the results of Shakespeare's continuing and expanding popularity among filmmakers, actors, and audiences. In this particular episode, the aliens confront Death. Hoping to shed some light on the subject, one of the aliens, called Harry, recites part of Hamlet's "to be or not to be" soliloquy.[3] Because Harry, the most awkward member of the group, assures his sister that he is repeating lines from a Mel Gibson film and not from a canonical literary work, the audience can understand his otherwise unbelievable ability to quote Shakespeare. The cultural commentary embedded in the joke suggests that for the alien with little education, high culture "literary" Shakespeare can be alienating indeed; but when mediated through Gibson, this same text becomes accessible even to an alien without a high school diploma.

In fact, "some Mel Gibson movie" is not an entirely false answer to an alien's question about authorship. For during the twentieth century's final decade, Shakespeare had incredible box office success. By the time the century ended, we had seen no fewer than ten Shakespeare films—not including the films related to Shakespeare and his plays. Indeed, Taylor also acknowledges this success, claiming that "Shakespeare has to make it in the movies . . . or he's not going to make it."[4] But what happens to Shakespeare when he is removed from the classroom and brought to the cinema? Does Hollywood teach Shakespeare any more effectively than high school teachers and university professors? In order to answer these questions, I shall examine one film's impact on the American imagination of a Shakespeare beyond the classroom.

In 1991 Franco Zeffirelli's *Hamlet* offered yet another reinvention of the melancholy Prince of Denmark. Through Mel Gibson, famous as Mad Max and Martin Riggs, two characters unafraid of actively seeking revenge, Hollywood treated audiences to an action-hero Hamlet. Appropriately, Zeffirelli's carefully crafted film omits most of the references to Hamlet's inaction. Gone, for example, are the Fortinbras subplot and the player's speech about Priam and Hecuba in which we get an image of Hamlet's own frozen action resumed and accomplished. Three Hollywood films made after Zeffirelli's *Hamlet* offer evidence of how this new incarnation of Shakespeare's most famous character has entered into the modern American imagination. Both *The Last Action Hero* (dir. John McTiernan, 1993) and *Renaissance Man* (dir. Penny Marshall, 1994) take on *Hamlet* in classroom settings and both films teach an action-hero version of the play. *Clueless* (dir. Amy Heckerling, 1995) offers Mel Gibson's *Hamlet* as part of Heckerling's extensive commentary on elite versus popular culture, which also acts as a captivating exploration of Shakespeare's place in contemporary education.

Danny, the youthful hero of John McTiernan's *The Last Action Hero*, is exposed to *Hamlet* in the classroom—a typical setting for an American interaction with a classic text. In his teacher's attempts to contextualize both Shakespeare's and Olivier's 1948 film version of *Hamlet*, the filmmakers reveal just how far removed these *Hamlet*s are from Danny's (and his peers') experience. Indeed, Danny prefers action films starring a stock action-adventure character played by Arnold Schwarzenegger. The film's audience should not be surprised, then, that Danny's preference for swift action and violence affects his engagement with Olivier's *Hamlet*. Zeffirelli's influence on McTiernan's *Hamlet* parody becomes apparent during Danny's interaction with Olivier's film.

We watch, with Danny and his classmates, a scene from Olivier's *Hamlet*, which has also been carefully crafted in the Zeffirelli film: Hamlet eavesdropping while Claudius attempts to pray. As Danny observes Claudius praying and Hamlet contemplating his moment for revenge, the camera juxtaposes the two figures of Danny and Olivier / Hamlet. We see Danny tense as he expects the action that Hamlet actually arrests with thought. When the action does not happen immediately—when Hamlet does not behave according to the standards of the action-hero—Danny refashions the film in his imagination, turning the black and white "classic" into a film-trailer advertising an action-figure Hamlet starring, of course, Schwarzenegger himself. Danny transforms the thoughtful Dane into a gun-toting hero who decides that Claudius is "not to be." Furthermore, Danny's audience learns through the voice-over in Danny's imagination that "Something is rotten in the state of Denmark, and Hamlet is taking out the trash."[5] This Hamlet gets the job done. In the end, however, so does Shakespeare's, and perhaps with just as much violence as any one of Arnie's usual characters. But in Shakespeare's play we have to wait.

In Shakespeare's play, Hamlet's hesitation in the church has a purpose; he wants to be sure that Claudius suffers for his sins. Shakespeare shares the moment's irony with the play's audience by making us privy to Claudius's confession that his prayers have failed. This irony, however, causes a significant difficulty for a filmmaker attempting to fashion an action-hero Hamlet. Indeed Zeffirelli makes Hamlet's inaction while Claudius prays acceptable to an audience more familiar with Mel Gibson's usual roles by removing the irony of the inaction: Claudius never indicates that his repentance is sincere, thus leaving him in a state of sin, fit only for hell. In *The Last Action Hero*, neither the film's audience nor Danny sees the scene's conclusion because in Danny's impatience for action, he loses interest in Olivier as soon as Hamlet's thoughts stop his dagger in mid-air.

Danny rewrites *Hamlet* according to his own impatience with Hamlet's inaction, perhaps representative of twentieth-century audiences accustomed to Schwarzenegger, Sylvester Stallone, and Gibson as actors playing men who act before they think. In fact, Gibson's Hamlet certainly spends less time thinking and talking than Shakespeare's Hamlet. But Danny seems to be doing more than just rewriting *Hamlet* according to his own expectations. He releases himself from what Taylor calls the "captive classroom" by turning himself into a "captivated audience." Danny may be "compelled" to study Shakespeare, but he escapes the "determined boredom" through several layers of Hollywood's influence.

Danny's fantasy version of *Hamlet* ends with an explosion when Hamlet destroys Elsinore in a storm of fire power. That shot then fades from the exploding castle into a Road Runner cartoon—from black and white to animated Technicolor violence. This new focus links Shakespeare with celebrity figures who may be more familiar to children (perhaps also to some adults) than are Arnie or Mel—Wile E Coyote and the Road Runner. Unlike most of *Hamlet*'s cast, this animated coyote survives from cartoon to cartoon in spite of several violent ends resulting from his basic ineptitude with explosives and other weapons. Schwarzenegger ruthlessly performs Hamlet's revenge by blowing up Elsinore. The coyote's survival of a similar explosion suggests that he will be back another day. This suggestion, that like the coyote and the Terminator, Hamlet will be back, echoes Barbara Hodgdon's reaction to Gibson's Hamlet's death:

> In spite of knowing that Hamlet *must* die, I feel an extra added shock because it is Mel Gibson who seems so surprised. When, in the film's last shot, the camera booms up, isolating Hamlet and Horatio together, surrounded (at a distance) by stunned courtiers, I experience a distinctly visceral loss. For I had thought that nothing bad could happen to a body so perfectly formed, so transparently whole. Although I know full well that *Hamlet* is merely a classical arabesque between *Lethal Weapon 2* and *Lethal Weapon 3*, . . . I am obsessed enough with this loss that I want to replace that last image with one from *Lethal Weapon 2*—aptly enough, a similar image, in which Gibson's Martin Riggs, badly wounded, is urged to live by his partner, Roger Murtaugh.[6]

And of course, Riggs lives not only for *Lethal Weapon 3*, but into *Lethal Weapon 4*. Zeffirelli may have allowed his Hollywood-icon Hamlet to die, but Danny won't do the same.

In *The Last Action Hero*, Hamlet becomes a man of action; in *Renaissance Man*, *Hamlet* is used to make men (and one woman) of action. Penny Marshall's film exploits several issues that grow out of Shakespeare's role in contemporary society: the suitability of Shakespeare as a subject for students of below-average abilities, the place of Shakespeare in "practical" matters, and the appropriation of Shakespeare by disempowered members of a society. Furthermore, the audience learns a lesson about the play through the film's use of *Hamlet* as "the perfect force for transforming wimps and misfit soldiers into the STRAK army company that concludes *Renaissance Man*."[7] Like Danny and his classmates, Bill Rago's (Danny DeVito) army recruit students encounter Shakespeare in a classroom. Instead of allowing Bill's students to refashion *Hamlet* for themselves, however, *Renaissance Man* presents *Hamlet* for the students as another victory tower like the structure used in training to improve physical fitness and self-confidence. And if Mel Gibson can act Hamlet, then United States soldiers can certainly understand him.

After advertising executive Bill Rago, a Princeton graduate, loses his job, he finds himself in a classroom on an army base, hired to teach a group of soldiers nicknamed the "double ds" (dumb-as-dog-shit). His teaching is designed to supplement their physical training, eventually making them better soldiers. But the disparity between Bill's and his students' education becomes immediately apparent. While Bill has a master's degree from Princeton (although we never learn in what subject), marking him as privileged in spite of his recent unemployment, his students are seven young men and one woman from underprivileged, unstable, and often unhappy homes. These underprivileged soldiers also represent the underclass in America: the majority of Bill's students are black; the white students are Southerners from trailer parks and broken homes. In the army, however, Bill's Princeton education seems to guarantee derision. For when the soldiers learn that he is a civilian, they accord him little respect. Eventually Shakespeare becomes the surprising tool that Bill uses to reach his students across their educational differences.

Hamlet makes its first appearance in the film when one of Bill's students asks what he is reading during their in-class reading time. The book he holds is impressive—in both its size and apparent age. Bill answers "*Hamlet*" and to their questions about its worth adds that it "pretty much beats the heck out of any book ever written,"[8] establishing the underlying assumption of the film—that *Hamlet* (as a work by Shakespeare) must be revered. Bill is reluctant to share his reading because he knows that when his students first encounter Shakespeare it may be too daunting for a class of soldiers who cannot identify a simile or metaphor. As he explains the story, however, he piques their interest with a Cliffs Notes version of *Hamlet*. As Bill continues to relate the plot, the soldiers immediately put the story into terms they understand: Hamlet's university education makes him a "rich kid"; Gertrude's marriage to Claudius mirrors the experience of one of the soldiers whose father left his mother to marry her sister. At the level of plot, at least, Marshall seems to demonstrate that while Bill's task remains daunting, these soldiers are indeed capable of handling Shakespeare. But so far they are only capable of handling Shakespeare's story.

Because the sketchy education that shaped his students is so alien to Bill's own academic experience, he is even more reluctant to share Shakespeare's words with the class. Nevertheless, his students persuade him to read something to them:

> Good Hamlet, cast thy nighted color off,
> And let thine eye look like a friend on Denmark.
> Do not for ever with thy vailed lids
> Seek for thy noble father in the dust.
> (*Hamlet*, 1.2.68–71)

Not only do the "double ds" lack a vocabulary for understanding Shakespeare's use of language and imagery, but Bill lacks a means for communicating these linguistic concepts to his students. They will not let him get away with simple answers, however. To his explanation of Gertrude's interaction with her son—"it just sounds better, that's why"—they respond, "C'mon, teach, teach us." So he begins with simile, metaphor, and oxymoron. Thus we watch Bill's first lesson in communicating with his students on their terms as he uses images they can understand to explain these rhetorical tools. Bill finally makes his point by using images from a farm setting to explain simile ("like a rooster with an itch") or popular culture to explain oxymoron ("girly man" from a *Saturday Night Live* comedy sketch). Bill successfully learns that he must find a common language in order to communicate the different kind of language the students will find in the play. At the end of the class, the audience realizes that this class is the first successful teaching experience that Bill has so far had with these students— because of *Hamlet*.

Marshall carefully constructs this success, however. The material the students choose to read as the scene begins instantiates the educational disparity between teacher and students. For Marshall juxtaposes *Hamlet* with comic books and *Sports Illustrated*. These cultural comparisons are hardly subtle. Instead, the audience cannot help but realize the distance between the literature accessible through a Princeton education and the comic books chosen by the "double ds." Even the materiality of the book housing *Hamlet* further demonstrates this disparity: Bill holds a large, aged, and most likely expensive volume while his students read from thin, cheap magazines. The audience must recognize the gap between students and teacher in order to understand how the filmmaker constructs Shakespeare's educational efficacy. Widening this gap, Marshall attempts to make the "double ds" eventual "success" that much more poignant.

Contemporary popular culture appropriates Shakespeare in the "double ds"'s own version of the play. In one of the most significant scenes in the film—significant because it underlines the students' understanding of the play—Bill arrives at the classroom to find it cleared of the desks and the soldiers engaged in a rap song that they have made from the play. In a moment reminiscent of Danny's interaction with *Hamlet*, Bill's captive classroom turns their teacher into a captivated audience. In fact, for the rap version of *Hamlet*, Bill's class uses the nickname given to them by the other soldiers as a means of empowerment—they are the "double d mc" now with their own verbal eloquence as the song's refrain suggests: "to be or not to be, the double d mc are letting it be." Though the students make their own meaning from Shakespeare's play, the song they create is based not upon the play, but upon the play as translated to them by their teacher. Whether or not the film's audience makes this distinction depends upon their own level of familiarity with the play. The audience of *Renaissance Man* is not expected to understand *Hamlet* as more than a means to an end—another challenge to be met by the men and women of the United States Army—whose motto is "be all that you can be." For Hamlet's question "to be or not to be"—which Schwarzenegger answers "not to be"—the army does not even offer the option not to be. In fact, the double d mc only *think* they are "letting it be."

The final exam provides the soldiers' final hurdle. The soldiers can choose to take the test, but if they fail, they will be out of the army. In typical feel-good fashion, of course, they all pass the exam—with one soldier remarking that at the end of *Hamlet*, in addition to silence, "all we got left is two guys: a soldier and a student." Furthermore, to underline this revelation, the scene is accompanied by the military marches usually reserved for the physical training scenes. The audience leaves with the impression that the soldiers are also meant to be scholars. With the successful graduation of the "double ds," we get the message that they have conquered Shakespeare and are now fit for the military. They, like Mel Gibson and Arnold Schwarzenegger, are action heroes through *Hamlet*.

But the film's heavily sentimentalized conclusion, which suggests that Shakespeare is accessible to all with hard work and proper training, masks the real outcome of the "double ds'" encounter with Shakespeare. Though the film attempts to demonstrate twentieth-century American notions of democratization—in spite of racial, class, and educational differences, Shakespeare becomes the property of these eight soldiers—the soldiers never really learn Shakespeare. For most of the film, we see their teacher reading Shakespeare to them; and instead of developing a sophisticated understanding of the play, they merely establish identifications with specific characters and their situations. Much like Hamlet and *Hamlet* are refashioned in other films to meet our needs in the twentieth century, so is the process of educating with Shakespeare as the primary tool. The soldiers understand a Shakespeare only as he fits into their own experiences—as Danny replaces Laurence Olivier with Arnold Schwarzenegger. In the end, they are soldiers who know the *story* of Hamlet, the Prince of Denmark, not the Renaissance men (and woman) the film title suggests.

Then to whom does the film's title refer? Of course, there are several meanings embedded within the film's name. Bill is one of the possibilities as he experiences his own rebirth during the course of his teaching duties; the selfish man who loses his job and then unwillingly accepts a teaching position gradually exhibits evidence of softening and becoming more of a humanist by the end of the film. His name is also an obvious reference to Shakespeare. Hamlet and Shakespeare are also Renaissance men, and there is Leon Battista Alberti, the fifteenth-century architect whom Bill describes to one of his students. But the film's primary message is that anyone can be a Renaissance man (or woman) if he or she simply works hard enough—climb the victory tower and read William Shakespeare's *Hamlet* and you yourself join the ranks of the educated and cultured or in this case, the United States Army.

I certainly do not condemn the work ethic suggested by the film—indeed, the notion that, through hard work, anyone can succeed is the cornerstone of American ideology. Instead, the film's ultimate failure lies in Marshall's attempt to exploit Shakespeare's cultural hegemony without challenging it. In spite of the students' initial challenge to Bill's authority because he is a civilian, none of Bill's students even suggests a challenge to Bill's insistence that *Hamlet* "beats the heck out of any book ever written." Furthermore, comparing the authority of the United States Army to that of the Western Canon suggests the same fantasy that yokes soldiers and scholars together. Good soldiers cannot be good scholars because they cannot challenge the authority of their teachers. And Bill was hired to make soldiers, not scholars—men whose actions are often more important than their thoughts.

As he was in *Third Rock from the Sun,* Mel Gibson is the explicit source for the "Shakespeare moment"[9] in Amy Heckerling's *Clueless,* a twentieth-century adaptation of Jane Austen's *Emma*. Although high school provides one important setting for this film, Shakespeare's appearances come to the audience mediated through texts other than his "own." In the characters' frequent mixture of high and popular culture icons lies evidence that Heckerling's film serves to comment extensively on that binary whose interstices often serve as a battleground for Shakespearean appropriation. Furthermore, the film provides a useful exploration of Shakespeare's place in contemporary education. Before turning to Shakespeare's role in the film, however, I shall take a closer look at the film's heroine, Cher Horowitz.

A Beverly Hills teenager, Cher is the most popular girl in her high school, home to students named after pop culture icons like Dionne Warwick, Elton John, and of course, Cher. Cher, while stereotypically self-involved, does not spend all her time worrying about her own hair, clothes, and makeup. In one scene, for example, we are treated to her notion of a makeover in which she undertakes the full improvement of her friend Tai, the new girl in school—an endeavor which prompts Cher's best friend, Dionne, to warn her that their "stock will plummet"[10] if they invest their time and energy in Tai. Cher focuses first on Tai's outward appearance but also concerns herself with Tai's speech, acting as a Beverly Hills Henry Higgins, saying, "We've got to work on your accent and vocabulary." In fact, Cher and her friends use a surprisingly impressive vocabulary. For example, she realizes her step-brother Josh has arrived home because she hears what she refers to as "the maudlin music of the university [radio] station," and after an unsuccessful attempt to seduce her gay friend Christian, she describes herself as "capricious" in her decision to lose her virginity. Dionne berates Josh for subjecting Cher to his "post-adolescent idealistic phase." Even Tai observes that Cher and her friends "talk like grownups." As an explanation for this phenomenon, Dionne offers, "This is a really good school." But in this film, school itself has little to do with their cultural and linguistic acumen.

A related part of Cher's program for self-improvement involves reading one "non-schoolbook" a week. Cher chooses to read *Fit or Fat* while Tai decides to read (as she says with the sort of reverence usually reserved for traditional canonical texts) *Men Are from Mars, Women Are from Venus*. Although Cher's suggestion that she and Tai will improve their minds via reading certainly tallies with high culture ideas of refinement, Cher unconsciously mocks this authority with her choice of reading material. Both books have certainly sold well, speaking to the late twentieth-century obsession with self-help books, but neither would find a place in Harold Bloom's Western Canon.

Cher's cultural capital, however, does not end with her notions of self-improvement through "literature." She also exhibits her exposure to the art world as she incorporates painters into her points of reference and her repertoire of insults. While photographing Tai as part of a plot to match her with Elton, one of their classmates, Cher flatteringly compares Tai to "one of those Botticelli chicks." Later, when reassuring Tai that Elton's new girlfriend, Amber, is not as pretty as Tai, Cher calls the girl in question "a full-on Monet." Tai, the "uneducated" friend needs an explanation: Amber looks good from a distance but up-close she is a "total mess." Here, Cher demonstrates her ability to assimilate the usually elite cultural symbols into her own experience. So far, however, Cher does not misappropriate. "Botticelli chicks" and a "full-on Monet" still refer directly to their points of origin— the painters who created a specific type of woman or style of painting. Although Cher makes no reference to her source for these comparisons— we do not know, for instance, if she is aware of each painter's specific biography or paintings—Cher's familiarity with their work becomes quite clear.

Finally, in another matchmaking effort, the subjects of which are two teachers in Cher's school, Shakespeare seems to appear for the first time in the film. Cher uses lines from Shakespeare's Sonnet Eighteen as the text of an anonymous love note she plants to begin her matchmaking process, which is actually part of a bid to renegotiate her grades. Dionne reads over Cher's shoulder, "Rough winds do shake the darling buds of May, / But thy eternal summer shall not fade." Shakespeare's identity, however, remains hidden in the exchange which follows:

Dionne. Phat. Did you write that?!
Cher. Duh. It's like a famous quote.

Dionne. From where?
Cher. Cliffs Notes.

We have no evidence that Cher recognizes Shakespeare as the author/poet, but we see the fame she attributes to these words. Cher does, however, attribute cultural authority to that pedagogical nightmare, Cliffs Notes, a study guide meant to help high school students understand "great litera-ture" but more often serving as their only exposure to the literature in ques-tion. Cher actually and unwittingly undermines the cultural authority usually reserved for Shakespeare by suggesting that Cliffs Notes are the original source for this "like . . . famous quote."

Students use Cliffs Notes because they are under the mistaken impres-sion that reading only a plot summary and accompanying simplistic com-mentary will save them time and effort. Just as Danny did not have the patience to wait for the end of the play to insert violence, Cher obviously did not read the sonnets for their own sake because Cliffs Notes presents the sonnets as the subject for an examination. Yet, Cher's use of the sonnet in the anonymous love note demonstrates an instinctive knowledge of a value—in this case, to woo a woman—beyond the examination process. Indeed, if a piece of text has made it into Cliffs Notes, it must be "good" because why else would students be expected to learn it? Cher's reliance on Cliffs Notes also points to the teachers' role in this film. For these teach-ers in Cher's school are portrayed as "clueless," almost secondary to the children's education. In many of the film's scenes, we hear a teacher lectur-ing underneath a voice-over in which Cher relays information important to the plot's development—details of her life that take precedence over what-ever material the teacher attempts to transmit. Nor are we to take the teach-ers seriously as authority figures, for we often see the students speaking on cell phones and searching for missing CDs during the class period without any interference from the teacher. Perhaps most disturbing to the modern educator, we see Cher and her father (a high-profile attorney) take pride in her ability to negotiate and manipulate her grades—based purely upon her power of persuasion. Indeed, these teachers are not actually useful as trans-mitters of information. Instead, they have been replaced by Cliffs Notes and, as we shall see, Mel Gibson's film career.

It should not be surprising, then, that Cher has found a means to incor-porate *Hamlet* into her own cultural vocabulary. In an exchange with her stepbrother's girlfriend concerning who in *Hamlet* actually says "To thine own self be true" (*Hamlet,* 1.3.78), Cher correctly identifies the speaker as "that Polonius guy." Cher's identification is accurate not because she has read the play but because, like Harry on *Third Rock from the Sun*, she has seen the film starring Mel Gibson.[11] The girlfriend, Heather, invokes *Ham-let* as a literary text to support her beliefs during an argument about a particular professor's teaching style. But Shakespeare actually does not appear in this moment—even in Heather's confidence that she knows *Hamlet*. If Heather really did know *Hamlet*, she would know that "To thine own self be true" is an ironic piece of advice because it is spoken by Polonius. Yet she takes these words out of context and tries to use them as a part of her argument. Cher corrects Heather not because she realizes that Heather's misappropriation of the text undermines her argument, but because Cher knows that Mel Gibson did not say those words. Given Cher's earlier demonstrations of an impressive cultural vocabulary, it is an ironic twist that Cher does not know—or at least does not name—the sources for the two Shakespearean moments in the film. And this ironic twist has made some critics uneasy:

> The popularization of Shakespeare on film, video, and television—which began inside the stalwartly liberal tradition of noblesse oblige attempting to bring culture to the masses—now finds itself, in America at least, in a strictly market-responsive milieu in which literary knowledge is in general a decidedly low capital, frequently mockable commodity, caught within the peculiarly American ambivalence about intellectualism, and therefore to be eschewed at all costs.[12]

But Cher and her friends have already demonstrated a respect for literary knowledge even if it is not in the form of canon-bound literature. Furthermore, the film's audience must recognize that Cher correctly identifies "that Polonius guy" as the speaker of "To thine own self be true" whether we have recognized Heather's mistake or not for the simple reason that Cher is right. For those members of the audience who may not realize that Cher is correct, Josh, the college student stepbrother, laughs, indicating that Cher has defeated Heather in the battle of wits. Presumably we know at least who Hamlet and Polonius are, but it is actually not necessary to know Shakespeare's version of the play to get the joke. It is, however, necessary to know that Mel Gibson really did play the Dane. The "Hollywoodization" of Shakespeare in this case makes it possible for Cher to know the Hamlet as played by Mel Gibson just as she knows the sonnet as transmitted by Cliffs Notes. Heckerling does not challenge notions of intellectualism; rather, she challenges the foundations of the canon itself. Because Cher correctly identifies other representatives of "high-status cultural currency"[13] in the names of Botticelli and Monet, her failure to identify Hamlet's words directly via the Shakespearean original signals a challenge to the status of that original.

In another, earlier challenge to that original, Cher's reaction to Dionne's question regarding the sonnet's authorship has two important stages: her incredulity that Dionne did not recognize the words as famous and her earnest assertion that the source she cites is the true source of the words.

These two reactions to her friend reveal, in ways that cannot be equaled by scholarly articles, the state of Shakespeare's position in the postmodern school and university. Shakespeare has been reduced to famous quotations and Cliffs Notes through an anxiety over his worth that began in the First Folio:

> ... it is not our prouince, who onely gather his works, and giue them you, to praise him. It is yours that reade him. And there we hope, to your diuers capacities, you will find enough, both to draw, and hold you: for his wit can no more lie hid, then it could be lost. Reade him, therefore; and againe, and againe: And if then you doe not like him, surely you are in some manifest danger, not to understand him. And so we leaue you to other of his Friends, whom if you need, can bee your guides: if you neede them not, you can leade your selues, and others. And such Readers we wish him.[14]

In order to avoid this "manifest danger" of misunderstanding the great poet, students look to sources that provide the right answers for their exams. If during an exam Cher were faced with an identification question regarding who says "to thine own self be true," Mel Gibson would also provide such a source.

On the other hand, if Cher needed to understand the irony of Hamlet's hesitation in the church, she, like Danny before her, would have no point of reference. Although Zeffirelli's *Hamlet* no longer provides this decade's only cinematic representation of Shakespeare's most famous character, the film's influence cannot be denied. Indeed, as these three films and one television program demonstrate, though we may be *getting* Shakespeare at the movies, it seems in many cases we are really only *seeing* Mel Gibson. Nevertheless, I share Gary Taylor's sentiments about Shakespeare's future resting in the hands of cinema directors. Mel Gibson's lasting influence as the melancholy Dane seen in such films as *The Last Action Hero* leaves me hopeful that Shakespeare will no longer inspire the awe which keeps him inaccessible. Indeed, although in line with critical theory's attempts to open the canon to new and culturally marginalized authors (or in fact, abolish it altogether), cinema provides us with the opportunity to redefine cultural ideologies in ways that literary criticism simply cannot. Audiences who know nothing about the literary theories that inform our work as critics and scholars, even those theories used in scholarly attempts to break down cultural assumptions, will have access to texts they once thought inaccessible—making Hollywood a surprisingly effective teacher.

In fact, we as teachers can learn our most useful lesson from Hollywood. For the films released in the last decade of the twentieth century do not rely upon some meaning embedded within the texts waiting to be released by the "right" reading, but rather upon the plurality carried by Shakespeare's name:

Shakespeare is a term with extraordinary currency in a wide range of discursive practices as a complex symbol of cultural value. It is widely used in vernacular idiom and throughout the genres of popular culture from advertising to situation comedies where it refers equivocally to a particular man, an author, a body of works, a system of cultural institutions, and by extension, a set of attitudes and dispositions. It defines taste communities and cultural positioning. But Shakespeare is not just a token of cultural worth and significance. The term has multiple and ambiguous valences, especially in its vernacular usage, where it may also signify privilege, exclusion, and cultural pretension.[15]

Instead of focusing on what Shakespeare means, we should also teach our students how "we mean *by* Shakespeare."[16] As Danny replaces Olivier with Schwarzenegger and the "double *d*s" mold "to be or not to be" into a rap-refrain, Cher also demonstrates what Terence Hawkes claims in his critical writing. In Cher's use of Shakespeare's sonnet to spark a love affair between two teachers, she constructs a new meaning with those words specifically for her teacher, Miss Geist, reversing if only for a moment, their roles. Furthermore, we watch Cher knowingly educate Tai through her extensive knowledge of their own cultural milieu. Indeed someday a Shakespeare, unmediated through Cliffs Notes and Mel Gibson, will become part of Cher's cultural vocabulary. Imagine the explanation Tai would require if Cher called someone a "full-on Hamlet": "Duh. Like he could *never* represent Nike." Even without knowing whose words she manipulates, Cher instinctively understands in a way that so many students do not, but so many filmmakers do, that Shakespeare, like Botticelli and Monet as cultural capital, is a tool for making meaning—even if in this moment she means only to renegotiate her grades.

NOTES

1. William Shakespeare, *Othello*, in *The Complete Works of William Shakespeare*, ed. David Bevington, updated 4th ed. (New York: Longman, 1997), 5.2.349. All subsequent references to Shakespeare's plays will follow this edition and be noted parenthetically in the text.

2. Gary Taylor, *Reinventing Shakespeare: A Cultural History from the Restoration to the Present* (London: Vintage, 1989), 384.

3. "Body and Soul and Dick," episode of *Third Rock from the Sun*, dir. Robert Berlinger and James Burrows II, 30 min., NBC television, 27 February 1996.

4. Gary Taylor quoted in David Gates, "The Bard Is Hot," 23 December 1996, 46.

5. *The Last Action Hero*, dir. John McTiernan, 2 hr. 11 min., Columbia Pictures, 1993, videocassette.

6. Barbara Hodgdon, "The Critic, the Poor Player, Prince Hamlet, and the Lady in the Dark," in *Shakespeare Reread:The Texts in New Contexts*, ed. Russ McDonald (Ithaca: Cornell University Press, 1994), 291–92.

7. Lynda E. Boose and Richard Burt, "Totally Clueless?: Shakespeare Goes Hollywood in the 1990s," in *Shakespeare, the Movie: Popularizing the Plays on Film, TV, and Video*, ed. Lynda E. Boose and Richard Burt (London and New York: Routledge, 1997), 9.

8. *Renaissance Man*, prod. and dir. Penny Marshall, 2 hr. 8 min., Touchstone Pictures, 1994, videocassette.

9. Boose and Burt, 9.

10. *Clueless*, dir. Amy Heckerling, 1 hr. 37 min., Paramount Pictures, 1995, videocassette.

11. Boose and Burt also point to this moment in the film in order to assess the effects of what they call the "Hollywoodization of Shakespeare" (8).

12. Boose and Burt, 12.

13. Boose and Burt, 8.

14. Henry Condell and John Heminge, "To the Great Variety of Readers," *The First Folio of Shakespeare, 1623*, ed. Doug Moston (New York: Applause Books, 1995), A3r.

15. Michael D. Bristol, *Big-Time Shakespeare* (London and New York: Routledge, 1996), ix.

16. Terence Hawkes, *Meaning by Shakespeare* (London and New York: Routledge, 1992), 3.

Works Cited

Boose, Lynda E., and Richard Burt. "Totally Clueless?: Shakespeare Goes Hollywood in the 1990s." In *Shakespeare, the Movie: Popularizing the Plays on Film, TV, and Video*. Edited by Lynda E. Boose and Richard Burt. London and New York: Routledge, 1997.

Bristol, Michael D. *Big-Time Shakespeare*. London and New York: Routledge, 1996.

Condell, Henry, and John Heminge. Preface to *The First Folio of Shakespeare, 1623*. Edited by Doug Moston. New York: Applause Books, 1995.

Evans, G. Blakemore. *The Riverside Shakespeare*. Boston: Houghton Mifflin, 1974.

Gates, David. "The Bard Is Hot." *Newsweek*, 23 December 1996, 41–47.

Hawkes, Terence. *Meaning by Shakespeare*. London and New York: Routledge, 1992.

Hodgdon, Barbara. "The Critic, the Poor Player, Prince Hamlet, and the Lady in the Dark." In *Shakespeare Reread: The Texts in New Contexts*. Edited by Russ McDonald. Ithaca: Cornell University Press, 1994.

Shakespeare, William. *Hamlet, Prince of Denmark*. In *The Complete Works of William Shakespeare*. Edited by David Bevington. Updated 4th edition. New York: Longman, 1997.

———. *Othello, the Moor of Venice*. In *The Complete Works of William Shakespeare*. Edited by David Bevington. Updated 4th edition. New York: Longman, 1997.

Taylor, Gary. *Reinventing Shakespeare: A Cultural History from the Restoration to the Present*. London: Vintage, 1989.

Films Cited

"Body and Soul and Dick." Episode of *Third Rock from the Sun*. Directed by Robert Berlinger and James Burrows II. 30 min. NBC Television, 27 February 1996.

Clueless. Directed by Amy Heckerling. 1 hr. 37 min. Paramount Pictures, 1995. Videocassette.

Hamlet. Directed by Laurence Olivier. 2 hr. 33 min. Paramount Pictures, 1948. Videocassette.

Hamlet. Directed by Franco Zeffirelli. 2 hr. 15 min. Warner Brothers/Nelson Entertainment, 1990. Videocassette.

The Last Action Hero. Directed by John McTiernan. 2 hr. 11 min. Columbia/Tri Star Pictures, 1993. Videocassette.

Renaissance Man. Produced and directed by Penny Marshall. 2 hr. 8 min. Touchstone Pictures, 1994. Videocassette.

The Film's the Thing:
Using Film in the Shakespearean Classroom

ANNALISA CASTALDO

THE ACADEMY AWARD WINNING FILM *SHAKESPEARE IN LOVE* (DIR. JOHN MADDEN, 1998) posits that Shakespeare's *Romeo and Juliet* began life as the formulaic *Romeo and Ethel, the Pirate's Daughter* and became the work we know today after Shakespeare fell in love and then experienced the loss of that love. The film tracks the development of the play, as both plot and verse are created out of Shakespeare's encounters with his muse, the well-born and unattainable Viola. In the end, the completed play captures the audience, including Queen Elizabeth and the clergyman, Makepeace, who originally called for the closing of the theaters, because it shows "the truth of love." The film goes on to suggest that other works (or at least *Twelfth Night*) will emerge directly from Shakespeare's relationship with Viola.

I begin with this film because, as a scholar not only of Shakespeare, but of Shakespearean film, I found that everyone I knew wanted my opinion of the film, and I discovered that a surprising number of people (including several with undergraduate degrees in English) wanted to know if that was how Shakespeare "really" wrote *Romeo and Juliet*. Historically, scholars know that Shakespeare, in fact, based his play on a popular poem by Arthur Brooke, called *Romeus and Juliet*, which, despite important differences, tells essentially the same story of young love tragically lost. Yet *Shakespeare in Love* obviously reflects a very real belief circulating in American culture: that Shakespeare's works exist outside the context of literature and history, and spring directly from his unique genius. The repeated question made me realize that Shakespeare's cultural centrality, especially through the way he is presented in secondary schools and universities, creates an aura of inevitability, of monolithic stability around the works. Shakespeare's reputation eclipses all questions of textual mutability, source material, or adaptation. The investment in the texts as stable and separate from the rest of culture is very high and actually helps to create Shakespeare's position.

As Michael Bristol points out, Shakespeare has become a celebrity, famous mostly for being famous.[1]

Of course, the texts are not stable, not originary, not a lot of things that they are accepted, and expected, to be. And while many professors and scholars feel that it would be wonderful to introduce the unstable text into the classroom, and to teach a Shakespearean play as a multilayered work connected to other texts, and part of an ongoing culture and history, the reality is that most of the time, classroom work needs to focus on close readings of the play in a modern edition. This is practically unavoidable at the high school and introductory university level (and sometimes beyond) because the language of the text itself is unfamiliar enough that simply getting students to read the text competently can take up most of a semester. On top of that is the question of coverage. With thirty-seven plays, no single class can do more than scratch the surface of Shakespeare's work (as opposed to many of his contemporaries, who either wrote less or whose works were partially lost). Spending time on texts or issues outside the actual plays often seems counterproductive when a semester can handle only six or seven plays in the first place. The result of these pressures is that students in Shakespearean classes continue to see the plays as they did before, *sui generis*, existing without equal or context.

Unfortunately, classroom practice mirrors more general ideological beliefs and each reinforces the other. This interplay would be less of a concern if the culture at large was not so deeply invested in the myth that Shakespeare is a solitary, original genius and that the plays are stable, singular creations. Roland Barthes usefully differentiates between a "work" and a "text," the former being authorized, singular, and fixed, the latter being open, variable, and multiauthored.[2] If the plays are admitted to be texts rather than works, Shakespeare's cultural placement is radically destabilized; a great part of the plays' value lies in the apparent fixity of their meaning. In fact, Shakespeare's plays hold the cultural position of a secular Bible; just as most people who read the Bible do not stop to think that the words are not only translated, but also pieced together from various fragments, and organized according to secular, historical needs, people who quote Shakespeare do not bother thinking about the tremendous amount of work that goes into creating the modernized text. For that matter, they rarely consider the plays as plays, where all the words spoken represent the views of characters, rather than the author's personal beliefs. This viewpoint is perhaps most obvious in the regular use of the quote, "To thine own self be true" as a piece of timeless wisdom, completely separated from its place within a tiresome lecture delivered by a meddling politician. This belief in the fixity of the text even extends to productions. Stage performances, for example, are often judged by how closely they conform not only to the words (which are themselves unstable), but also to the supposed spirit or meaning of the original, which is considered inherent and therefore unchangeable.[3] Because the plays are supposed to represent universal wisdom, Shakespeare's authority, and thus the authority of his interpreters (from students and teachers to directors and editors), rests on discovering the meaning of single, knowable, stable work.

To maintain the fiction that the plays have always been exactly the same is to willfully ignore the very important cultural work that goes into creating and maintaining Shakespeare's position of centrality. In fact, it often seems that ignoring the underground work is a necessity to maintaining Shakespeare's status. As Jean E. Howard and Marion F. O'Connor put it, "somewhat like a Dior suit, Shakespeare never ages and eludes all historical implication."[4] This appears true, but in fact the reason Shakespeare wears well is because he can be accessorized; he is fluid in both text and performance, allowing almost infinite alterations while appearing to remain completely fixed. Culture can keep reinventing Shakespeare to suit its needs, all the while pretending nothing has changed.

Shakespeare's very fluidity has led him to become his own adjective. Foucault argues that an author is not the real person who wrote the texts; rather, the "author function" always works at a remove from the reality of the writer.[5] But Shakespeare has stepped beyond even the author function, into a sort of "cultural function." By that, I mean that the name itself, "Shakespeare," along with a fragmented knowledge of certain parts of the texts circulate free from the texts themselves, recognizable but flexible. The value that culture attaches to Shakespeare's name remains no matter where the plays are encountered or how far from the actual text the use travels. Linda Charnes gives an excellent description of this cultural function:

> "Shakespeare"—like "Willie Horton"—has become a general equivalent, a medium of exchange, pure (that is, so saturated with itself as to signify nothing but "itself") ideological value available to authorize whatever "structures of feeling" are being promoted . . . Shakespeare the playwright is superseded by Shakespeare the paradigm.[6]

The very fact that today most people barely recognize the name "Willie Horton" or assign it special significance, while Shakespeare is as recognizable as ever, further proves the latter's status.

Shakespeare thus circulates freely in popular culture, so that most people (and especially university students) feel familiar with the works and their meaning. But even as they circulate in an amazing variety of forms, the cultural function creates an apparent stability and fixity that leads to a belief in and acceptance of the plays' universal meaning and value. In classic Derridian terms, the plays are always already understood: their meaning is known long before they are read, so the reading is always an (unnecessary) rereading.

Given the level of wisdom and stability ascribed to the texts, it is no wonder that students often actively resist any suggestion that these same texts might be partial, unstable, multiple, or altered. The very first time I raised the issue of textual variation in an introductory Shakespeare class, a student raised his hand and said "I'm very uncomfortable with this idea." Indeed, he was so uncomfortable that he went in search of biographical material that would help him factually decide—apart from any of the ideological constraints I had described—which variants were correct. Even when students are not this overtly resistant to the idea of textual variation or source material they often simply ignore its existence as soon as it is no longer required that they consider it. In this, they simply follow the familiar cultural path that separates the plays and Shakespeare himself from all context.

Given cultural and practical pressures, how then can any instructor successfully introduce the ideas of textual variation, multiple authorship, source material, and cultural alteration of the text's meaning, without waiting until the class consists purely of senior English majors with an interest in editing theory and adaptation? I propose that film can be at least a partial answer to this conundrum. Most instructors already use film clips in their classes, if only to engage the interest of their students. On the whole, however, film use generally stops at providing examples of competing interpretations, or helping students understand the importance of the nonverbal aspect of the plays. While these are valid and important uses of film in the Shakespeare classroom, film can be used in many other ways because film itself, as a medium, can help students overcome their cultural expectations of Shakespeare.

The value of film lies in the often overlooked fact that it has already prepped our students for the issues we wish to teach them. Films exist in a world that is self-referential, especially films that are most familiar to high school and college students in the mid to late nineties. Postmodern ironic stances lead to regular overt homages (or rip-offs), breaking of the fourth wall, and parodies. A film such as *The Last Action Hero* (dir. John McTiernan, 1993), which includes a brief segment of Arnold as Hamlet, relies for its humor on the audience's knowledge of the stock character Arnold regularly plays, and the often ridiculous parameters of action movies as a genre (the hero being able to outrun bullets and escaping with only "minor scratches").

Films are also generally accepted as multiauthored, something equally true but usually hidden in the field of literature—even when that literature is drama. While a heavily edited edition of Shakespeare is still "Shakespeare's," a film, depending on the target audience, will be variously identified by the actors, the director, the screenwriter, and even the producer or studio. There may be a defining personality in a project, but no attempt is made to suggest that a film is the creation of single person. In fact, such an attempt to maintain complete control, as in the case of Orson Welles or George Lucas with *Star Wars: Episode I—The Phantom Menace* (1999), is so rare as to be remarked upon (and usually not favorably). Students who are uncomfortable with the notion of editors changing even a single word of the Shakespearean text are familiar with and even expect last-minute rewrites by new screenwriters, cuts to please the ratings board, and altered endings after poor results from test audiences. Furthermore, all of these changes tend to be discussed in the media as they happen; thus films are openly and publicly created by committee.

Finally, film in the current age regularly exists in multiple forms. On the most basic level, practically every film made today is transferred to videotape, and the majority of those are not transferred to "wide-screen" but are "formatted to fit your television." Films that are shown on network TV are further changed because of stricter regulations concerning sex and violence, or simply cropped to allow for a specific viewing time. And now, with laserdisc and DVD, more and more films come to the home viewing market in several forms, such as a "director's cut," including scenes that were originally edited out of the final product, with commentary, with enhanced special effects not previously available, remastered, and so on. Films thus closely mirror Renaissance theater in both form and creation: both are mutable, multiauthored creations that blur the line between entertainment and art.

For all these reasons, films condition students to view works of entertainment (and perhaps also art) in precisely the ways we would like them to view Shakespeare's plays. By expanding the ways in which we, as instructors, use film in the classroom, we can introduce fairly sophisticated concepts—from editing theory to precopyright views of authorship—to students in a way they can easily grasp. The value of this, I have found, lies not only in a painless way to teach extratextual matters I consider important. Without fail, I have also found that once students understand and are comfortable with the unstable and polysemous nature of the text, their readings and interpretations of that text are strengthened, ever-liberated. Most students, especially those not yet at ease with the language, view the plays as the literary equivalent of a marble statue: unchanging and unchangeable. Too often students approach the text looking for a single "correct" reading that they feel they must find in order to be successful. At best, this results in uncertain, quiet students who parrot back the instructor's words or, at worst, plagiarism of any authority they can find. When the text instead appears as fluid, unstable, and multiauthored, students more readily accept that there might be multiple acceptable readings, that readings depend on context, and that their task is not to decipher a code with inadequate tools, but to engage in an ongoing debate using creativity as well as facts.

☆ ☆ ☆

As I discussed in the beginning of my essay, many people, even those with experience in literature, view Shakespeare as an originator of plots. This may seem like a minor issue—who really cares if Shakespeare was the first one to write about Romeo and Juliet or Macbeth or King Lear? It is, after all, the verse that has earned him his place in the canon, and that is where the focus of study should be, not in a comparison of plots and characters with earlier texts. Despite the obvious practicality of this focus, this is a problematic approach for precisely the reasons that lead students to seek the one true interpretation of a text. Sources provide a corrective, a way of better defining Shakespeare's place within the span of English literature. Too often, with courses and semesters devoted entirely to his works, Shakespeare loses his part in the conversation between writers. Even in introductory drama or Great Books courses, Shakespeare often stands alone to represent the early modern period. Sometimes medieval literature is entirely skipped, giving the impression that between the Romans and Shakespeare exists a thousand-year wasteland. At the furthest extreme, he becomes a conduit for something greater than humanity and civilization itself, passing on archetypal stories, rather than emerging as a gifted but merely human creator himself. Then the meaning of the plays is again locked into a single timeless story, a demonstration of a universal truth about human nature.

Sources allow students to compare Shakespeare's work with what came before, which not only gives Shakespeare context, but also helps students to understand what it is that makes Shakespeare worth studying. One of the easiest and best ways to demonstrate where Shakespeare's creativity lies is to compare his work to his sources. The creation of Falstaff, the decision to end King Lear with the deaths of Lear and Cordelia instead of a restoration of the old order, the preservation of Isabella's chastity through the bed trick, all of these things are Shakespeare's. Since it is highly unlikely that students will be familiar with other early modern works, let alone earlier texts, studying the sources points out where Shakespeare actually was innovative, how changes in details make a great difference, and how Shakespeare's language differed from (or was similar to) other writers of the time. All of these elements ground students' readings of the plays and thus help them to produce more textured interpretations.

By introducing Shakespeare's sources into a discussion of the plays, we can begin to break down the artificial divisions that have isolated and elevated Shakespeare from the rest of English literature. However, reading another complete text along with each Shakespearean play is usually too time consuming for a regular classroom, especially in an introductory course. And using excerpts of texts, often in a form that creates visual inferiority compared with the modernized Shakespearean text, does not give students a real chance to compare Shakespeare to his sources. The natural tendency is simply to dismiss the sources as inferior. Film, which itself uses Shakespeare as a source, can help open up a discussion about sources by introducing an adaptation that is as much or more powerful than Shakespeare's text. Students who can articulate a modern director's changes of Shakespeare's play will more easily be able to make the same connections between Shakespeare and his sources.

Every film made of a Shakespearean play varies from its source, even if only in terms of the textual cuts. In addition to cuts, there are often alterations in scene order, lines are reassigned, and occasionally new lines are written. Finally, many directors use silent but extratextual scenes to help modern audiences understand cultural values that are four centuries old. Thus each film, no matter how traditional and complete it attempts to be, varies from the source just as Shakespeare (with a great deal less concern than most modern directors) varied from his. A focus on the reasons behind these changes opens the door for a discussion of the changes Shakespeare himself made and helps cast Shakespeare in the role of adapter. A wonderful example of this, and a way to breathe life into a too familiar play, is to discuss the ways in which Baz Luhrmann recreates *Romeo and Juliet*.

As Patricia Lennox eloquently puts it, Luhrmann functions, in his creation of the film, as a *bricoleur*. "Luhrmann is not mounting a new production of Shakespeare's play as much as he is recycling the myth of the story of Romeo and Juliet."[7] *Romeo and Juliet* is the perfect play with which to investigate the relation of adaptation to original since no play, not even *Hamlet*, is so successfully and completely embedded in the culture of contemporary America, and so familiar to students at all levels. "Romeo" of course no longer functions as a proper name, but as a definition of a certain type of young man. The bare outlines of the story—lovers divided—is used regularly as shorthand for a wide array of shattered romantic dreams, not only for young lovers who commit suicide after they are separated by the feud between their families. Instead, any two people can be seen as modeled after Shakespeare's lovers.

Luhrmann's method in creating his version is to assume audience familiarity with both the plot and the culturally mythic elements of the story, like the balcony scene, for instance. Based on this familiarity, Luhrmann then feels free to reconstruct the play by using the mythic elements as a way to ground the audience while immersing them in a dense collage of visual references. Rather than attempting to create a visual world in line with the highly rhetorical poetry of the Elizabethan play, Luhrmann plays up the conflict and uses it to call attention to what the audience thinks it knows about Shakespeare. This deliberate disruption of the audience's prior knowledge is perhaps most apparent in the death scene. In Luhrmann's version, Juliet awakes before Romeo dies, but after he has doomed himself by drinking the poison. This ending actually reaches back beyond Shakespeare's immediate source, to earlier Italian sources: Da Porto, Clitia, and Bandello. It is highly unlikely that Luhrmann realized he was recovering the original version of the story. In light of Luhrmann's extensive background in opera, he may have been familiar with the Victorian stage tradition which (when it did not rewrite the ending all together) allowed the lovers one last farewell before death; but it seems to me that rather than gesturing toward the existence of sources before (or after) Shakespeare, Luhrmann is playing with audience expectations. Most of the viewers are in no doubt as to the end of the story, and, in fact, Luhrmann has not hidden the end by removing or cutting the opening chorus, as Zeffirelli does in his *Romeo and Juliet* (1968). Yet the faint movements of Juliet's fingers and eyelids as Romeo says his farewell lead to the belief that possibly, this time, things will be different. Maybe they *will* get out alive. In fact, the Hollywood romance genre dictates that the lovers will succeed against impossible odds and ride off into the sunset. Two sets of expectations are brought directly into conflict and because the power of Hollywood is so strong and the adaptation so free ranging, it is just conceivable for an audience—even an audience familiar with the ending of Shakespeare's play—to think that this time the ending might be a happy one.

Posing the question of what such a change gains, or, to put it another way, why Luhrmann would want to make this change, forces students to confront their own expectations of the text, including the belief that its form cannot change. In fact, the ending of *Romeo and Juliet* is one of the most mutable aspects of the play in adaptation. A "Romeo and Juliet" type story need not end with both lovers committing suicide; one alone can die, as in the musical *West Side Story*, or they can both live, albeit separated. Luhrmann's shifts of narrative emphasis result in a new way of reading the familiar lines. When Juliet says "Thy lips are warm," she is not discovering the fact that Romeo has been dead only seconds, but ironically commenting on the inevitable change about to take place. And Romeo's "Thus with a kiss I die" is no longer a romantic choice he makes; he is a helpless pawn in Juliet's attempt to join him in death. By unsettling expectations, Luhrmann forces the viewer to discover the text anew.

Although Shakespeare's language is often considered difficult and strange by students, it is much more easily digested than that of his sources, especially early modern texts such as Brooke, which do not benefit from the modernized translations often used for Green and Latin texts. And with a play as familiar as *Romeo and Juliet*, it would be a rare student indeed who would not automatically find

"O welcome Death" quoth she, "end of unhappiness,
That also art beginning of assured happiness
Fear not to dart me now, thy stripe no longer stay,
Prolong no longer now my life, I hate this long delay." (2773–76)[8]

inferior to the much more familiar and direct "Yea, noise? Then I'll be brief. O happy dagger, / This is thy sheath! There rust and let me die!"[9] However, if the only result of reading source texts is to reiterate how much obviously better the Shakespearean version is, there is little use in the effort. By introducing the idea of alternate routes via film (usually more attractive to students than text), a door is opened to question what Shakespeare's approach and changes do to the text. Once students are comfortable with this idea, Brooke's text can be discussed more closely. A number of students will find Luhrmann's version of the ending more effective because of the tension it evokes and the way in which it unsettles expectations. They are thus prepared for the heretical thought that not everything Shakespeare wrote was perfect in every way. If students understand that Brooke was practically as popular in his time as Shakespeare has become, they will be able to question why Shakespeare would have made the changes he did and discuss whether or not these changes were effective.

One such change that might be discussed is the way in which Shakespeare removed religious issues from the actions and thoughts of the two lovers. Romeus's final thought, for example, is not of Juliet, but his own soul: "'Take pity on my sinful and my poor afflicted mind! / For well enough I know, this body is but clay, / Nought but a mass of sin, too frail, and subject to decay'" (2678–80). Shakespeare, like Brooke, lived in a deeply religious world and yet he systematically removed religious doubts and concerns from the love story (or, as with "If I profane," dialogue transmuted religion into a romantic symbol). Modern American students, who live in a very different world and are deeply familiar with Shakespeare's version, might well automatically assume that Brooke is the oddity and dismiss his overly religious slant; but the lack of condemnation for the lovers' actions (especially suicide) may very well have been problematic for Shakespeare's contemporary viewers. Luhrmann actually injects religion back into the play, drenching the visual field with crosses, statues of Jesus and Mary, and other religious imagery. Together, Brooke and Luhrmann can defamiliarize Shakespeare's version of the story and allow aspects such as the religious element to be studied with fresh eyes.

Rather than asking students to compare two texts (one labeled "Shakespeare," and therefore clearly the superior), working from film to play and then back to source allows for greater equality. The film's extraordinary popularity and the natural impact of seeing a scene acted out rather than read provides a counterbalance to the power of Shakespeare's reputation. Even a film that doesn't star Leonardo DiCaprio usually has a greater emotional impact than a text. This emotional impact and the inevitable changes create an easy way to lead into discussing the alterations Shakespeare made to his source, just as Luhrmann and other directors have done four centuries later.

☆☆☆

A much more difficult issue for students to grasp than the value of source study is that of textual instability and the concurrent theory of editing that text. Even when students accept that the texts have been heavily modified by a series of editors, they are often unable or unwilling to see that this makes any real difference in interpreting the text. Intent on finding the correct reading, they continue to demand the "correct" text. In fact, students are often angry at their "wasted" close readings when they first learn of the texts' unstable nature, since the instability suggests that not all of the words are Shakespeare's. But the flexible nature of film and the variety of film forms can help students understand that there is no single correct text, only choices based on context, and studying the choices made in various editions is as important and valuable as studying the words themselves.

The film that perhaps best parallels the state of the Shakespearean text, while remaining accessible to students, is *Blade Runner* (dir. Ridley Scott, 1982). Based very loosely on a novel by Philip K. Dick, the film's first release featured regular, explanatory voice-overs by the main character and a happy ending in which the hero and his android lover escape to the still pristine wilderness. When the film was released on video, a "director's cut" version removed the voice over and replaced the happy ending with a much more ambiguous version of possible but fleeting escape. The first version has the authority of major release and was in fact created because of test audience dissatisfaction and confusion with the director's version. But the second version has become the one that has gained respect by casual and serious viewers alike.

While we have no "director's (author's) cut" of *Hamlet* (or of any play by Shakespeare), we do have a surprisingly similar situation in terms of good and bad quartos. "Bad" quartos are, of course, illegitimate versions supposedly taken down in shorthand or written from memory by bit actors to sell for quick cash. They were unsanctioned by the playhouse and, presumably, by Shakespeare himself. But like the first version of *Blade Runner*, these versions offer a more direct link to the actual productions of the

Elizabethan stage than their "good" counterparts. If bad quartos are, in fact, written down from memory by actors, then they are closer to what the audiences saw than the versions taken from Shakespeare's foul papers, probably even closer than those transcribed from the prompt book. Editors recognize this by using the often more descriptive stage directions of bad quartos even when they will not consider the text itself as legitimate.

As with the first version of *Blade Runner*, the bad quarto of *Hamlet* (the 1602 Quarto, hereafter Q1) may well be the text that provides scholars with the best clues for what the first audiences saw and what they liked or disliked in what they saw. Q1 differs substantially in several places, places hard to ascribe to memory error by actors. For example, there is an entire scene in Q1 between Horatio and Gertrude, where he tells her of Hamlet's return and she pledges her full support to Hamlet. This builds on a much less ambiguous closet scene in which the Queen declares "But as I have a soul I swear by heaven / I never knew of this most horrid murder" and promises "I will conceal, consent and do my best / What stratagem soe'er thou shalt devise."[10] There is no doubt, in Q1, that Gertrude is innocent of both adultery and murder. There is also a significant shift in the placement of the nunnery scene, which is moved from 3.1 to just after the fishmonger scene of 2.4, so that the testing of Hamlet takes place in one long stretch. In this scene, Hamlet's behavior towards Ophelia is explained by his certain knowledge of their being overheard. Both of these changes make the play simpler, more straightforward. Did the original audience object to the complicated script Shakespeare penned and demand a rewrite for clarification, as the test audiences did with *Blade Runner*? Or was it the other way around, with Shakespeare's second version, which made it much harder to "pluck out the heart of [its] mystery"—the version that won acclaim?

It is difficult to put aside the knowledge of the modern conflated *Hamlet* and discuss the possible reasons for the Q1 variations. Viewing the placement of the nunnery scene in Olivier's version of *Hamlet* can help, again because film provides a powerful visual appeal, which can counterbalance the natural authority of the modern text. While Olivier does not go so far as to shift the whole of the nunnery scene, he does move "to be or not to be" from before Hamlet's encounter with Ophelia to afterwards. This change creates the natural conclusion that Hamlet's depression and despair, unexplained when he soliloquizes at the beginning of 3.1, are a result of Ophelia's betrayal. In Olivier's version, rather than an abrupt, off-stage shift from the excitement of the Mousetrap plot to the despair of "to be or not to be," there is a natural progression from anxiety at speaking to his previously unavailable beloved through anger at her betrayal (in Olivier's film, as in Q1, made clear by extratextual business) to depression at the apparent collapse of both his plans and his romance.

After viewing the scene and reading the placement of the scene in both the modernized conflated edition and Q1, discussion can begin as to why one version might be considered more valuable than the other and why. The discussion can then focus on what the second version (which in each case is actually the earlier version) has to offer. At least one writer, Maxwell E. Foster, argues that Q1 is actually a superior drama because of the internal coherence of the hero and the pacing of the action. As with *Blade Runner*, one version, apparently the version favored by or at least shown to early audiences, privileges clarity and explanation over ambiguity and length. And although the conflated Q2/F version has the weight of authority (both Shakespeare's and history's), Olivier's version shows that it is not so sacrosanct that it must be considered flawless. If students keep in mind the idea of quartos as various versions released to the public, rather than letting the labels of "good" and "bad" prejudge them, an interesting discussion can ensue.

Students most often object to the realities of editing because they are uncomfortable with the idea that Shakespeare's plays, which they have always considered unchangeable, are in fact multiauthored and exist in a variety of forms. Films such as *Blade Runner* or *Little Women* (dir. Gillian Armstrong, 1994), which had a movie tie-in novel selling next to the original text, help students become more at ease with the idea that there is no original, single version of any work, especially a Shakespearean play.

☆☆☆

As a final example, I would like to discuss adaptation. This is not often a subject of introductory Shakespearean classes, but I believe it would be useful to include it more often. As stated earlier, Shakespeare is often presented to students without any context, separate from the rest of both literature and history. The works naturally assume an unchanging, timeless quality that is quite distant from the truth. There are enough adaptations of Shakespeare to provide the substance of several courses (and many academic works). It is valuable for students to recognize this proliferation of different versions early; it allows them the flexibility to bring their own interpretations to the table, rather than attempting to mimic authorities. A question rarely raised but infinitely interesting is where the line of adaptation is drawn, where a production is no longer a play by William Shakespeare and becomes "based on" or "adapted from" that play. Where to draw that line and what it even means to do so helps clarify issues of authority and value. Is it the words that define Shakespeare or is it something less definite? While many academics would claim that without the words Shakespeare wrote, an adaptation cannot be Shakespeare's work, these same academics value the films of Akira Kurasawa, for example, as somehow

"Shakespearean," and consider them truer to the spirit of the original than more popular versions of Shakespeare's plays, such as the films of Zeffirelli. There are almost infinite ways to approach this question of what constitutes an adaptation by using films. Zeffirelli's 1967 version of *The Taming of the Shrew*, for instance, might be compared to the recent adaptation *10 Things I Hate about You* (dir. Gil Junger, 1999) as well as the musical *Kiss Me, Kate* (dir. George Sidney II, 1953). Numerous versions of *Romeo and Juliet* exist for comparison viewing. For the purposes of this essay, however, I would like to suggest using Orson Welles's *Chimes at Midnight* (1966) as a provocative way to discuss the Henriad.

1 Henry IV is a text often read in college Shakespeare classes. It provides a compelling story and wonderful characters, along with an extraordinarily neat structure that makes it a joy to teach. Sherry Bevins Darrell, in fact, makes a compelling argument for *1 Henry IV* as the best possible choice when an instructor can teach only a single Shakespearean play in a class.[11] However, the very name of the play indicates that it is part of something, incomplete on its own (although the play works well on its own, it is not until the "sequel" *2 Henry IV* that the true closure of Hal's ascension and Falstaff's rejection are presented). And as a history, the play is already clearly an adaptation of a previous source, in this case, actual events. In *Chimes at Midnight*, Welles takes the hint provided by the continuous storyline of the Henriad and completely abandons the structure of the single Shakespearean text, drawing instead on bits of four separate plays to create an almost new work with the character of Falstaff at the center. The film is generally recognized as cinematically brilliant, but is often slighted by Shakespeareans and rarely shown in classrooms, and I would like to suggest that this is due to its existence on the border between adaptation and interpretation; therefore, scholars (and audiences) are unsure of how to react to the product displayed. Is it Shakespeare? Is it Welles? And, finally, does it matter?

The multiple names under which the film travels beg similar questions. The film first had a Spanish title—*Campanadas a Medianoche*—which ties it to the filming location as well as the funding. The second title, *Chimes at Midnight*, is a direct quote from *2 Henry IV*, but the basis for the title is not easily available since that play is rarely read and usually seen as a companion to the more popular *1 Henry IV* rather than a work in its own right. While *Chimes at Midnight* is a wonderful title, evocative of the themes of change, loss, age, and regret that predominate in the film, it is unsurprising that at its preview at the 1966 Cannes Film Festival, it was already being called *Falstaff*. The film was released in America under that name and thus is the only English-language Shakespearean film to be marketed under two titles. This issue of naming leads back to Shakespeare's own adaptation of history and his renaming of "Oldcastle" as Falstaff. Just as Welles's titles were eventually out of his control, Shakespeare was forced to rename his character in order to avoid political retribution. Welles and Shakespeare both found themselves at the intersection of what might appear to be fact and fiction, but this threshold was more accurately described as the intersection of fiction and adaptation. Welles, of course, was reworking the fictionalized account of history created by Shakespeare. The problem, however, was that Shakespeare did not use historical documents in the same way modern historians do. He accepted Holinshed's words as fact, but rather than simply reproducing them, he used them as raw material (just as Welles does). Similarly, it is important to recognize that Welles was not simply filming his own ideas and calling the finished product "Shakespeare." He made plenty of films without using a literary source, starting, obviously, with *Citizen Kane* (1941). It is the melding of Shakespeare's existing cultural meaning with Welles's own ideas and interests that make this film so textured and fascinating. By using Shakespeare, Welles is deliberately investigating the concerns of adaptation. Just as Hal moves away from and beyond Falstaff, so Welles's Shakespearean adaptations step away from their source in terms of the theme conveyed, yet never forget or cease to regret that necessary distance.

Welles understood that the two parts of *1 Henry IV* have different moods, so he chose to cast the mood of the second part back over the entire piece. Because both *1 Henry IV* and especially *Henry V* are much better known than *2 Henry IV*, Welles is deliberately going against the accepted and expected interpretation of Shakespeare's second teratology. In fact, by melding bits of four of Shakespeare's plays, Welles expands the bounds of experiencing the plays. While scholars are familiar with cross-play reference and often write about more than one play at a time, this is a difficult thing for students to do with any sophistication. *Chimes at Midnight* helps them by modeling the ways in which a director (or interpreter) can find intersections and common themes in a variety of plays. Moreover, Welles, by remaking the plays to fit his own structure and meaning, pushes students to investigate the boundaries of interpretation.

The way in which Welles chooses to unify his structure in terms of mood provides an example of his method. Shakespeare's *1 Henry IV*, although it has some contemplative or tragic moments (the King upbraiding Hal, Hotspur's death), the mood in general is one of comedy. *2 Henry IV*, on the other hand, is a much more melancholy play, with an odor of disease, decay, and rejection permeating the action and the verse. *Henry V* presents a third mood, the triumphant. Welles takes the melancholy and spreads it out over the entire Henriad. This begins at the very opening of the film. First on screen are Falstaff and his partner Silence, framing their story as a requiem for their memories, memories that are not part of any Shakespearean play. Through the placement of their reminiscing, it is possible to see at least the first part of the film as an extended flashback of their memories, rather than of Shakespeare's play. The barren, cold landscape intensifies the idea that this is a sad, memory-driven work, a very different opening than the *in media res* of King Henry's court.

Welles continues his opening with a line of soldiers marching across the screen. They are a ragtag bunch, barely recognizable as military personnel, except for a few pikes and helmets. One even leaves his march to run after his escaped hat. The soldiers and their march is unexplained, mere background to the credits, but they provide a visual link to the very beginning of *1 Henry IV* and Westmorland's report of the wars against the Welsh. They also resonate with Falstaff's conscripts, "food for powder, food for powder" (4.2.58–59). The audience is treated to proof that they will "fill a pit as well as better" (4.2.59) as the scene ends and several corpses are shown hanging from gallows.

Welles is clearly creating an adaptation, rather than strictly following Shakespeare's play. But the version he creates is true to several important elements emphasized in Shakespeare's work. How then to react to his film? Knowing that Hal rejects Falstaff at the end of *2 Henry IV*, it is hard to read even *1 Henry IV* as comic, let alone the earlier scenes of the sequel. If Welles chooses to cast that mood over his entire production, it does not go against the spirit of the Henriad, which begins with Richard II giving up his crown and ends with the Chorus reminding viewers that Henry V's accomplishments will be destroyed soon after his death. Adaptation can be a way of discussing not only how plays fit together with other plays, but how Shakespeare's cultural influence continues to be felt, lived, and realized.

☆☆☆

These are only a few examples of the way film can be used to destabilize the Shakespearean text and invite students to participate in the ongoing conversation that is scholarship, rather than simply seeking the right answers. Many other pedagogical suggestions are contained in the rich intersection of Shakespeare and cinema. Encountering adaptations encourages students to push even further towards a discussion of what constitutes the boundaries of the Shakespearean text. A professionally edited and printed version of the plays seems to provide clear and unalterable boundaries, but even here the edges are ambiguous. *The Two Noble Kinsmen* is now generally accepted as "by" Shakespeare and is granted that status by being included in editions of the complete works, but for centuries the opposite was true. Often 1 *Henry IV* and 2 *Henry IV* are listed as two separate plays, but they are also read and studied together. The question of the sanctity of cultural boundaries provides even more provocative points for discussion when posed from within the contemporary classroom. The recent *Twelfth Night* (dir. Trevor Nunn, 1996), for example, can be used to discuss changing expectations about the complex relationship between sexuality, gender, and spectacle. Issues of race in seventeenth-century England and contemporary culture can be elicited by comparing Oliver Parker's *Othello* (1995), the first major production to cast an African American in the lead role, with either the Olivier or the Welles versions, both of which feature a white actor in blackface. In the end, there is almost no limit to the range of possibilities film opens up for pedagogical initiatives and discoveries.

Shakespeare's cultural authority has, in the twentieth century, grown to the point where the mere phrase "To be or not to be" or even Shakespeare's name alone conveys a body of tradition and meaning. More than any other writer, Shakespeare operates and exists on many levels and is deeply embedded in the everyday culture of America. This validates the attention paid to him in both high school and university English departments (more so than the focus on his universal greatness), but students deserve to be introduced to all the levels of Shakespearean scholarship and investigation. Film can be the medium that allows students to excavate the many layers of this extraordinary universe.

NOTES

1. Michael D. Bristol, *Big-Time Shakespeare* (London and New York: Routledge, 1996), 3.

2. Roland Barthes, "From Work to Text," in *Image-Music-Text*, trans. Stephen Heath (New York: The Noonday Press, 1977).

3. W. B. Worthen, *Shakespeare and the Authority of Performance* (Cambridge: Cambridge University Press, 1997).

4. Jean Howard and Marion O'Connor, eds., *Shakespeare Reproduced: The Text in History and Ideology* (London and New York: Methuen, 1987), 6.

5. Michel Foucault, "What Is an Author?" in *The Foucault Reader*, ed. Paul Rabinow (New York: Pantheon Books, 1984), 112.

6. Linda Charnes, *Notorious Identity: Materializing the Subject in Shakespeare* (Cambridge: Harvard University Press, 1997), 15

7. Patricia Lennox, "Baz Luhrmann's *William Shakespeare's Romeo + Juliet*" (paper presented at the annual meeting of the Shakespeare Association of America, Washington, D.C., April 1997), 2.

8. Arthur Brooke, *Brooke's Romeus and Juliet*, ed. J. J. Munro (New York: AMS Press, 1970). For an extensive analysis of the relationship between Luhrmann's film and Brooke's poem, see Courtney Lehmann, "Strictly Shakespeare? Dead Letters, Ghostly Fathers, and the Cultural Pathology of Authorship in Baz Luhrmann's *William Shakespeare's Romeo + Juliet*," *Shakespeare Quarterly* 52 (forthcoming).

9. William Shakespeare, *Romeo and Juliet*, in *The Norton Shakespeare*, ed. Stephen Greenblatt et al. (New York and London: W. W. Norton, 1997), 5.3.168–69. All subsequent references to Shakespeare's plays will refer to this edition and be noted parenthetically in the text.

10. Maxwell E. Foster, *The Play behind the Play: Hamlet and Quarto One* (Portsmouth, N.H.: Heinemann, 1998), 3.4.91–92, 105–6.

11. Sherry Bevins Darrell, "If Only One, Then *Henry IV, Part I* for the General Education Course," in *Teaching Shakespeare Today: Practical Approaches and Productive Strategies*, ed. James E. Davis and Ronald E. Salomone (Urbana, Ill.: NCTE Press, 1993).

WORKS CITED

Barthes, Roland. "From Work to Text." In *Image-Music-Text*. Translated by Stephen Heath. New York: The Noonday Press, 1977.

Bristol, Michael D. *Big-Time Shakespeare*. London and New York: Routledge, 1996.

Brooke, Arthur. *Brooke's Romeus and Juliet*. Edited by J. J. Munro. New York: AMS Press, 1970.

Charnes, Linda. *Notorious Identity: Materializing the Subject in Shakespeare*. Cambridge: Harvard University Press, 1997.

Darrell, Sherry Bevins. "If Only One, Then *Henry IV, Part 1* for the General Education Course." In *Teaching Shakespeare Today : Practical Approaches and Productive Strategies*. Edited by James E. Davis and Ronald E. Salomone. Urbana, Ill.: NCTE Press, 1993.

Foster, Maxwell E. *The Play behind the Play:* Hamlet *and Quarto One*. Portsmouth, N.H.: Heinemann, 1998.

Howard, Jean E., and Marion O'Connor, eds. *Shakespeare Reproduced: The Text in History and Ideology*. New York: Methuen, 1987.

Lehmann, Courtney. "Strictly Shakespeare? Dead Letters, Ghostly Fathers, and the Cultural Pathology of Authorship in Baz Luhrmann's *William Shakespeare's Romeo + Juliet*." *Shakespeare Quarterly 52*. Forthcoming.

Lennox, Patricia. "Baz Luhrmann's *William Shakespeare's Romeo + Juliet*." Paper presented at the annual meeting of the Shakespeare Association of America, Washington, D.C., April 1997.

Shakespeare, William. *1 Henry IV.* In *The Norton Shakespeare*. Edited by Stephen Greenblatt et al. New York and London: W. W. Norton, 1997.

———. *Romeo and Juliet*. Edited by Stephen Greenblatt et al. New York and London: W. W. Norton, 1997.

Worthen, W. B. *Shakespeare and the Authority of Performance*. Cambridge: Cambridge University Press, 1997.

FILMS CITED

Blade Runner: The Director's Cut. Directed by Ridley Scott. 1hr. 57 min. Warner Brothers, 1982. DVD.

Chimes at Midnight (Falstaff). Directed by Orson Welles. 1 hr. 55 min. Arthur Cantor Films, 1966. Videocassette.

Hamlet. Directed by Laurence Olivier. 2 hr. 33 min. Paramount, 1948. Videocassette.

Last Action Hero. Directed by John McTiernan. 2 hr. 10 min. Columbia Pictures, 1993. Videocassette.

Shakespeare in Love. Directed by John Madden. 2 hr. 2 min. Miramax Films/Universal Pictures, 1998. DVD.

William Shakespeare's Romeo + Juliet. Directed by Baz Luhrmann. 2 hr. TwentiethCentury Fox/Bazmark Films, 1996. Videocassette.

Afterword:
T(e)en Things I Hate about Girlene Shakesploitation Flicks in the Late 1990s, or, Not-So-Fast Times at Shakespeare High

THE LATE 1990S WITNESSED AN ONSLAUGHT OF HOLLYWOOD "TEENSPLOITATION" movies, remarkable both for the R-rated transgressive behavior of the characters ("these teenagers have more sex, take more drugs, and are a whole lot slicker," as two movie critics put it) and for the cruelty the popular characters, especially the young women, display toward innocent nerds [1] Many of these teensploi films constitute a subgenre of what I call "Shakesploitation" flicks. They either cite Shakespeare, as in the following teen movies: *High School High* (dir. Hart Bochner, 1997), *Whatever* (dir. Susan Skoog, 1997), *Can't Hardly Wait* (dir. Deborah Kaplan and Harry Elfront, 1998), *Jawbreaker* (dir. Darren Stein, 1999), *The Rage: Carrie 2* (dir. Robert Mandel and Katt Shea, 1999), *Cruel Intentions* (dir. Roger Kumble, 1999), *200 Cigarettes* (dir. Risa Bramon Garcia, 1999), *American Pie* (dir. Paul Weitz, 1999), *Outside Providence* (dir. Michael Corrente 1999); or, they adapt Shakespeare's plays: *10 Things I Hate about You* (dir. Gil Junger, 1999) is based on *The Taming of the Shrew*, *Never Been Kissed* (dir. Raja Gosnell, 1999) on *As You Like It*, and *O* (dir. Tim Blake Nelson, 2001) on *Othello*.[2] These Shakesploi flicks tread the path blazed by earlier 1990s teen films that adapted Shakespeare for a youth market, such as Baz Luhrmann's *William Shakespeare's Romeo + Juliet* (1996), Lloyd Kaufman's *Tromeo and Juliet* (1996) and, in an overtly pedagogical vein, Al Pacino's *Looking for Richard* (1996).[3]

I find Shakesploi flicks, particularly the four on which I will focus in this essay, *Jawbreaker*, *The Rage*, *10 Things*, and *Never Been Kissed*, of critical interest for three reasons. First, they overtly thematize both the "dumbing down" of Shakespeare seen in earlier high school movies such as *Porky's 2* (dir. Bob Clark, 1986) and the figure of the loser that emerged in early nineties mass culture.[4] Yet these newer films oppose female intelligence and loserdom so that Shakespeare literacy and receptivity by girls are allied with not smoking or drinking (drugs nearly go unmentioned), safe sex (both to prevent pregnancy and the transmission of STDs), waiting until you're ready for sex (not being a "slut"), and so on. (Rock and roll, even starting a band, however, seem to be O.K.) The loser is not a figure with whom teen girls are permitted to identify except insofar as they can hope to reject him. Second, Shakesploi flicks focus on what I call "lesbosocial" relations: a girl and often a group of girls occupy the film's romantic center, with the heroine poised between bad girls who are sexually active (sluts) and good girls who are (naive) virgins.[5] The flicks project a cinematic fantasy wherein the ugly duckling, intelligent Cinderella-like heroine will triumph over her (usually) hotter but dumber rivals, not only winning the hunky guy but ending up with a far better relationship than the superficial rivals would ever be able to manage. "Girls," these films call out, "you can stay a sober virgin, and he'll still be into you!" In dividing teen girls off from the loser, these films invite, if not force, feminist critics to revisit the longstanding divide between feminists over female sexuality and over the bad girl.[6] Third, the subgenre of Shakesploi flicks breaks down into two genres, horror films like *Jawbreaker* and *The Rage* and romantic comedies like *10 Things I Hate about You* and *Never Been Kissed*.

These two genres are, of course, necessarily intermixed because they are defined against each other: romantic failure equals horror (and the female grotesque—Josie's nickname in *Never Been Kissed* is "Josie Grossie"—and tragedy) while romantic success equals comedy.[7] (One expects a film that fuses the genres of horror and romantic comedy out any day now entitled *A Midsummer Night's Scream*.)[8] What is striking, however, are the differences between the genres: the horror film allows for greater attention to lesbosocial relations—girl/girl rivalry and girl/girl friendship—than to heterosexual coupling (in the lesbosocial world of horror films, men are boy toys, trophies, or arm rests, a means to success rather than the be-all and end-all); and the more the focus is on same-sex rivalry, the less fully thematized Shakespeare is in the film. In *Jawbreaker* and *The Rage*, moral and literary intelligence either extricates the good girl from a hermeneutic relation to Shakespeare or marks romantic outcomes for loser girls as necessarily disastrous failures.

In the remainder of this essay, I will offer a critique of the four Shakesploi flicks under discussion, particularly the romantic comedies, as instances of conservative feminism. Late nineties Shakesploi films use Shakespeare's cultural authority to legitimate a rather repressive notion of female intelligence, one that divides women yet again into (smart) good girls and (stupid, if somewhat prettier and hotter) bad girls. This construction of female intelligence infantilizes rather than liberates teen girls, and one could rightly regard these extremely similar films as a conservative reaction to the more transgressive role pop stars like Madonna played in relation to teen girl Madonna wanna-bes in the 1980s with music videos like "Express Yourself."

Rather than make this critique in the name of materialist feminism, however, I want to explore the possibility of loser feminism (some might call it bimbo feminism) and loser romance, or "dumb love."[9] Any feminist attempt to redeem Shakesploi flicks from loserdom, I will maintain, remains bankrupt insofar as it lacks a positive account of romantic love and reproduces yet another version of the contentious, competitive split between women that these teen films consistently put on display, this time playing out the good girl/bad girl opposition as a conflict between conservative and materialist feminists.[10]

☆☆☆

Late nineties Shakesploi flicks, particularly the adaptations, leave the language of the plays almost entirely behind. These films dumb down Shakespeare in fulfilling manufactured preteen fantasies about being popular (romantically successful) in high schools, which are divided into losers and hotties. (The central fantasy in all of the teensploi films is that one can cross over from being a nerd to a hottie and vice versa: cool guys may fall for nerd girls, nerd guys may get hot girls, and seemingly cool guys and girls may turn out to be losers.)[11] While late nineties Shakesploi flicks dumb down Shakespeare insofar as they leave the language of the plays behind, they also resist the celebration of dumbness and stupidity so marked as a guy thing in loser films like *Tapeheads* (dir. Bill Fishman, 1988), *Bill and Ted's Excellent Adventure* (Stephen Herek, 1989), *Wayne's World* (dir. Penelope Spheeris, 1992), and *Dumb and Dumber* (dir. Peter Farrelly, 1994). (*Clueless* and *Romy and Michelle's High School Reunion* [dir. David Mirkin, 1996] were the exceptions to the "guy as loser" rule.)[12] Instead, Shakesploi flicks articulate a fantasy about the nerdy girl who is unpopular because she is basically smarter than her classmates. Unlike Cher in *Clueless*, who has seen the Franco Zeffirelli 1990 film of *Hamlet* but not read Shakespeare's play, these newer heroines know their literary Shakespeare. To be sure, Rachel in *The Rage* is a loser outcast, and the heroines of *10 Things* and *Never been Kissed* are each branded early on in their respective films with loser status. In *10 Things*, Bianca (Larisa Oleynik) twice calls Kat (Julia Stiles), a character based on Shakespeare's Katherina Baptista, a loser, and Josie Geller (Drew Barrymore), the heroine of *Never Been Kissed*, accidentally prints the word "loser" on her forehead, making herself a figure of public ridicule who is greeted by students with comments like "Hi loser." Josie is thereafter known by her peers as "the loser" until her brother helps her become popular. Yet the teen girl leads in romantic comedies are not, in the end, losers, and even the heroine of a horror film like *The Rage: Carrie 2* can elevate her loser status insofar as she can be written into the role of Shakespeare's Juliet.[13]

This shift in the new Shakesploi flicks to girl-centered plots either with heroines who are literate, nonloser identified readers of Shakespeare or with a heroine who can be taught the meaning of love with the help of her nonloser boyfriend and Shakespeare is no doubt due in part to the fact that the major part of the audience is made up of teen and preteen girls, or girlenes, as I like to call them in my own dumb way, a phenomenon that film execs took notice of after it became clear that much of the success of James Cameron's *Titanic* (1997), pitched by Cameron as "*Romeo and Juliet* on a sinking ship," was due to repeat ticket sales by girl spectators.[14] Both films have novelizations, clearly directed at a young, girl market of readers (the assumption being that girls are more likely to read than boys).[15] Mandella, Kat's friend in *10 Things*, knows passages from Shakespeare by heart and at the end of the novelization urges the reader to go on to read Shakespeare's play. It is not only the marginal, somewhat nerdy couple, Michael and Mandella, who closely identify with Shakespeare. Kat also loves her English teacher's assignment to imitate Shakespeare's Sonnet 141. Similarly, the focus of *10 Things* is on Kate. The referents of "I" and "You" in the film's title are ambiguous, the title is open to being read as either Patrick hating Kat or the reverse. Yet both the movie poster and the soundtrack CD-cover gender the title's meaning by drawing a line in the right side of "u" in "you" with an arrow pointing down at Patrick, thereby making the "I" who is doing the hating Kat, not Patrick.[16] In a shift away from the more male-centered films like the *Porky's* and *Revenge of the Nerds* series or *Weird Science* (dir. John Hughes, 1985) and the 1994 television series it spawned, loser guys in current teen films generally look callow, are sometimes villains as in *The Rage*, or are recast as losers, as in *Can't Hardly Wait*.[17] Male leads from Shakespeare are now largely in tragedies such as *Hamlet*, *Othello*, and *Titus Andronicus*, all of which put male misogynistic anxieties about female sexuality on display. Along similar lines, references to Romeo are to (loveable) loser boys, as in *Can't Hardly Wait* and *200 Cigarettes*.[18] The movie poster for *10 Things* interestingly placed a tag line at the bottom which read "Romeo, Oh Romeo, get out of my face." The poster reads the film's adaptation of *Taming* as an anti-Shakespeare backlash against the current cinematic vogue for Shakespeare's *Romeo and Juliet*.[19] Shakespeare, then, is marked as a girl thing in the newer teensploi films.

The central questions raised by these new Shakesploi flicks are whether or not the loser figure works for young women as well as it did for young men and whether knowing their Shakespeare gets these teen girls anywhere feminist critics might want them to be. While I would happily concede that there is nothing of interest in Shakesploi teen mall films when it comes to formal complexity, I nevertheless want to propose that their pop, light-weight status in conjunction with the way they position Shakespeare as a high culture icon provides the means to construct a genuinely dialectical relation between the films and feminist critique. Shakesploi flicks are particularly valuable, in my view, because of the resistance they offer to existing versions of feminism, exposing some of their limitations and blind spots by bringing teen girls into conjunction with the loser. In particular, they make it difficult for feminists of whatever kind to treat mall Shakesploi films either as just plain stupid or as cleverly promoting a sexist, reactionary notion of stupidity, as if their own vantage point was securely in critical knowledge free of philosophical concerns about the relation between knowledge and ignorance. For it was the teen mall film *Clueless* that forcefully destabilized the relation between the primary, original Shakespeare play and the secondary, film adaptation as it simultaneously destabilized the opposition between intelligence and stupidity. Cher is both dumber *and* smarter than her college student rival when she correctly attributes "To thine own self be true" to Polonius because she has seen Franco Zeffirelli's *Hamlet* starring Mel Gibson, not read the play. In the romantic economy of *Clueless*, less is more.[20] Materialist feminist critical practice breaks down, I submit, in response to the issue of female stupidity raised by Shakesploi flicks, either trying to recuperate "stoopidity" as transgressive, or eschewing it as a male, adolescent pose, which serves only the interests of men. What demands attention in recent Shakesploi films, then, is the way they attempt—I think in conservative fashion—to restabilize the oppositions destabilized in *Clueless*, divorcing teen girlene literacy from (adolescent male) loserdom.

☆☆☆

Of the four Shakesploi flicks under discussion, *Jawbreaker* is most concerned with lesbosocial girl/girl rivalry, and its one reference to Shakespeare is the least thematized. *Jawbreaker* is a story about four girls, Courtney Shayne (Rose McGowan), Julie Freeman (Rebecca Gayheart), Macie Fox (Julie Benz), and Liz Purr (Charlotte Lopez) who are members of an elite trendsetting group known as the Flawless Four, three of whom accidentally murder one of their members, Liz, who chokes on a jawbreaker Courtney stuffs into her mouth and then prevents her from spitting out by duct taping her mouth shut and tying her up. The three girls then replace Liz with a nerdy girl, Fern Mayo (Judy Greer) after Fern stumbles onto their secret, effectively using the lure of popularity to bribe her so she won't tell on them. The film has an early scene in an English class discussion of *Macbeth*, though the play is unnamed (we also see a picture of Shakespeare on the wall). The class discussion, led by a woman English teacher (Rachel Winfree), focuses on Lady Macbeth. The three "bad girls" resemble the three witches initially, and two of the three girls bear a likeness to Lady Macbeth: as the ringleader, Courtney resembles Lady Macbeth near the beginning of the play—she's ambitious and manipulative—and Macie resembles Lady Macbeth late in the play as she begins to go insane. The good girl, Julie, who breaks with bad ringleader girl Courtney, is increasingly distanced from *Macbeth*. Though Julie gets exiled from the group by Courtney, she manages a comeback at the prom, and Courtney is exposed and humiliated. She is the only one to couple, though her boyfriend is an undeveloped character who takes the backseat to her plotting. *Jawbreaker* gags on Shakespeare. The girls are relatively distanced from him. Significantly, in the class discussion of *Macbeth*, the teacher does all the talking.

The Rage: Carrie 2* is less focused on lesbosocial relations than *Jawbreaker* and uses Shakespeare more extensively, rewriting *Romeo and Juliet*, foregrounding the issue of female literacy with regard to Shakespeare and romantic success. *Romeo and Juliet* is the model for the two main heterosexual, romantic relationships in the film, both involving loser girls who are also close friends. Near the beginning of the film, there is a class discussion about the play involving the students. Rachel (Emily Beryl), the loser outcast and telekinetic heir to Carrie, comments from the back of the room, "I don't know if I believe in it." "What's that?" the teacher asks her. "Love," she answers. She is quickly taunted with another student's rhetorical question, "Who'd love her?" but Jesse Ryan (Jason London), the hunky, cool, popular guy in school and a quarterback, soon falls for her. Their initials, R and J, mark Rachel and Jesse as lovers like Romeo and Juliet, and this scene not only sets the two teens apart from their peers but also sets up Jesse's break from his vicious, misogynistic jock friends, who have a contest to determine who can sleep with the most girlfriends before school lets out. *Romeo and Juliet* also serves as the model for another romantic relationship between Rachel's one and only friend at school, Lisa (Mena Suvari). After being dumped by a guy named Brad (Justin Urich) she has slept with once, and who is one of the jocks participating in the contest, she kills herself by jumping off a school building rooftop. (In the trailer for the film, the class discussion is intercut with the scene of Lisa going up to a roof at school and jumping off.)

Similar to the original *Carrie* (dir. Brian De Palma, 1976), *The Rage's* Rachel dies at the end at a postprom party in which she is humiliated and deceived into thinking that Jesse didn't really love her, sleeping with her only to win the contest (secretly filmed videotape of them having sex is shown to the group on several large-screen television sets). She then takes her revenge by destroying everyone in sight. But Jesse, whose arrival at the party has been delayed by his jealous and predatory former girlfriend, gets there in time to prove to Rachel that he does in fact love her, and she heroically uses the last of her powers literally to throw him out of harm's way rather than save herself. Modeling itself on the sensational ending in the Luhrmann *William Shakespeare's Romeo + Juliet*, wherein Juliet awakes while Romeo is still alive, *The Rage*'s prom scene includes clips from the analogous scene in *Carrie*, making it clear that *The Rage* is rewriting the original to give Rachel a happier romantic relationship, even if it is distressingly brief, than Carrie managed. Rachel is redeemed from her loser status, that is, both from her origins in white-trash foster parents and in a crazy biological mother who was carted off to the looney bin when Rachel was a child.[21]

This rewrite of *Carrie*'s ending depends on teaching being gendered male earlier in *The Rage*, with the twin plots about Lisa and Rachel suggesting that with the help of a male canonical author and a male teacher, a boyfriend can teach his loser (because damaged by her childhood) girlfriend about love, trust, and faith. Hence, Rachel can rescue her boyfriend from Romeo's fate. (By contrast, women in *The Rage* are unable to save each other: Rachel fails to save Lisa or herself from Juliet's fate, and Sue Snell [played by Amy Irving in both films], Carrie's friend in the original and now the high school counselor in the sequel, fails, like the gym teacher who dies in *Carrie*, to save Rachel.) Rachel and Lisa are compared as kind of dumb with regard to romantic love, the former teachable, the latter not. Both girls have problems reading boys: just as Lisa overreads Brad's note to her, so Rachel misreads the video and the book with Jesse's signature in it at the big party. But Rachel can be taught how to read love correctly, even if she shares her friend's fate: Rachel's suicide is a sacrifice made out of love and the knowledge of being loved, unlike Lisa's more hopeless death. The epilogue to *The Rage* undoes even this optimistic fusion of Shakespeare and male pedagogical authority in Rachel's case, however.

The epilogue begins with Jesse studying alone in his room, having fallen asleep, but study here is not a way out of the impasse of teen disaster. He appears to awake when Rachel appears to come back to life and return to him, but, after a short pause, she takes nightmarish form, and he truly awakens to find himself painfully alone. Female sexuality remains nightmarish insofar as it remains outside the control of the boyfriend, and, by extension, of the teacher and male author. Jesse's nightmare cancels out his fantasy that she has died at peace, that he can mourn Rachel's death by incorporating her as a lost love object. The epilogue also undoes the optimistic use of Shakespeare by inverting the gender equivalences between the principal characters in both plots. Jesse ends up occupying the role played in *Carrie* by Carrie's sympathetic girlfriend, Sue Snell, and this inversion is quietly signaled throughout the film by Jesse and Rachel's initials in that they mark an identification with Shakespeare's lovers as cross-gendered, Rachel corresponding to Romeo, Jesse to Juliet.[22]

☆☆☆

In contrast to these two horror Shakesploi flicks, the two romantic comedies *10 Things* and *Never Been Kissed* link the heroines' literacy and knowledge of Shakespeare to their achievement of romantic success. The two romantic comedies differ markedly, however, in the way they conceive of adapting Shakespeare. *10 Things* thematizes adaptation in terms of an aural register, using the cover song and the register of sound to create a series of cynical puns that invite us to read the film as a cover of *Taming*. By contrast, *Never Been Kissed* thematizes adaptation as going undercover, using the visual register of disguise as a means by which the writer's voice can be read rather than heard. The conception of adaptation as aural or visual has significant consequences for the ways these two films both revise gender issues in Shakespeare's plays and revise the teensploi films with which they compete: *10 Things* reads itself as a cheap trick, a prostitution of Shakespeare; by contrast, *Never Been Kissed* reads itself as saving itself for Shakespeare, the heroine refusing to prostitute herself for the sake of getting a newspaper story.

10 Things updates *The Taming of the Shrew*, setting Shakespeare's farce in present-day Seattle at Padua High School. Sisters Katarina and Bianca Stratford and male hunk Patrick Verona (Heath Ledger) are the principals; Cameron James (Joseph Gordon-Levitt) is Lucentio; Michael Eckman (David Krumholtz) is Hortensio; Joey Donner (Andrew Keegan) is Gremio; and the widow is bifurcated into two girls, each a friend of one of the sisters: Mandella (Susan May Pratt) is Kat's friend, who is "involved" with Shakespeare, and the inaptly named Chastity (Gabrielle Union) is Bianca's best friend. Chastity, not Bianca, turns out to be the real shrew. In a series of pairings that are neater than those of Shakespeare's play, Cameron hooks up with Bianca, Mandella with Michael, Joey with Chastity, and Kat with Patrick.

In order to update *The Taming of the Shrew*, *10 Things* has to radically revise the play, making it feminist in many respects, most notably in the characterization of Katarina Stratford. Kat is made quite literally a feminist critic of the English and American literary canon taught in her high school. She nails Ernest Hemingway, whose *Sun Also Rises* is being discussed in class, as an alcoholic and abusive misogynist, and she asks that the class discuss instead Sylvia Plath, Charlotte Brontë, or Simone de Beauvoir. When Joey teases her for being "a self-righteous hag," he is rebuked by the teacher, but the teacher, who remains neutral in all such class disputes, in turn caustically trumps Kat by mocking her "suffering" as a middle-class suburban female, reminding her that her oppression pales in comparison with his own as a black man: there are no black male writers in the school curriculum either, he points out. (The set design backs them both up: all the writers on posters in the classroom are white, and all but one are male.)

When sent to the counselor, where Ms. Perky (Allison Janney) tells her she is regarded by her classmates as a "heinous bitch" and then accuses her of terrorizing the class, Kat rightly says that expressing one's opinion is not terrorism and proves her intelligence and wit by supplying Ms. Perky, who writes romance novels on her laptop while counseling students, with various words and phrases for erect penises such as "tumescent" and "quivering member." This positive view of her intelligence is confirmed when we learn that she has been accepted for admission into Sarah Lawrence College. Kat is also portrayed sympathetically for being into the Riot Grrrl music of the Raincoats, Bikini Kill, even though it is Letters to Cleo (not a Riot Grrrl band but a kind of No Doubt knockoff with a hot blonde lead singer) who she goes to see play at the local Club Skunk.[23]

The film takes a feminist turn as well in several other respects. It revises the relations between the two sisters, making it one of deep friendship rather than competition. Although the father, Dr. Walter Stratford (Larry Miller), says that Bianca cannot date until Kat does, Kat does go to a party just so Bianca can as well, and later in the film, Kat similarly goes to the prom for her sake, not because Patrick asks her out.[24] The play is also stripped of male bravado and male authority over women. For example, the film has a number of penis size jokes, all of which are made at the expense of the boys. When Patrick first appears, we see him at Ms. Perky's office, sent there to discuss an incident in which he had publicly used a bratwurst sausage as if it were his penis, and Perky comments skeptically: "A bratwurst, Patrick? You wish." Kat is sent to Perky's office as well, in her case for kneeing some guy in the balls, and, at the prom, Bianca similarly knees Joey in the balls after socking him three times in the face. Moreover, Kat confides to Bianca that Joey never told anyone he had slept with Kat because she threatened to tell everyone that he has "a really small dick" if he did.

Further undermining male authority, Patrick's character is denied Petruchio's sexist domination of Kate. Kat is not kept from food, sleep, or clothing; indeed, unlike Kate, there is no taming of Kat at all. Instead, Patrick merely saves her from her potentially Sylvia Plath-like self-destructive impulses. Though Patrick's attempts to keep her from getting drunk or his refusal to kiss her in his car contain echoes of the scene at Petruchio's

house where he prevents Kate from eating and sleeping and where he with-
holds sex on their wedding night, Patrick's behavior arises out of his gentlemanly concern for Kat's well-being, not his desire to assert control over
her. His refusal to kiss her in the car, we may infer, stems from his being
put off both by residual barf in Kat's mouth and her still somewhat drunken
state. Similarly, even the father's patriarchal authority is softened in the
film. Walter Stratford may be overbearing, overprotective, and controlling
when it comes to his daughters going out on dates with boys, but he's portrayed as being rightly concerned about teen pregnancy, and he does relent
and let the girls go to Bogey Lowenstein's party, then to the prom. Similarly, he lets Kat go to Sarah Lawrence rather than force her to stay in
Seattle and attend the University of Washington as he wants her to do.

   10 Things revises heterosexual romance in *Taming* so that it no longer
involves "right" male "supremacy" and hierarchy of husbands over wives
but instead involves reciprocity and equality. Going so far as to invert the
play's (at least official) account of gender relations, *10 Things* tells a story
about the taming of male desire. Teen boys are tamed either through having their private parts symbolically cut down to size, so to speak, though
the ball kneeing does seem to potentially literalize the metaphor, or by
cleaning up their act—no smoking or drunkenness—and, in a very un-
Shakespearean move, bonds between boy and girlfriend are made by breaking bonds between boys. Along the same lines, Kat is made morally superior
to Patrick. He lies to her, but she does not lie to him (or anyone else). And
all of Petruchio's transgressive behavior is denied Patrick and given over to
Kat. What remains of Petruchio's wooing process is hardly transgressive at
all; Petruchio's public flattery of Kate before he takes her back to his house
is what is emphasized in Patrick's wooing of Kat. Furthermore, unlike Richard Burton's drunken Petruchio in Franco Zeffirelli's *Taming of the Shrew*,
Patrick is seen only once in a bar nursing a beer, and he is perfectly sober.
In contrast, Kat is the one who gets drunk, and she even barfs very near if
not on Patrick. No speech is demanded from Kat on wifely (or girlfriendly)
obedience, and none is delivered by her. At the end of the film, Patrick is
the one who has "messed up" by lying to her about why he wanted to take
her to the prom, and he is the one who has to ask for forgiveness from Kat.
Domestic violence is euphemized, shrunk to the lovers harmlessly and joy-
fully throwing paint at each other in an amusement park.

   Yet, as perhaps has already become clear, *10 Things*'s feminism, such as
it is, comes at the price of harnessing it to a conservative idealization of the
good girl. The film neuters Shakespeare's play, taking a Nancy Reagan-
like "just say No" position on the problems said by conservatives and reac-
tionaries to have been caused or at least exacerbated by the high divorce
rate in the U.S., namely, premarital teen sex, teen drinking, and teen smoking. We never see the two couples consummate their relationships. Though

we learn from Bianca that Kat wears black undies (because she wants to have sex) and though Kat tells Bianca that she has lost her virginity, Kat explains that she had sex only once because she wasn't ready and counsels her sister to wait. Here she takes the place of her father and is overprotective of her the same way he is of both of his daughters. Despite the subtle reference to Cleopatra in the band name Letters to Cleo, Kat is no budding, sexually active Cleopatra. The only transgressive things Kat does are to flash her breasts at a teacher, knee a student in the balls, back her car into Joey's car, and kick a soccer ball at Patrick, and the only transgressive things Patrick does are pay the marching band to back him up as he performs a cover of Frankie Valli's "Can't Take My Eyes Off of You" while he publicly serenades Kat, and drill a hole in Cameron's French class textbook. Rumors that Patrick has spent a year in jail, set a state trooper on fire, and so on, all prove to be untrue. In fact, he spent a year in Australia caring for an ailing grandfather. When Kat gets drunk downing shots of tequila at a party and konks her head on a chandelier after table dancing for fellow revelers, he catches her and then does so again several times when she nearly faints. Although Patrick "saves" Kat, she "saves" him back by getting him out of detention.

Along similarly conservative lines, *10 Things* also enlists Shakespeare's cultural authority in the service of exclusively heterosexual romance. Bianca makes it clear to Cameron that Kat is not a lesbian (her resistance to Patrick's advances have nothing to do, that is, with same-sex desire), and gay references are brought in in relation to Michael and Cameron several times, but only to be tossed aside as jokes or disavowed. In one of several "blooper" outtakes included as the credits roll at the end, for example, Michael jumps Cameron, declaring his love for Cameron in the party scene just after Cameron has been dumped by Bianca for Joey. Similarly, Michael cites the first line of Sonnet 56, "Sweet love, renew thy force," when attempting to encourage Patrick to continue pursuing Kat. But Patrick quickly rebuffs him and tells Michael not to speak that way to him. In a non sequitur that enables Michael to disavow any homoerotic desire for Patrick or in Shakespeare's sonnet, Michael in turn tells Cameron not to speak that way to Patrick. At an earlier moment, Cameron says to Patrick that he and Michael are buddies but not in "a prison movie kinda way."

Although *10 Things* leaves behind Shakespeare's language and radically rewrites his plot, the film also foregrounds Shakespeare's status as cultural icon. Shakespeare is made into a kind of currency, the means by which the film's brand of conservative feminism gets its authority and value. Though the one hundred dollar bills given by Joey to Patrick no doubt have Ben Franklin on them, their close-up display nevertheless calls to mind Shakespeare's portrait (both guys have long hair and receding hairlines). More directly, if less literally, the film sets up Shakespeare as *the* cultural authority to quote, as a model for students to imitate. The teacher says, for example, that Shakespeare "knows his shit," even if he is white and male. This shared appreciation of Shakespeare transcends their earlier disagreement about the canon. The teacher reads the first five lines of Sonnet 141 as if rapping them, translating them into urban African-American mass culture. The first five lines also become the model for Kat's poem—which is not a sonnet at all—and for the title of the film:

> Love is my sin, and thy dear virtue hate,
> Hate of my sin grounded on sinful loving.
> O, but with mine compare thou thine own state,
> But 'tis my heart that loves what they despise,
> Who in despite of view is pleased to dote

Shakespeare is unsurprisingly made the ultimate authority on romantic love. We are to appreciate the depth of Kat's love for Patrick and the damage he has done her by lying to her when she reads the following (quite atrocious) poem aloud in class:

> I hate the way you talk to me
> and the way you cut your hair.
> I hate the way you drive my car.
> I hate it when you stare.
> I hate your big dumb combat boots
> and the way you read my mind.
> I hate you so much it makes me sick.
> It even makes me rhyme.
> I hate the way you're always right.
> I hate it when you lie.
> I hate it when you make me laugh,
> Even worse when you make me cry.
> I hate it when you're not around
> and the fact that you didn't call.
> But mostly I hate the way I don't hate you,
> Not even close, not even a little bit,
> Not even at all.

Similarly, Mandella and Michael connect romantically when they both cite a line from *Macbeth*, and Mandella, who has a picture of Shakespeare in her hall locker, says she is not just a fan of his but "involved" with him. Michael leaves Mandella a prom dress and a note inviting her to the prom signed "William S," and Michael shows up at the prom dressed as him. Mandella is a Goth chick, so here Shakespeare is read as an authority even for "alternative" kids like her and Kat who are not initially interested in going to proms.

Yet if the film uses Shakespeare's cultural authority to produce a conservative feminism where the price of avoiding domestic abuse is the repression of women's sexual freedom and the price of teen interest in Shakespeare is the radical dumbing down of his writings, the film also produces an account of its own process of adapting Shakespeare in terms of the cover. With the closer relation between MTV, film, and video, spinoff soundtracks are crucially important to gaining a market for teensploi films, and some of the allusions to Shakespeare in these films are made through soundtracks. Sound clips from Dire Straits' love song "Romeo and Juliet" play on *Can't Hardly Wait* and *200 Cigarettes*, for example, and a clip from the Cardigans' pop hit "Lovefool," on the soundtrack of Luhrmann's *William Shakespeare's Romeo + Juliet*, is played for the virgin Annette Hargrove (Reese Witherspoon) by Sebastian Valmont (Ryan Phillippe) in *Cruel Intentions*, thereby suggesting that he is no Romeo looking for eternal love and marriage but a Don Juan interested only in one-night (or afternoon, as the case may be) stands. (He does become Romeo by the end of the film.)[25]

10 Things does not simply allude to Shakespeare through the use of a sound clip but thematizes its status as a teen adaptation of a literary classic both by gendering rock music and by using the cover song to reflect as well on its relation to similar teen films. The film begins by representing Kat's relation to her female peers in terms of a war between pop songs. Kat is differentiated from other girls from the start by her interest in (bad) girl rock and roll. The movie begins conventionally enough with unlocated soundtrack music, Barenaked Ladies' "One Week," heard as the credits roll while the camera pans right from a shot of the Space Needle and skyline to kids arriving at school. This song (by an all-guy band) is then located in a car radio, with four girls in the car listening happily to the music. As Kat pulls her car up beside theirs, "One Week" is drowned out by Kat's car radio, playing Joan Jett's "Bad Reputation." And this song in turn becomes the unlocated soundtrack as the credits continue to roll. Music is similarly used to contrast scenes with the two couples coming back from Bogey Lowenstein's party. Angry music plays as Kat leaves her date's car and walks into the house while happy music plays as Bianca leaves her date's car. (In a lapse of gentlemanly etiquette, the guys don't get out of the car to escort the girls to the door.)

In thematizing a teen adaptation of Shakespeare in terms of the cover, *10 Things* also foregrounds teen music itself as a form of adaptation by using a number of cover songs. As we have seen, Patrick covers Frankie Valli's "Can't Take My Eyes Off of You," and a cover of Nick Lowe's pop song "Cruel to Be Kind" by Letters to Cleo plays on Kat's car radio as Patrick drives Kat home from Bogey Lowenstein's party. At the prom, a red-haired woman singer sings a cover of "Shout," and Letters to Cleo then covers "Cruel to Be Kind," with the lead singer coming onto the floor to address both Patrick and Kat. The film ends as we hear a cover of Cheap Trick's "I Want You to Want Me," also by Letters to Cleo, and the film cuts to them playing on the roof of the school building as the credits roll.[26] These covers explore cross-gender possibilities for performance and also suggest a model for understanding what kind of reception teen audiences may give Shakespeare.[27] All of the songs covered by women were originally sung and written by men. Only Patrick covers a song written by a person of the same gender. At the prom, this gender inversion is also reinforced as the male brass players dance like female backup singers. Though some critics might conclude that cross-gendered covers of male songs allow women greater freedom, the opposite, I suggest, is actually the case. For one thing, the covers by the women are nearly identical to the originals except for the gender of the voices. By contrast, Patrick's cover of Valli is quite different, performed at the high school stadium, sung first without accompaniment and then, when he gets to the refrain, with the high school marching band as his orchestra.

Rather than simply closing down feminist possibilities, however, the film invites a critique of its own Shakesploi version of teen romance. The title of the last cover song—"I Want You to Want Me"—and the name of the band performing it—Cheap Trick—activate a series of puns that bear on the cover song as a model for teen adaptations and the way Shakespeare is made into a currency in the film. The cover of this band in particular invites one to read the film's resolution and the film itself as a "cheap trick" in which one kind of desire is converted into another: the film *10 Things I Hate About You* is exchanged for the similar sounding play *The Taming of the Shrew*, and the novelization of the film is similarly exchanged for the play as literature. The cover of Cheap Trick's "I Want You to Want Me" comes on just after Kat and Patrick make up and invites a critique of the film's own cheap tricks, particularly with regard to the happy ending. When Kat learns accidentally that Joey paid Patrick to take her out, Patrick repairs the damage done to his relationship and the hurt he has caused Kat by using the money Joey paid him to take her out on a date to buy her a Fender Stratocaster guitar (which he had seen her, unobserved by her, play in a music store). She'd also told him earlier that she should start a band. They kiss and she protests, "You can't just buy me a guitar every time you mess up, you know." He replies, "I know. But there's always drums, the bass, and maybe even someday a tambourine." They kiss again and she starts to protest again—"And don't just think you can . . ."—but he silences her by kissing her. The cover of Cheap Trick's "I Want You to Want Me" then comes on.

The film's "cheap trick" undermines, if not entirely cancels, the conservative feminism and reformation of heterosexual male desire the film wants to shore up by licensing the institution of a new economy in romantic relationships: in moving the wager at the end of the play to the beginning of the film, *10 Things* effectively turns Patrick into a gigolo. According to this new romantic economy, the guy can still treat his girlfriend as a Joan: he can "mess up" but then clean things up by paying the girlfriend off. Whatever Patrick has done that may have harmed Kat is translated, in the logic of this romantic economy, into a loss recoverable with interest: whatever she loses will come back to Kat in the form of something she wants. This economy licenses male transgressions against romantic love, although in the film's soft-pedaled teen fantasy there are no real transgressions (such as cheating) to speak of: Patrick is not interested in Bianca, nor is he interested in any other woman (he never even looks at any). *10 Things* regards Kat and its audience as tricks to be cheaply turned. It reveals its own use of Shakespeare's high cultural authority to exchange an earlier Shakespearean form of feminized sexism for a nineties form of sexist feminism that, ultimately, is itself a form of prostitution, a cheap(ening) trick.[28] To be sure, the film may hold out some hope by suggesting a link between the singer of Letters to Cleo and Kat, the singer anticipating what Kat plans to become. The end furthermore heightens the connection between Kat and the singer by echoing the play's Induction (as the credits roll, the outtakes show us how the film was made, what was cut, what didn't work); the cross-dressing ambiguities raised by the page dressed as Christopher Sly's wife are here played out in terms of the cover as a vocal transvestism. Yet, as we have seen, the cover song here covers over the (rebellious) female voice, limiting it to being the copy-Kat, as it were, of the male voice, conceived of as much freer and originary.

In contrast to *10 Things'* thematization of teensploi adaptations of literary classics in terms of the cover song, *Never Been Kissed* goes undercover and thematizes Shakespeare in terms of the visual register of disguise. While more high-minded, *Never Been Kissed* is, in my view, actually the cheaper film. It undoes the feminist and homoerotic potential of *As You Like It*, turning the theme of disguise in the play into a means by which heterosexual love can discover itself. The film revises the standard teensploi plot about a nerdy girl, Josie Geller (Drew Barrymore), who finds true love with a hunky guy, into a pastoral comedy in which an adult can go back to high school to undo her traumatic experiences there. When Josie walks into her English class, her teacher, Sam Caulson (Michael Vartan) says "Welcome to Shakespeare's *As You Like It*." The film offers a humanist, thematic reading of the play:

> Sam. "All the world's a stage, and all the men and women merely players." Anyone have any idea what Shakespeare meant by that? It's about disguise, playing a part. It's the theme of *As You Like It*. Can anyone tell me where we see that?

Aldys. Well, Rosalind disguises herself as a man and escapes into the forest.
Sam. Right. And it's when she's in costume that she can finally express her love
for Orlando. See, Shakespeare's making the point that when we're disguised,
we feel freer. We can do things we wouldn't do in ordinary life.

Josie later answers Sam's question about the meaning of pastoral comedy:
"Pastoral means set in the country, originally seen in the *Eclogues* of Virgil.
It's from the Latin 'pascere,' 'to graze.'"

Citations from *As You Like It* and commentary on it register Josie's transition from shit girl loser to it girl celebrity. While reciting Rosalind's lines
in class from act 5, scene 2—"No sooner had they met but they looked; no
sooner looked but they loved; no sooner loved but they sighed"—she lapses
into a reverie of reading in high school a poem she had written to a boy
named Billy on whom she had had an unrequited crush:

Does he notice me?
Does he hear my heart screaming his name?
O Sometimes it's so loud I think
The gods can hear my pain.
His voice is so mellifluous,
Oh, to get just one small kiss.

Josie's abject humiliation at being brutally rejected by Billy (who pretended
to ask her out, then threw an egg at her when he drove by to pick her up) is
put in the past as Josie identifies increasingly with Rosalind. She writes an
essay on the play, part of which she reads aloud in class: "And so it is
Rosalind, in disguise, who is best able to see through the disguise of others.
To say to Phoebe, 'Mistress, know yourself,' to look at love from every
angle, and to realize, finally, that she is in love with Orlando.'" Her successful transformation is displayed forcefully at the prom when she goes
dressed as Rosalind and her date, Guy (Jeremy Jordan), goes dressed as
Orlando. At the prom, she foils a plot hatched by the three popular girls to
throw Alpo dog food on a nerdy girl, and she then delivers a lecture to the
assembled students that is comparable to Rosalind's lecture in which she
sorts out the various lovers into couples.[29]

Like Rosalind, then, Josie is able to find a romantic partner by temporarily taking on a disguise, thereby transforming not only her high school
status as loser but also moving herself up from copy editor to undercover
reporter for her newspaper.[30] The play's theme of cross-dressing is translated into being able to control the way one is read. Significantly, Josie's
success is signaled in visual terms: as she takes on a disguise like
Shakespeare's Rosalind, she also moves from being an undercover newspaper human interest story writer to being a reporter who wears a hidden
camera to being the subject of a story televised by other reporters. The

move from disguise and undercover reporter to television reporter/celebrity suggests that by controlling the ways in which she is read, the Cinderella girl can occupy both sides of any given teen girl fantasy or behavior. Girls, you can have it both ways, the film implies, when it comes to popularity, taking drugs, and having sex. Josie gets stupid stoned on ganja cake and wows the audience of a band when she dances on stage, but she takes the drug accidentally, without knowing that the cake is spiked. She's a virgin, but she's rumored by her brother to be sexually active and a femme fatale who has dumped really hot boys in popular rock bands. Similarly, she becomes popular and is crowned prom queen, but she then throws it all away at the prom because she is morally above being superficially concerned about proms and popularity.

Yet the film's focus on the visual register of disguise has significant implications for Josie's voice and hence for any feminism one might want to claim for the film. The (very humanist) plot is centrally about Josie finding her voice, and it might seem, at first glance, that the film moves out of the visual register of disguise and deception into the aural and vocal register of (naked) truth. Josie reads aloud from the play in class, which recalls her earlier moment of reading a poem aloud in class, and then she reads her paper on *As You Like It* aloud as well. Later in the film, she reads aloud her story in the newspaper in a voice-over, and she speaks to the assembled crowd and television cameras with a microphone as she waits for Sam to show up to kiss her. Yet *Never Been Kissed* actually folds the aural register into the visual, reducing the former to silence. Moreover, Josie turns the hidden camera off in order to talk with Sam privately about her feelings for him. To this extent, it might be thought that she controls how she is seen and by whom. Yet the medium of the newspaper poses a problem in readability: although it is published, Josie's story may be missed, discarded as trash, by its readers, as when Sam doesn't see it while he packs up to leave town. The film supplies Josie's story to the audience through a voice-over, and her use of a microphone at the baseball field suggests a further need for a prosthetic supplement to her voice. (It's never clear why Sam comes after all, whether he has read Josie's story after all or heard about it.) Furthermore, the displacement of her newspaper story by a story filmed live by television cameras reinscribes her voice in a medium where she herself is seen and finally silenced. When Sam, like Orlando, shows up late for his romantic rendezvous, after Josie has given up and, significantly, dropped her microphone (hence lost her voice), Josie does not rebuke him. Indeed, she says nothing, simply grateful he has come to kiss her.[31] In strikingly sexist terms, the film equates romantic success for a woman with losing her voice, at best allowing her to gain it only in order to lose it.

Never Been Kissed's brand of conservative feminism can also be measured by the way it makes Josie far less central than Rosalind and gives her far less freedom from male authority figures than Shakespeare gives his romantic heroine. While Josie chooses the prom theme, "Couples from History Who Were Made for Each Other," Guy gives her permission to choose it, and he then approves her choice (the other students follow his lead). And while she expresses her desire for Sam quite publicly, she waits to be kissed by him rather than going off to find him and then kiss him. She depends at a key moment on her brother Rob to help her become "cool." Moreover, by displacing her spacey and much younger date, seventeen-year-old Guy, as untaught Orlando with the older teacher Sam as the taught Orlando, the film invests Josie's male lover with an authority Orlando does not have at all in Shakespeare's comedy. (To be sure, Sam does think he has much more power over her when he believes she is only seventeen, and he withdraws from her once he learns her real age. His desire for her is tied up in his ability to "pull strings" to help her get into Dartmouth.) Further-more, in a riff taken from *The Truman Show* (dir. Peter Weir, 1998), Josie has to wear a camera so that her editor, who, in another allusion to the play, is called "the Duke," can make sure she gets her story. She is under the surveillance of her male boss and a male reporter. No figure in the film corresponds to the female deity Hymen in Shakespeare's comedy.[32]

The homoerotic potential of the play is also neutralized, made into two small jokes, one by Sam about a football player who, when wearing a uni-form (like a disguise in the play), touches other men's butts and another by Josie at Sam's expense when she returns his compliment that she makes a beautiful prom queen with an apparently unironic rejoinder, "so do you." Any lesbian potential in the relationship between Rosalind and Celia is gutted by the substitution of Rob for Celia.[33] The gender and erotic ambi-guities of the play's epilogue are similarly displaced by a scene of purely heterosexual romance in which age differentials become the site of poten-tial transgression (a young girl develops a crush on Josie's brother and wants to have sex after they leave the prom). Their kiss serves as *the* ex-ample to be followed mimetically by everyone else. Once Sam shows up to give her a kiss, most of the couples in the live audience begin kissing as well. The only transgressive elements in the film are the teacher-student relationship (the teacher thinks she is only seventeen when he develops a major crush on her) and the fact that Josie has not lost her virginity at age twenty-five. Josie's elevation to romantic winner and star reporter goes hand in hand with a notion of her virginal innocence.

Never Been Kissed's conservative feminism can also be seen in the way it yokes Shakespeare and mass media, especially television journalism, to a very straightlaced notion of female sexuality. Like the other Shakesploi flicks under discussion, *Never Been Kissed* turns on a division between the girl characters, and in this case models that division on a corresponding division between high literary culture and low mass culture. Knowledge of

Shakespeare's *As You Like It* is the means by which Josie's superiority over her female rivals gets confirmed. The three popular girls, Kristen, Kirsten, and Gibe, are shown up (somewhat unfairly, I would add, since Rosalind and Orlando are not immediately recognizable characters, the way Hamlet is) as embarrassingly stupid and ignorant when they can't figure out which historical couple Josie and Guy have come to the prom dressed up as:

> *Kirsten*. Who are you guys?
> *Gibby*. Please don't tell me you're Medieval Barbie.
> *Josie*. Rosalind and Orlando.

When Kirsten and Gibby look blank, Josie adds, "From *As You Like It*?" When they still don't get it, she adds, "Shakespeare?" But they still draw a blank. In contrast to Josie, the three girls have come to the prom dressed as different versions of Barbie: proto-Stepford wife clones, Kirsten gets angry with Kristen, claiming that Kristen has stolen the idea from her. Barbie, we are to infer, is a bad role model for girls from a feminist point of view. Shakespeare, by contrast, is where it's at.[34] Yet Josie also gets the better of these girls by virtue of the fact that she is a reporter, her final triumph being her performance in front of cameras. The film articulates a preteen girl's fantasy of romance which, it has to be said, is quite timid: after all, the film is called *Never Been Kissed*, not *Never Been Fucked*. Despite the baseball field setting, where Josie waits to be kissed, it is clear that while Josie may be ready to play, she is not ready to ball. The film's erotic focus is a kiss, not sex, a kiss that perhaps takes a Monica Lewinsky, exhibitionistic direction, as the fantasy of being the star of the romance, fit for media consumption, is fulfilled here. But the fantasy, of course, falls far short of Josie winning her teacherly kneepads. (Even when asked for a date by Guy in her teen bedroom at a party with no parents around and with both of them sitting on her bed, neither one attempts to kiss the other.)

☆☆☆

Taken together, the four Shakesploitation flicks I have examined reveal a dialectical contradiction between dumbing down Shakespeare and making him a genius (and, by extension, making those who appreciate him intelligent and morally superior). This dialectical contradiction returns us to the question of how these films might transform current feminist critical practice. One could assimilate the Shakesploi flicks' use of Shakespeare's cultural authority to an equally conservative one like the right-wing feminism of the Catherine MacKinnon antisex sort (which has sometimes held hands with the likes of the right-wing, antisex Christian Coalition). Along similar lines, feminist critics might want to read the Shakesploi flicks against the grain, valuing *10 Things* above *Never Been Kissed,* or the horror films and the female grotesque in *Jawbreaker* and *The Rage: Carrie 2* over and against the sugar-and-spice girls in the two romantic comedies. Alternatively, one could celebrate the films that work against Shakespeare or use him minimally rather than those that thematize his plays and harness his authority. Consider the teensploi flick *Whatever.* This film is the most clearly lesbosocial of any of the films I have mentioned. It focuses on a friendship between two high school girl dropouts and models itself on *Thelma and Louise* (dir. Ridley Scott, 1991). In this context, the unnamed citation of Antony's funeral oration in *Julius Caesar* might be read as a fantasy about assassinating the hated male English teacher and male writers generally.

Yet this film does not really resolve the problems we have seen in the other Shakesploi conservative romantic comedies. Even here the two girls are contrasted as "good" bad girl to "bad" bad girl. One girl is a virgin, romantic, and an art student, and the other gets drunk and is a "slut" who lets boys use and abuse her. Some critics might then conclude that Shakespeare is the problem and prefer another literary authority such as *Dangerous Liaisons* (dir. Stephen Frears, 1988) and the hotter, R-rated teensploi spinoff, *Cruel Intentions.* Yet this film too comes out at the same place with respect to romance and the bad girl. Kathryn Merteuil (Sarah Michelle Gellar) is punished for being beautiful and smart. She can't keep guys from dumping her for stupider girls. Though Kathryn is the hotter chick, she is in effect a "bitch" incapable of love who is ultimately humiliated for her destructive nastiness. By contrast, Sebastian and Annette triumph as variations of Romeo and Juliet. The recent adaptation of *Great Expectations* works similarly, with Paltrow's Estella being just another ice queen femme fatale stereotype.[35]

In a last-ditch effort to salvage something progressive in the bad girl, some materialist feminist critics might want to dispense with literary authority altogether and attempt to locate a nonliterary mass culture icon as a standard bearer for a "Don't call me 'babe,'" bad girl feminism.[36] Yet even more transgressive films such as *Tank Girl* (dir. Rachel Talalay, 1995) and *Barbwire* (dir. David Hogan, 1996) keep their heroines either asexual or strictly heterosexual. Whether or not that is because film producers fear that mainstream audiences won't see transgressive films about sexually active lesbians is really beside the point, since a more transgressive film using Shakespeare—say, for example, Kaufman's *Tromeo and Juliet*—will reproduce sexist stereotypes about the sexually voracious "bad" girl, just as a film that doesn't use Shakespeare or any other literary authority will too. And insofar as the heroine's "badness" is appealing, it will be said that this kind of bad girl is being marketed to boys anyway, regardless of whether she is straight or lesbian.[37]

Instead of trying to locate the truly transgressive option in mass culture, then, we might do better to consider the possibility that the two brands of feminism—conservative good girl and materialist bad girl—are not as different as feminists of either stripe might like to think. Materialist feminism always recuperates the bad girl, viewing her as in effect good bad and putting her transgressions of bourgeois decorum and convention on the side of political progress and critical intelligence.[38] Similarly, neither kind of feminism values romantic love: conservatives view it as antifeminist because it is a male-centered con; being in a relationship with a hot guy is made the (false) measure of a (presumptively heterosexual) woman's happiness, not her job or career, not her relationships with other women or with male friends. Materialist feminists tend to read romantic love negatively as a mystification created by consumer capitalism.[39] The most pointed resemblance between conservative and materialist feminisms concerns the theme of lesbosocial relations in Shakesploi films, namely, conflicts between (even feminist) women.[40] Shakesploi teen films give local habitation and a name to the fantasy that cultural literacy can be the vehicle for romantic triumph, and this fantasy is dearly held, I think it is fair to say, not only by conservative feminists but by liberal pop feminists (some of whom, dare I say it, are academic feminists too) and materialist feminists as well. All share fantasies about the progressive effects cultural criticism and a negative, demystifying media critique can have on teen girls.[41] For example, in her book *Where the Girls Are: Growing up Female with the Mass Media*, Susan Douglas criticizes the mass media for getting young girls to think that they can only attract boys by pretending to be dumber than they are, for making these girls think that only bimbos can be sexy hotties.[42] In this view, the loser figure has nothing to offer teen girls but more sexist oppression since it reinforces the equation between sexiness and stupidity, leaving the girls just as obsessed about how fat they are, whether their boyfriends think another girl is prettier, and turning them into consumers of products they don't really need such as cosmetics, fashion magazines, plastic surgery, and so on.

Is it an overstatement to say that the ugly duckling Cinderella fantasy informing so many of these girl-oriented teen flicks assuages anxieties about the other, sexier woman from which feminists themselves are not immune, no matter how sexy and bright they may be? Are feminist viewers more likely to reject or to share the fantasy that sexy women (as defined by the likes of blonde-haired Pam Anderson Lee, say), which many heterosexual men find appealing, are really bad, ugly on the inside, and dumb? Ditto for the fantasy that if you're smart and if you play your cards right, you can show those hotties up for the losers they really are and leave them eating your dust, taking your man in tow (who, of course, would never even think of looking at Pam Anderson).[43] Instead of radically departing from conservative feminism, then, its analysis of Shakesploi flicks in particular and teensploi films in general reveals that materialist feminism ends up mirroring its conservative opposite in many crucial respects, and it does so most deeply, I think, by defining success for teen girls and young women in terms of a radical divide between intelligence and stupidity, between winners and losers.

A fuller engagement with stupidity and the loser in mass culture might profoundly transform materialist feminist criticism and its account of the bad girl; conflicts between women driven by rivalry over men; female sexuality; mass culture; cultural literacy for teen girls; and so on. Such an engagement might open up a new perspective on the datedness of materialist feminism as presently practiced, and open up reflection on the generational specificity of this criticism as well. Perhaps *10 Things*, for example, is really aimed at forty-year-old-and-over mothers with teen daughters. Can we really believe that a contemporary teen feminist would read books like *The Bell Jar* and *The Feminine Mystique* and wear hippie clothes, rather than read magazines like *Bust* and *Bitch* and wear makeup and cute T-shirts with "Porn Star" written on them? By extension, materialist feminism might consider itself to be a variation of loser criticism. The issue would no longer be men in feminism but couples (and coupling) in feminism. This would involve an analysis of heterosexual romance not only from the viewpoint of loser feminism but as loser romance, what I call "dumb love." But this would be another project, one that would entail reading the way that another story, *Lolita*, has rivaled if not yet displaced *Romeo and Juliet* as the foundational plot for post–Cold War American romance.[44]

Notes

I would like to thank Laurie Osborne for her characteristically thoughtful responses to an earlier draft of this essay and to José Ramón Díaz Fernández for giving me the opportunity to present a much shortened version of it at Shakespeare on Screen: The Centenary Conference, held in Malaga, Spain, in September 1999.

1. See Veronica Chambers and Yahlin Chang, "High School Confidential," *Newsweek*, 1 March 1999, 63. They point out that as many as one teensploi film a week was released in the first part of 1999. See also, Stephen Holden, "A New Rule: The Bad and the Beautiful," *New York Times*, 28 February 1999, 13, and Bruce Newman, "Can't Read the Classic? See the Teen Movie," *New York Times* 28 February 1999, 13, 22.

2. The convergence of these films and Shakespeare was notable in the trailers. The night I went to see *Jawbreaker*, trailers played for *10 Things*, *The Rage*, and *Never Been Kissed*, all of which highlighted Shakespeare. There's a citation of *Macbeth* in *High School High*, *Julius Caesar* in *Whatever*; a reference to *Henry the Fourth, Part One* in *American Pie,* and to *Hamlet* in *Outside Providence.* For a discussion of *High School High*, see Rich-

ard Burt, *Unspeakable ShaXXXspeares: Queer Theory and American Kiddie Culture*, 2d ed. (New York: St. Martin's Press, 2000), 210–11. Also aimed at the teen market, though keeping Shakespeare's text, is a remake of *Hamlet* (dir. Michael Almereyda, 2000) set in modern-day New York starring Ethan Hawke as Hamlet and Julia Stiles as Ophelia. *Beautiful Girls* (dir. Ted Demme, 1998), about a high school reunion of forty-somethings, one of whom has a thing for a very young girl, has two references to the balcony scene in *Romeo and Juliet*. For an earlier teen comedy citing Shakespeare, see *Eight Days a Week* (dir. Michael Davis, 1997). A character named Peter (Joshua Schaefer) camps out below the balcony of a girl he likes named Erica (Kerri Russell), whom he initially fails to win over. After his grandfather dies, his best friend Matt (R. D. Robb) says to him, "You're just in a crappy mood because you realize that this Romeo act is a dumb-ass idea"; and in the romantic comedy *Down to You* (dir. Kris Isacsson, 2000), with Julia Stiles, a guy who stars in porn movies is said later to be doing *Macbeth*. In the body of the paper, I note the references to Shakespeare in the other teensploi films I discuss.

    3.   The turn to Shakespeare was also part of a more general turn to literary classics in teensploi films such as *Emma* (dir. Douglas McGrath, 1997), with Gwyneth Paltrow, itself modeled on *Clueless* (dir. Amy Heckerling, 1995), an earlier adaptation of Jane Austen's novel, and whose lead actress, Alicia Silverstone, played a Shakespeare-citing heroine in that film and was then cast to star as Rosaline in Kenneth Branagh's *Love's Labour's Lost* (2000); *Great Expectations* (dir. Alfonso Cuaron, 1997), also with Paltrow in the lead; *Cruel Intentions* (dir. Roger Kumble, 1999), an adaptation of Choderlos de Laclos's epistolary novel, *Dangerous Liaisons*; and *She's All That* (dir. Robert Iscove, 1999), an adaptation of George Bernard Shaw's *Pygmalion*. On *Clueless* and Shakespeare, see Richard Burt, *Unspeakable ShaXXXspeares*, xv, 7–9, 11, 26, 210, 214, 282, and Lynda E. Boose and Richard Burt, "Totally Clueless: Shakespeare Goes Hollywood in the 1990s," in *Shakespeare, the Movie: Popularizing on Film, TV, and Video* (London and New York: Routledge, 1997), 8–22.

    4.   For a discussion of these earlier films, see Richard Burt, *Unspeakable ShaXXX-speares*, 44–47.

    5.   Unsurprisingly, the flip side of the turn to sexually active teens in some teenploi flicks was a turn to virgins in others. See A. J. Jacobs and Jessica Shaw, "Virgin Spring," *Entertainment Weekly*, 2 April 1999, 10–11. My use of the term "lesbosocial" is indebted to Eve Sedgwick's term, "homosocial" and to her exploration of relations between men in which women are objects of exchange. Lesbosocial rivalry is not driven in Shakesploi horror films, however, by a girlene lesbophobia. See Eve Sedgwick, *Epistemology of the Closet* (Durham, N. C.: Duke University Press, 1989), and *Between Men: English Literature and Male Homosocial Desire* (New York: Columbia University Press, 1985).

    6.   On the deep-seated, lasting problem female sexuality has posed inside feminism, see Cora Kaplan's brilliant essay, "Wild Nights," in *Sea Changes: Culture and Feminism* (London: Verso, 1986).

    7.   On the female grotesque, see Mary Russo, *The Female Grotesque* (New York: Routledge, 1995). This necessary generic inmixing has been heightened by the fact that current teensploi films draw their box office power in part based on the casting of actors who became successful in teen slasher films (for example, the lead actor, David Arquette, in *Never Been Kissed* appeared in *Scream* [dir. Wes Craven, 1996] and *Scream 2* [dir. Wes Craven, 1996]; similarly, Drew Barrymore appeared in a cameo in *Scream;* moreover, *Never Been Kissed* explicitly cites *Carrie*). Rather oddly, *Macbeth* spills over in *10 Things* in a romantic context, as if the film were implying it could dissolve the threat of the horror genre. Michael and Mandella connect over a shared citation from the play: "Who could refrain, / That had a heart to love," Michael says, and pauses. Mandella takes her cue and completes the quotation from *Macbeth*, though neither mentions the play by name: "and in that heart / Courage to make his love known" (2.3.113–15). This is, of course, part of

Macbeth's justification for killing the grooms after Duncan's corpse is discovered, certainly an inapt quotation, though in the film it is entirely stripped of its meaning in the play.

8.   By contrast, the Shakespeare films starring Julia Stiles (as Kat in *10 Things*, Ophelia in *Hamlet*, and Desdemona in *Yo, What's Up with Iago*) have been elevated above the usual teen horror fare by virtue of their more explicit use of Shakespeare and of an actress who plays the central female Shakespearean roles in all three.

9.   *Dumb Love* is the title of a book I am cowriting on twentieth-century American loser culture with my wife, Elizabeth Burt (Power). The title is hers.

10.   My critique will focus on materialist feminism, as I consider it to be the dominant academic feminist practice. For negative critiques of romantic love from this perspective, see Linda Charnes, "What's Love Got to Do with It? Reading the Liberal Humanist Romance in Shakespeare's *Antony and Cleopatra*," *Textual Practice* 6, no. 1 (1992): 1-16, and Barbara Hodgdon, *The Shakespeare Trade: Performances and Appropriations* (Philadelphia: University of Pennsylvania Press, 1998).

11.   The production of these films also involves a dumbed-down Shakespeare. Disney handed out Cliffs Notes to the stars *of 10 Things I Hate about You*. See Jessica Shaw, "Good Will Hunting," *Entertainment Weekly*, 12 February 1999, 9. Similarly, in an MTV interview, Joseph Gordon-Levitt, a regular on the sit-com *Third Rock from the Sun* who plays Cameron James (a character based on Lucentio) in *10 Things*, admitted that no one in the cast read the play. (However, Julia Stiles, who pays Kat, claims to have read it.) It is also worth pointing out that Shakespeare has cachet in mass culture consumed by a youth market not because a particular teen film can cite Shakespeare but because it can cite Shakespeare *in* and *as* mass culture (for example, films like the Luhrmann film of *Romeo + Juliet* or the Zeffirelli film of *Hamlet*); moreover, teen-oriented Shakesploi flicks have cachet in the teen market because they cite contemporary mass culture in general, mostly MTV heavy rotation music videos, but also mass culture icons like Barbie, cartoons like *Josie and the Pussycats*, films like *Carrie* (dir. Brian De Palma, 1976), and indie rock bands like Bikini Kill and the Donnas.

12.   And *Romy and Michelle* effectively undoes the loser thing by making the women much smarter and successful than their male counterparts.

13.   On the loser, see Burt, *Unspeakable ShaXXXspeares*, 14–22, 239–46.

14.   Connie Brown and David Ansen, "Rough Waters," *Newsweek*, 15 December 1997, 66. Similarly, the wave of classic adaptations was begun by *Clueless* and *Emma*.

15.   For the novelizations, see David Levithan, *10 Things I Hate about You* (New York: Scholastic Ink, 1999), and Cathy East Dubowski, *Never Been Kissed* (New York: Harper Entertainment, 1999). All the film reviews on Amazon.com are written by girls. Essentialist feminists might be interested to know that the screenplay of *10 Things* was written by a woman, Karen McCullah Lutz, and the screenplay of *Never Been Kissed* was written by a woman and a man, Abby Kohn and Marc Silverstein. Personally, I think the gender of the writer is meaningless, in and of itself, since a woman writer can be antifeminist.

16.   Rather ineptly, however, the arrow points down to Bianca in the video and DVD covers.

17.   Of course, some of these films persist in the nineties, and in the eighties there were directors like Amy Heckerling and John Hughes who were more sensitive to girls' issues.

18.   Similarly, "Romeo" is also called a "stupid dunce," and in a song entitled "Local God" by Evercleer the singer says to a character named Romeo "you look so stupid in love." Both songs are featured on the first soundtrack of the Luhrmann film, *William Shakespeare's Romeo + Juliet*.

19.   Patrick stands at an even greater remove from Shakespeare, never once quoting him. (Indeed, when Michael quotes to Patrick the first line of Sonnet 56, "Sweet love, renew thy force" in order to encourage Patrick in his quest to take out Kat, Patrick tells him not to speak like that, as if Michael were making a pass at him.) See also *Jerry MacGuire*

(dir. Cameron Crowe, 1996) for a reference to Romeo as a stalker and *Beautiful Girls* for a reference to a Humbert Humbert-like Romeo.

20. For a more detailed discussion of *Clueless*, see Burt, *Unspeakable ShaXXXspeares*, 7–9.

21. Female rewriting (either of *Carrie* or *Romeo and Juliet*) also seems impossible in *The Rage*. As she rages, her body begins to become auto-tattooed, as a kind of tattoo barbwire encircles her forehead, her arms, and so on. The tattoo writing disappears when she dies. Her body becomes a kind of text when she rages but is no longer readable as she finally learns the meaning of love.

22. This is true of James Cameron's *Titanic* as well, the main characters being named Rose and Jack.

23. To be sure, Kat's feminist line is also undercut throughout the film. It is so dated and clichéd (we see her reading *The Bell Jar*, not *Gender Trouble*) that it is easily parodied by Bianca and her friend, who finish her predictable sentence for her.

24. Similarly, in a scene at Club Skunk, nearly all the people present are women, and we see Kat dancing with another woman to music performed by Letters to Cleo. Bianca beats up Joey after he decks Cameron at the prom; she first kisses Cameron; and Kat moves to kiss Patrick in the car.

25. The soundtrack of the Luhrmann film made it into the top 10 in the U.S. and the U.K., furthering the identification of the song with the film.

26. This sequence was part of the trailer for the film as well.

27. It is worth pointing out that Lauryn Hill covered the Valli song, rearranging it significantly, on her CD *The Miseducation of Lauryn Hill* (Sony/Columbia, 1998). Joan Jett got her fame from covering "I Love Rock and Roll" and covered it for *Wayne's World*. Sandra Bernhard's many covers in the film *Without You I'm Nothing* (dir. John Boskovich, 1990) also play out the cross-gendered, same-sex possibilities, as in "Me and Mrs. Jones."

28. In an essay on Shakespeare's *Shrew*, I argue that the play enacts a new kind of male authority—charismatic rule—to legitimate rather than subvert patriarchal authority. See Richard Burt, "Charisma, Coercion, and Comic Form in *The Taming of the Shrew*," *Criticism* 26 (1984): 295–311.

29. The reference is activated by the fact that Josie brought up this scene earlier in the film when she read from her paper aloud in class.

30. The film also links Josie to Shakespeare's Jessica. Josie cites one of her lines from act 5 of *The Merchant of Venice* at the prom. When Guy asks Josie what she is thinking of, she replies "Shakespeare. How he described a night like this: 'Look how the floor of heaven is thick inlaid with patinas of bright gold.'"

31. To be sure, one can easily understand why she is silent here, especially since she is the one who is apologizing.

32. A music video for the theme song of the film, Swirl 360's "Candy in the Sun," further writes Barrymore and her character into a traditional female role, the groupie. Drew Barrymore plays a chauffeur who drives the Hanson soundalike band, comprised, similarly, of cute guys who play guitar and sing. A group of identically dressed and coifed Barrymore/Josie look-alikes stalk the band and follow them into a skyscraper to the roof, but the guys manage to escape in a helicopter. The song was featured on the trailers.

33. Josie's friend at work is closer to the crude Audrey than she is to Celia.

34. The film also ridicules the students for having their superficial knowledge of mass culture. They don't know who hockey player Gordie Howe was, but they do know Tiger Woods. Similarly, Aldys does not know who Josie and the Pussycats were. And when the novelization of *10 Things* ends with Mandella advising the reader to go read the play on grounds that it tells the story better than she can, we may presume that no reader is expected to appreciate the metafictional moment here: a story based on a film based on a play has a

character refer to the play source as if it were written after, not before, both the film and the novelization of the film.

35. It is not clear that using an American literary authority would make a difference. Consider the film *Pleasantville* (dir. Gary Ross, 1998). In it, American literature such as *The Catcher in the Rye* and modern European art are the means by which a town is liberated from its stultifying, patriarchal, black-and-white, mass media limitations; but the film celebrates its own special effects to colorize people who become humanized and liberated.

36. On bad girl feminism, see Linda Kaufman, *Bad Girls and Sick Boys: Fantasies in Contemporary Art and Culture* (Berkeley and Los Angeles: University of California Press, 1998), Catharine Lumby, *Bad Girls: The Media, Sex, and Feminism in the Nineties* (London: Allen & Unwin, 1997), and Marcia Tucker, ed., *Bad Girls* (Cambridge: MIT Press, 1994).

37. The same would inevitably be true in any production, I would argue. I am cowriting a screenplay with Kristin Brenna entitled *Titus Androgynous* set in New York in the 1990s, in which Lavinia sees herself as a tank-girl-inspired Riot Girl. The point would be precisely that her punk-rock-stripper-slut-wear would still leave her vulnerable to the likes of the brothers. She could get her revenge, of course, by anally raping the brothers with her stumps.

38. It is worth recalling that many feminists did not think that Madonna was a feminist in her late 1980s incarnations.

39. See, for example, Charnes and Hodgdon.

40. On this issue, see Marianne Hirsch and Evelyn Fox Keller, *Conflicts in Feminism* (New York: Routledge, 1990). This volume, to my mind, enacts on the academic front the very kinds of problems it seeks to resolve.

41. The politics of the romance has been a matter of long-standing debate among feminists. For the debate, see Richard Burt, "No Holes Bard: Homonormativity and the Gay and Lesbian Romance with *Romeo and Juliet*," in *Shakespeare without Class*, ed. Don Hedrick and Bryan Reynolds (New York: St. Martin's Press, 2000). For fascinating accounts of Shakespeare's citation in romance novels, see Laurie Osborne, "Romancing the Bard," in *Shakespeare and Appropriation*, ed. Christy Desmet and Robert Sawyer (London and New York: Routledge, 1999), and Laurie Osborne, "Sweet, Savage Shakespeare," in Hedrick and Reynolds, *Shakespeare without Class*.

42. Susan Douglas, *Where the Girls Are: Growing up Female with the Mass Media* (New York: Times Books, 1994).

43. There have some attempts to occupy this bad girl position from a feminist perspective. See, for examples, Joannna Freuh, *Erotic Faculties* (Berkeley and Los Angeles: University of California Press, 1996), and Jane Gallop, *Feminist Accused of Sexual Harrassment* (Durham, N.C.: Duke University Press, 1997). But these examples are, to my mind at least, pathetically failed attempts to be hot. This is not to say, of course, that there are not hot feminist critics, only that even the hottest will share the anxiety that another (feminist) woman—generally younger—is even hotter (hotness being defined not only as sexy looking but sexy thinking), hence competition, hence a rival rather than an ally. For a further critique of bad-girl feminism, see Richard Burt and Jeffrey Wallen, "Knowing Better: Sex, Cultural Criticism, and the Pedagogical Imperative in the 1990s," *Diacritics* 29, no.1 (1999): 72–91.

44. The two works come together in the film *Beautiful Girls*.

Works Cited

Boose, Lynda E., and Richard Burt. "Totally Clueless: Shakespeare Goes Hollywood in the 1990s." In *Shakespeare, the Movie: Popularizing on Film, TV, and Video.* Edited by Lynda E. Boose and Richard Burt. London and New York: Routledge, 1997.

Brown, Connie, and David Ansen. "Rough Waters." *Newsweek,* 15 December 1997, 66.

Burt, Richard. *Unspeakable ShaXXXspeares: Queer Theory and American Kiddie Culture.* 2d ed. New York: St. Martin's Press, 2000.

———. "No Holes Bard: Homonormativity and the Gay and Lesbian Romance with *Romeo and Juliet.*" In *Shakespeare without Class.* Edited by Don Hedrick and Bryan Reynolds. New York: St. Martin's Press, 2000.

———. "Charisma, Coercion, and Comic Form in *The Taming of the Shrew.*" *Criticism* 26 (1984): 295–311.

Burt, Richard, and Jeffrey Wallen. "Knowing Better: Sex, Cultural Criticism, and the Pedagogical Imperative in the 1990s." *Diacritics* 29, no. 1 (1999): 72–91.

Chambers, Veronica, and Yahlin Chang. "High School Confidential." *Newsweek,* 1 March 1999, 62–64.

Charnes, Linda. "What's Love Got to Do with It? Reading the Liberal Humanist Romance in Shakespeare's *Antony and Cleopatra.*" *Textual Practice* 6, no. 1 (1992): 1–16.

Douglas, Susan. *Where the Girls Are: Growing up Female with the Mass Media.* New York: Times Books, 1994.

Dubowski, Cathy East. *Never Been Kissed.* New York: Harper Entertainment, 1999.

Freuh, Joanna. *Erotic Faculties.* Berkeley and Los Angeles: University of California Press, 1996.

Gallop, Jane. *Feminist Accused of Sexual Harrassment.* Durham, N.C.: Duke University Press, 1997.

Hirsch, Marianne, and Evelyn Fox Keller. *Conflicts in Feminism.* London and New York: Routledge, 1990.

Hodgdon, Barbara. *The Shakespeare Trade: Performances and Appropriations.* Philadelphia: University of Pennsylvania Press, 1998.

Holden, Stephen. "A New Rule: The Bad and the Beautiful." *New York Times,* 28 February 1999, 13, 22.

Jacobs, A. J., and Jessica Shaw. "Virgin Spring." *Entertainment Weekly,* 2 April 1999, 10–11.

Kaplan, Cora. "Wild Nights." In *Sea Changes: Culture and Feminism.* London: Verso, 1986.

Kaufman, Linda. *Bad Girls and Sick Boys: Fantasies in Contemporary Art and Culture.* Berkeley and Los Angeles: University of California Press, 1998.

Levithan, David. *10 Things I Hate About You.* New York: Scholastic Ink, 1999.

Lumby, Catherine. *Bad Girls: The Media, Sex, and Feminism in the Nineties.* London: Allen & Unwin, 1998.

Newman, Bruce. "Can't Read the Classic? See the Teen Movie." *New York Times,* 28 February 1999, 13, 22.

Osborne, Laurie. "Romancing the Bard." In *Shakespeare and Appropriation.* Edited by Christy Desmet and Robert Sawyer. London and New York: Routledge, 1999.

——— . "Sweet, Savage Shakespeare." In *Shakespeare without Class.* Edited by Don Hedrick and Bryan Reynolds. New York: St. Martin's Press, 2000.

Russo, Mary. *The Female Grotesque*. London and New York: Routledge, 1995.

Shaw, Jessica. "Hey Kids! "Teensploitation!: Inside Hollywood's Box Office Boom." *Entertainment Weekly*, 12 March 1999, 22–24.

———. "Good Will Hunting." *Entertainment Weekly*, 12 February 1999, 9.

Tucker, Marcia, ed. *Bad Girls*. Cambridge: MIT Press, 1994.

FILMS CITED

Carrie. Directed by Brian De Palma. 1 hr. 38 min. MGM, 1976. DVD.

Clueless. Directed by Amy Heckerling. 1 hr. 37 min. Paramount, 1995. DVD.

Cruel Intentions. Directed by Roger Kumble. 1 hr. 37 min. Columbia, 1999. DVD.

Jawbreaker. Directed by Darren Stein. 1 hr. 27 min. Tri-Star,1999. DVD.

Never Been Kissed. Directed by Raja Gosnell. 1 hr. 48 min. Twentieth Century Fox, 1999. DVD.

The Rage: Carrie 2. Directed by Robert Mandel and Katt Shea. 1 hr. 45 min. MGM, 1999. DVD.

10 Things I Hate about You. Directed by Gil Junger. 1 hr. 37 min. Touchstone, 1999. DVD.

Whatever. Directed by Susan Skoog. 1 hr. 35 min. Columbia-Tristar, 1997. Videocasette.

William Shakespeare's Romeo + Juliet. Directed by Baz Luhrmann. 2 hr. Twentieth Century Fox/Bazmark Films, 1996. DVD.

Notes on Contributors

RICHARD BURT is Professor of English at the University of Massachusetts, Amherst. He is the author of *Unspeakable ShaXXXspeares: Queer Theory and American Kiddie Culture* and *Licensed by Authority: Ben Jonson and the Discourses of Censorship*; editor of *Shakespeare after Mass Media: A Cultural Studies Reader* and *The Administration of Aesthetics: Censorship, Political Criticism, and the Public Sphere*; and co-editor of *Enclosure Acts: Sexuality, Property, and Culture in Early Modern England* and *Shakespeare the Movie: Popularizing the Plays on Film, TV, and Video*. He is currently working on two books, *Ever Afterlives: Reanimating the Renaissance and the Loss of History* and *Dumb Love*.

ANNALISA CASTALDO is Visiting Assistant Professor of English at Temple University. She is currently working on an essay called "What Dreams are Made On: The Character of Shakespeare in the Sandman comics" for *Shakespeare after Mass Media: A Cultural Studies Reader*, edited by Richard Burt.

SAMUEL CROWL is Trustee Professor of English at Ohio University. He is the author of *Shakespeare Observed* and numerous articles and reviews of Shakespeare in performance on stage and film. He is completing a book on all the recent Shakespeare films called *Shakespeare at the Cineplex: Kenneth Branagh and the Revival of Shakespeare on Film*.

ELIZABETH A. DEITCHMAN is a Ph.D. candidate in the Department of English at the University of California, Davis. Her essay in this volume is drawn from her M.Phil thesis for Queen Mary and Westfield College, the University of London, entitled "Some Mel Gibson Movie: Shakespeare, Cinema, and Authenticity in the 1990s." She also played Snap the Constable in a one-night, all-female performance of *Damon and Pythias* (dir. Richard Edwards) at the Globe Theater in London during its prologue season in 1996.

233

COURTNEY LEHMANN is Assistant Professor of English and Film Studies at the University of the Pacific and co-editor of *Spectacular Shakespeare: Critical Theory and Popular Cinema*. She has published articles on all of Kenneth Branagh's Shakespeare films. Her most recent essay is "Strictly Shakespeare? Dead Letters, Ghostly Fathers, and the Cultural Pathology in Baz Luhrmann's William Shakespeare's *Romeo + Juliet*." She is currently co-editing, with Lisa S. Starks, a volume entitled *The Reel Shakespeare: Alternative Cinema and Theory* (Fairleigh Dickinson University Press), and she is completing a book called *Shakespearean Projections*.

LISA HOPKINS is Senior Lecturer in English at Sheffield Hallam University and editor of Early Modern Literary Studies. Her publications include *John Ford's Political Theatre, The Shakespearean Marriage: Merry Wives and Heavy Husbands,* and *Christopher Marlowe: A Literary Life*. She is currently working on a project tentatively entitled *The Lady's Tragedy: Female Heroes in English Renaissance Drama*.

DOUGLAS LANIER is Associate Professor and the Coordinator of Graduate Studies in English at the University of New Hampshire. He has published articles on Shakespeare, Jonson, Marston, Milton, the Jacobean masque, literary pedagogy, and Shakespeare on film in many journals and collections. His most recent essay is "WSHX: Shakespeare and American Radio." He is currently working on a book on Shakespeare and popular culture.

ALFREDO MICHEL MODENESSI is Professor of English and Comparative Literature at the Universidad Nacional Autonoma de Mexico. He has published books on American drama and popular culture, as well as essays on Shakespeare, Shakespeare on screen, and Elizabethan and American theatre. He translates and adapts plays for the stage and is currently preparing his versions of Marlowe's *Edward II* and Shakespeare's *Love's Labour's Lost* for publication.

LAURIE OSBORNE is Associate Professor of English at Colby College. She has published *The Trick of Singularity: Twelfth Night and the Performance Editions* as well as several essays on Renaissance audiences and Shakespeare in film and popular culture. Her current work includes "Sweet, Savage Shakespeare" in *Shakespeare Without Class* and an essay on pedagogy entitled "Shakespeare and the Construction of Character."

MARGUERITE HAILEY RIPPY is Assistant Professor of Language and Literature at Marymount University. She has published articles on representations of women in performance from Shakespearean drama to classic

Hollywood cinema. Her current projects include an analysis of Orson Welles's mass media adaptations of the works of novelist Charles Dickens.

Lisa S. Starks is Assistant Professor of English at University of South Florida St. Petersburg and co-editor of *Spectacular Shakespeare: Critical Theory and Popular Cinema.* She has published on film, Shakespeare, and Marlowe in books like *Shakespeare and Appropriation* and *Marlowe, History, and Sexuality* and journals such as *Literature and Psychology, Post Script,* and *Theatre Journal.* Starks has also guest-edited two special issues of *Post Script: Essays in Film and the Humanities* on Shakespeare and Film. She is currently co-editing, with Lehmann, *The Reel Shakespeare: Alternative Cinema and Theory* (Fairleigh Dickinson University Press).

Index

237